SUPPORTING Gender Identity AND
Sexual Orientation Diversity
IN K-12 SCHOOLS

PERSPECTIVES ON SEXUAL ORIENTATION AND GENDER DIVERSITY

Maria Lucia Miville, Series Editor

SUPPORTING Gender Identity AND Sexual Orientation Diversity
IN K–12 SCHOOLS

EDITED BY
Megan C. Lytle and
Richard A. Sprott

 AMERICAN PSYCHOLOGICAL ASSOCIATION

Published by
American Psychological Association
750 First Street, NE
Washington, DC 20002
https://www.apa.org

Order Department
https://www.apa.org/pubs/books
order@apa.org

In the U.K., Europe, Africa, and the Middle East, copies may be ordered from Eurospan
https://www.eurospanbookstore.com/apa
info@eurospangroup.com

Typeset in Meridien and Ortodoxa by Circle Graphics, Inc., Reisterstown, MD

Printer: Gasch Printing, Odenton, MD
Cover Designer: Beth Schlenoff, Bethesda, MD

Library of Congress Cataloging-in-Publication Data

Names: Lytle, Megan C., editor. | Sprott, Richard A., 1965- editor.
Title: Supporting gender identity and sexual orientation diversity in K-12 schools /
  edited by Megan C. Lytle and Richard A. Sprott.
Description: Washington, DC : American Psychological Association, [2021] |
  Series: Perspectives on sexual orientation and gender diversity |
  Includes bibliographical references and index.
Identifiers: LCCN 2020024318 (print) | LCCN 2020024319 (ebook) |
  ISBN 9781433832956 (paperback) | ISBN 9781433833205 (ebook)
Subjects: LCSH: Gender identity in education. | Sexual minority
  youth—Education. | Transgender students—Social conditions.
Classification: LCC LC212.9 .S92 2021 (print) | LCC LC212.9 (ebook) |
  DDC 371.826/6—dc23
LC record available at https://lccn.loc.gov/2020024318
LC ebook record available at https://lccn.loc.gov/2020024319

https://doi.org/10.1037/0000211-000

Printed in the United States of America

10 9 8 7 6 5 4 3 2 1

CONTENTS

CONTRIBUTORS

Austin R. Anderson, MPA, PhD, University of Southern Indiana, Evansville, IN, United States

Clinton W. Anderson, PhD, American Psychological Association, Washington, DC, United States

Judy Chiasson, PhD, Los Angeles Unified School District, Los Angeles, CA, United States

Gabriel DeLong, BA, Wayne State University, Detroit, MI, United States

Sam E. Greenberg, MPP, Sharp Insight, LLC, Kensington, MD, United States

Julie C. Herbstrith, PhD, Texas Woman's University, Denton, TX, United States

Sarah Kiperman, PhD, Wayne State University, Detroit, MI, United States

Megan C. Lytle, PhD, University of Rochester Medical Center, Rochester, NY, United States

Amie R. McKibban, PhD, University of Southern Indiana, Evansville, IN, United States

Emily S. Meadows, PhD, Lehigh University, Bethlehem, PA, United States

Joel Meyers, PhD, Georgia State University, Atlanta, GA, United States

Jeremy D. Shain, EdS, Oregon State University, Corvallis, OR, United States

Jana E. Sharp, MPH, Sharp Insight, LLC, Kensington, MD, United States

Richard A. Sprott, PhD, California State University, East Bay, Hayward, CA, United States

Peter S. Theodore, PhD, AIDS Project Los Angeles, Los Angeles, CA, United States

Kris Varjas, PsyD, Georgia State University, Atlanta, GA, United States

SUPPORTING Gender Identity AND
Sexual Orientation Diversity
IN K-12 SCHOOLS

Introduction

Moving From Research to Policy and School Interventions

Megan C. Lytle and Richard A. Sprott

We should indeed keep calm in the face of difference, and live our lives in a state of inclusion and wonder at the diversity of humanity.

—GEORGE TAKEI (2013)

The journey of a thousand miles begins with one step.

—LAO TZU (BBC, n.d.)

Throughout the process of creating the *Resolution on Gender and Sexual Orientation Diversity in Children and Adolescents in Schools*, the working group of which we were a part was mindful and intentional about planning out next steps to ensure that the recommendations made in the Joint Resolution could be applied within school districts across the country (American Psychological Association & National Association of School Psychologists, 2015). Soon after the Joint Resolution was adopted, we worked with a team of scholars and researchers to develop a series of fact sheets to provide additional information to school administrators, educators, and staff. We quickly realized that a book like this was needed to help break down barriers and facilitate implementation. Amid constantly changing laws, legalized discrimination, evolving terminology, gaps in knowledge and services, as well as struggles with finding resources, we worked with experts across the country to move beyond talking about change to walking you through strategies and examples of how to make schools affirming, safe, and enjoyable for gender and sexually

https://doi.org/10.1037/0000211-001
Supporting Gender Identity and Sexual Orientation Diversity in K–12 Schools, M. C. Lytle and R. A. Sprott (Editors)

diverse (GSD) students! Similarly, as we wrote sections of this book and reviewed each chapter, it has become glaringly obvious that significant gaps in research remain, especially when it comes to learning about the distinct needs of GSD youth across various age groups, ethnicities, and intersecting identities.

EDUCATION AND HEALTH DISPARITIES

Before we sift through the empirical literature about disparities in educational and health outcomes for GSD students, we must mention that the disproportionate burdens endured by so many GSD youth is a reflection of the chronic discrimination they face, most of which can be ameliorated or prevented if societal biases are significantly reduced or altogether removed. The majority of programs and resources discussed throughout this book should be used to fight against the cisnormative and heteronormative assumptions that manifest into prejudice and discrimination. However, a few programs have been developed to support GSD youth with overcoming societal biases.

In terms of educational outcomes, research suggests that the victimization GSD students experience is directly associated with missing school (Kosciw et al., 2015), and 3.4% of GSD youth were not sure if they would graduate from high school, compared with fewer than 1% of students in the general population (Palmer et al., 2016). Both educational and health disparities are usually linked to negative school environments (Palmer et al., 2016). However, Black, Hispanic, and White youth who identify as lesbian, gay, and bisexual (LGB) had greater odds of reporting suicide ideation than their White heterosexual peers regardless of whether they had been bullied or not (Mueller et al., 2015). In comparison with their cisgender peers, transgender students were more likely to feel unsafe at school, attempt suicide, use substances (e.g., alcohol, cigarettes, inhalants), and have intercourse before 13 years of age (Johns et al., 2019). When compared with heterosexual youth, LGB students each had greater odds of feeling unsafe at school, using substances (e.g., cocaine, inhalants), and attempting suicide (Johns et al., 2018). The majority of research has focused on the experiences of GSD youth in middle school and high school, and few studies have addressed the unique needs of GSD students in elementary school. Indeed, grade school administrators, teachers, and staff often struggle to implement affirming changes, such as using the correct pronouns, even after receiving training (Smith & Payne, 2016).

PURPOSE OF THE BOOK

This book provides an overview of efforts as well as challenges in the translation and implementation of theory and research into programs, interventions, and initiatives addressing the equitable education of GSD children, youth, and families in the context of schools. We asked our contributing authors to examine how laws, policies, and programs can bolster GSD children and adolescents; how stigma and minority stress affect school performance among GSD children and adolescents; and how GSD-affirming school policies and interventions reduce high-stakes, risk-taking behavior. Our contributors also cover bullying and the challenges encountered by antibullying efforts, advocacy strategies to create safe and welcoming schools, and the need for training of school personnel around gender and sexual orientation diversity. Throughout the book, authors integrate examples of educational and health challenges and what successful interventions "look like" in action.

We developed this book as a resource for counseling and psychological helping professions (e.g., school counselors, psychologists, social workers, student affairs leaders), education administrators, and school boards that need the scientific background, practical interventions, and model policies to address issues of equitable education for GSD children, youth, and families. Faculty and graduate students in education and the helping professions are also important target audiences for the text. According to Smith and Payne (2016), despite training elementary school teachers about GSD-specific vocabulary and how to make schools more inclusive of transgender and gender diverse youth, evidence suggests that staff struggle with shifting away from a binary perspective of gender and fixate on safety (e.g., fear over what happens if a cisgender boy has a crush on a transgender girl). Perhaps if the next generation of administrators, teachers, helping professionals, and staff are trained to not only consider safety but also learn how to create inclusive and welcoming schools, GSD youth can thrive within any school environment.

After identifying gaps in knowledge (e.g., how to apply research and interventions in diverse school settings), we reached out to the Society for the Psychology of Sexual Orientation and Gender Diversity of the American Psychological Association for feedback and suggestions. From the start, we envisioned a resource that would address a broad range of topics with a focus on diversity as well as intersecting identities. We also envisioned creating something that the interdisciplinary teams could use on the front lines (i.e., not just teachers but also school counselors, health professionals, administrators, students, parents, and others). We originally conceptualized GSD students as youth who ranged from elementary school-age children through emerging adults who were in college (Arnett, 2007). Our rationale for considering such a wide age range was that emerging adulthood is critical time for identity development, and, for some GSD youth, it is their first opportunity for individualization and living authentically (Arnett, 2007; Lytle, De Luca, & Blosnich, 2014). However, because of the significant differences between youth in K–12 grades and those in higher education, we opted to narrow the focus of this book. We are considering working on another book about the distinct needs of GSD college students.

THEORETICAL LENS

The primary lens for this book is an integration of the three pillars of positive psychology with minority stress theory. As you read each chapter, we invite you to consider how you can create positive social institutions (e.g., all-gender restrooms, inclusive policies), foster positive subjective experiences (e.g., inclusive language, curricula with GSD role models), and identify GSD character strengths (e.g., recognize fairness and advocacy as GSD strengths, promote creativity) that will help youth thrive as well as ease adverse outcomes (Lytle, Vaughan, et al., 2014; Seligman & Csikszentmihalyi, 2000). These pillars of positive psychology can neutralize the minority stress experienced by GSD communities due to the cisnormative and heteronormative expectations that are so prevalent within our school systems.

All too often, researchers and scholars focus on the negative outcomes that GSD individuals experience without thoroughly exploring how minority stress stems from chronic discrimination that is additive to the everyday stressors we all deal with (Hendricks & Testa, 2012; Meyer, 2003). Based on minority stress theory, individual (e.g., character strengths, positive subjective experiences) as well as community (e.g., positive institutions) resources can ameliorate the physical and mental health outcomes associated with distal (e.g., prejudice, discrimination) and proximal (e.g., internalized stigma, fear of rejection) experiences of societal biases (Hendricks & Testa, 2012; Meyer, 2003). In addition, the socioecological theory complements this integrated framework by understanding how the bidirectional relationship between different systems (e.g., individual, family and school, community) may foster discrimination and minority stress (Bronfenbrenner, 1977). However, this theory can also inform administrators, teachers, staff, and school boards on how they can implement programs at different system levels to create positive institutions and positive experiences as well as reduce minority stress.

OVERVIEW OF THE CHAPTERS

In Chapter 1, we (Lytle and Sprott) use the *Resolution on Gender and Sexual Orientation Diversity in Children and Adolescents in Schools* (American Psychological Association & National Association of School Psychologists, 2015) as a foundation to review some of the most accessible programs and interventions available to school psychologists, administrators, teachers, and community stakeholders.

In Chapter 2, Judy Chiasson reviews historical legal decisions that have helped to bolster the rights of GSD students. Through her personal experience as program coordinator for the Office of Human Relations, Diversity, and Equity at the Los Angeles Unified School District (LAUSD), she describes the development of the Project 10 student support group, gay prom, and Models of Pride. Chiasson demonstrates how the fight for education civil rights for Black students serves as a template for advocacy on behalf of GSD students. Although legal discrimination continues to leave many GSD youth vulnerable, the example of LAUSD provides many practical strategies for protecting students within your school district.

In Chapter 3, Emily S. Meadows and Jeremy D. Shain provide accessible recommendations for not only creating safe spaces but also supporting GSD youth in socially conservative school environments. On the basis of empirical evidence and personal experience, they describe how trusted adults may help protect against potential risks and disparities (Eisenberg & Resnick, 2006; Hatzenbuehler et al., 2014). Indeed, although the 2017 Gallup Poll suggested that approximately 4.5% of Americans (and 8.2% of Millennials) identify as lesbian, gay, bisexual, and transgender (LGBT), 24% of 12- to 14-year-olds who died by suicide were LGBT (Ream, 2019). Therefore, it is imperative to help schools, community stakeholders, and families recognize how dire the consequences are for youth who do not have the necessary supports and resources they need to thrive. As Meadows and Shain note, numerous resources are available to help school counselors, teachers, and administrators to create a safe and inclusive environment for all students.

Using the socioecological theory (Bronfenbrenner, 1979), Peter S. Theodore and Judy Chiasson describe how GSD youth not only experience bullying from their peers, but large proportions of students hear their teachers, administrators, and school staff making homophobic and transphobic remarks. In Chapter 4, these authors review such outcomes of bullying as psychological distress and engaging in risky behaviors and discuss in depth the advantages and disadvantages of various techniques to end bullying. Specifically, antibullying interventions at the individual level (e.g., what students and teachers can do) as well as at the systems level (e.g., GSAs, an acronym that has referred to "gay–straight alliances" but more recently refers to "gender and sexuality alliances" or "genders and sexualities alliances"; inclusive curricula; public policies; advocacy) are presented along with recommendations.

Coming out is among the unique experiences that GSD youth face, but determining if, how, and when to do so should be a personal decision. Unfortunately, there are instances in which GSD youth feel forced to disclose their gender identity or sexual orientation to their parents and guardians so they can receive services (e.g., engage in therapy, participate in research). In Chapter 5, Sarah Kiperman, Gabriel DeLong, Kris Varjas, and Joel Meyers review different strategies for obtaining informed consent, informed assent, and waived consent to meet the needs of GSD youth regardless of their level of outness. Such strategies as identifying when youth can be considered "mature minors" or "emancipated minors" are important especially because recent legislation at the state level (Harper, 2018) has been proposed to out youth to their parents, and federal guidelines are not always clear (Ettinghoff, 2013). Therefore, it is essential to educate administrators, counselors, psychologists, social workers, teachers, and researchers about the rights of GSD youth and how to best support these students by connecting them to the services they need and protecting their privacy.

In Chapter 6, Julie C. Herbstrith uses the ecological systems perspective to translate basic science into interventions and practices in K–12 schools that support GSD families. Specifically, she addresses systems-level issues that families headed by GSD parents face, including educators' lack of knowledge about GSD communities, school climate with elements of heteronormativity as well as cisnormativity, and prejudice directed against GSD families. Herbstrith goes on to describe evidence-based strategies that have been found to reduce prejudice (e.g., intergroup contact and invocation of social norms), and how these strategies can be applied to better support GSD families.

The American Psychological Association's *Respect Workshop: Preventing Health Risks and Promoting Healthy Outcomes Among Lesbian, Gay, Bisexual, Transgender and Questioning Students* (Rosenbaum et al., 2018) is an additional resource for school districts, state professional organizations, and individuals across disciplines who are interested in preventing health risks and promoting health outcomes among GSD youth. In Chapter 7, Sam E. Greenberg, Jana E. Sharp, and Clinton W. Anderson provide an overview of the *Respect Workshop*, participant outcomes, and how this program can be adapted to meet the diverse needs of school districts across the country. This training is available in two formats (online and in person), and participants gain access to additional training materials.

In Chapter 8, Amie R. McKibban and Austin R. Anderson describe how legislation (e.g., laws that require GSD inclusive curricula) and school policies (e.g., enumerated antibullying and harassment policies) can address issues of health disparities for sexual and gender minority students. Specifically, they discuss policies around curricula, school sports, and gender-related spaces (e.g., locker rooms, bathrooms) in relation to how each of these procedures can ameliorate minority stress as well as improve the health and well-being of GSD students. In addition to exploring these concerns, the authors provide numerous resources and strategies to help schools implement more affirming policies.

In Chapter 9, we (Sprott and Lytle) review how existing efforts are starting to address gaps in service and note that, despite these efforts, additional research as well as program development are needed to make educational environments safer and more affirming for all students. We also discuss what lessons have been learned about implementing interventions, programs, and policies for GSD youth. On the basis of these lessons learned, we propose an agenda for research and future advocacy in response to the gaps in knowledge.

KEY TERMS

The language and terminology used to describe GSD individuals is constantly changing and expanding. Regardless, we consider all school populations to be diverse, meaning inclusive of the entire spectrum of genders and sexual identities. However, throughout this book, authors do use the term *gender and sexually diverse* to mean primarily those children and adolescents who identify as lesbian, gay, bisexual, transgender, and queer or questioning (LGBTQ). The term *gender and sexually diverse* is often used as a more strength-based and inclusive umbrella term because not all individuals identify with the terms in the LGBTQ acronym. For instance, some gender-expansive or non-binary individuals do not identify as transgender because the cisnormative expectations of gender as a binary concept are often forced on transgender communities. When referring to research literature, chapter authors may specify subgroups or spell out only LGB, for example, because the research sample included only individuals identifying as lesbian, gay, or bisexual, and no participants identified as transgender, queer, or questioning.

Additional terms such as "cisnormative" and "heteronormative" are also used throughout this book. *Cisnormative* refers to the assumption that all individuals are *cisgender* (i.e., the gender assigned at birth aligns with their gender identity) because this is the expected "norm." Between cisgender privilege and cisnormative beliefs, individuals who identify as or are perceived to be transgender and gender diverse are frequently misgendered, their pronouns are assumed or ignored rather than respected, and they endure harmful microaggressions associated with *transnegativity/transphobia* (i.e., bias and prejudice toward transgender and gender diverse individuals). Similarly, *heteronormative* is the assumption that all individuals are *heterosexual* (e.g., a cisgender male is attracted to a cisgender female), and, again, this is the expected "norm." Heterosexual privilege in combination with heteronormative beliefs often leads to assumptions about whom students should be attracted to and how health education classes should be taught, and influences forms, policies, and *homonegative/homophobic* (i.e., bias and prejudice toward lesbian, gay, bisexual, and questioning individuals) cultures within school systems. Beliefs about sexual orientation often stem from cisnormative expectations and may contribute to conflated presumptions about gender identity and sexual orientation.

HOW TO USE THIS BOOK

Use this book as a guide and an inspiration for how you can make your school safe, affirming, and inclusive for GSD students across cultures; enhance professional development for you and your students; educate or suggest talking points for elected officials (e.g., superintendents); and for students and parents to prepare their school system for the unique needs of GSD families. Each chapter addresses how suggested research, programs, laws, and policies can be adapted or implemented within the school system. In addition, please refer to the *Takeaways and Opportunities* section at the end of each chapter; there, key content points are summarized in bullet list form, and readers are given at least one question for reflection or suggestions for actions you can take to better "walk the walk" for GSD students in your schools and districts.

In addition to the resources discussed throughout the book, an Appendix provides a list of resources organized by topic. And, to help you easily find the information you are looking for, some of the resources are listed under more than one topic.

We hope this book inspires you to become a champion for GSD students in your schools and districts. Education is a basic human right, and all students should be able to thrive at school. It should not be a student's responsibility to make their school safe and affirming. That is our job. As mental health professionals, teachers, administrators, and staff, please use this resource to identify what steps you can take to ensure that GSD students have a safe and affirming place to learn and grow.

REFERENCES

American Psychological Association & National Association of School Psychologists. (2015). *Resolution on gender and sexual orientation diversity in children and adolescents in schools*. https://www.apa.org/about/policy/orientation-diversity

Arnett, J. J. (2007). Emerging adulthood: What is it, and what is it good for? *Child Development Perspectives, 1*(2), 68–73. https://doi.org/10.1111/j.1750-8606.2007.00016.x

BBC. (n.d.). *Lao Tzu*. http://www.bbc.co.uk/worldservice/learningenglish/movingwords/shortlist/laotzu.shtml

Bronfenbrenner, U. (1977). Toward an experimental ecology of human development. *American Psychologist, 32*(7), 513–531. https://doi.org/10.1037/0003-066X.32.7.513

Bronfenbrenner, U. (1979). *The ecology of human development: Experiments by nature and design*. Harvard University Press.

Eisenberg, M. E., & Resnick, M. D. (2006). Suicidality among gay, lesbian and bisexual youth: The role of protective factors. *Journal of Adolescent Health, 39*(5), 662–668. https://doi.org/10.1016/j.jadohealth.2006.04.024

Ettinghoff, E. (2013). Outed at school: Student privacy rights and preventing unwanted disclosures of sexual orientation. *Loyola of Los Angeles Law Review, 47*, 579–617.

Harper, B. (2018, June 28). *Proposed Ohio law would force teachers to "out" transgender youth*. WCPO Cincinnati. https://www.wcpo.com/news/state/state-ohio/proposed-ohio-law-would-force-teachers-to-out-transgender-youth

Hatzenbuehler, M. L., Birkett, M., Van Wagenen, A., & Meyer, I. H. (2014). Protective school climates and reduced risk for suicide ideation in sexual minority youths. *American Journal of Public Health, 104*(2), 279–286.

Hendricks, M. L., & Testa, R. J. (2012). A conceptual framework for clinical work with transgender and gender nonconforming clients: An adaptation of the minority stress model. *Professional Psychology, Research and Practice, 43*(5), 460–467. https://doi.org/10.1037/a0029597

Johns, M. M., Lowry, R., Andrzejewski, J., Barrios, L. C., Demissie, Z., McManus, T., Rasberry, C. N., Robin, L., & Underwood, J. M. (2019). Transgender identity and experiences of violence victimization, substance use, suicide risk, and sexual risk behaviors among high school students—19 states and large urban school districts, 2017. *Morbidity and Mortality Weekly Report, 68*(3), 67–71. https://doi.org/10.15585/mmwr.mm6803a3

Johns, M. M., Lowry, R., Rasberry, C. N., Dunville, R., Robin, L., Pampati, S., Stone, D. M., & Mercer Kollar, L. M. (2018). Violence victimization, substance use, and suicide risk among sexual minority high school students—United States, 2015–2017. *Morbidity and Mortality Weekly Report, 67*(43), 1211–1215. https://doi.org/10.15585/mmwr.mm6743a4

Kosciw, J. G., Palmer, N. A., & Kull, R. M. (2015). Reflecting resiliency: Openness about sexual orientation and/or gender identity and its relationship to well-being and educational outcomes for LGBT students. *American Journal of Community Psychology*, *55*(1–2), 167–178. https://doi.org/10.1007/s10464-014-9642-6

Lytle, M. C., De Luca, S. M., & Blosnich, J. R. (2014). The influence of intersecting identities on self-harm, suicidal behaviors, and depression among lesbian, gay, and bisexual individuals. *Suicide & Life-Threatening Behavior, 44*(4), 384–391. https://doi.org/10.1111/sltb.12083

Lytle, M. C., Vaughan, M. D., Rodriguez, E. M., & Shmerler, D. L. (2014). Working with LGBT individuals: Incorporating positive psychology into training and practice. *Psychology of Sexual Orientation and Gender Diversity, 1*(4), 335–347. https://doi.org/10.1037/sgd0000064

Meyer, I. H. (2003). Prejudice, social stress, and mental health in lesbian, gay, and bisexual populations: Conceptual issues and research evidence. *Psychological Bulletin, 129*(5), 674–697. https://doi.org/10.1037/0033-2909.129.5.674

Mueller, A. S., James, W., Abrutyn, S., & Levin, M. L. (2015). Suicide ideation and bullying among U.S. adolescents: Examining the intersections of sexual orientation, gender, and race/ethnicity. *American Journal of Public Health, 105*(5), 980–985. https://doi.org/10.2105/AJPH.2014.302391

Palmer, N. A., Greytak, E. A., & Kosciw, J. (2016). *Educational exclusion: Drop out, push out, and the school-to-prison pipeline among LGBTQ youth*. GLSEN.

Ream, G. L. (2019). What's unique about lesbian, gay, bisexual, and transgender (LGBT) youth and young adult suicides? Findings from the National Violent Death Reporting System. *Journal of Adolescent Health, 64*(5), 602–607. https://doi.org/10.1016/j.jadohealth.2018.10.303

Rosenbaum, L., Anderson, C., Christopher, D., & Wright, T. (2018). *The Respect Workshop trainer manual* (3rd ed.). American Psychological Association.

Seligman, M. E. P., & Csikszentmihalyi, M. (2000). Positive psychology: An introduction. *American Psychologist, 55*(1), 4–14. https://doi.org/10.1037/0003-066X.55.1.5

Smith, M. J., & Payne, E. (2016). Binaries and biology: Conversations with elementary education professionals after professional development on supporting transgender students. *Educational Forum, 80*(1), 34–47. https://doi.org/10.1080/00131725.2015.1102367

Takei, G. (2013). *Lions and tigers and bears: The internet strikes back. Oh myyy!* Limited Liability Company.

1

Resolving to Fix Social Injustices for Gender and Sexually Diverse Youth

Starting Points

Megan C. Lytle and Richard A. Sprott

This chapter begins with an overview of the *Resolution on Gender and Sexual Orientation Diversity in Children and Adolescents in Schools*, referred to hereafter as the Joint Resolution because it provides a road map for moving from a large research base toward implementing interventions and programs that ameliorate stress from societal prejudice and support gender and sexually diverse (GSD) students in school (American Psychological Association [APA] & National Association of School Psychologists [NASP], 2015). After reviewing the Joint Resolution process and statement, we explore the current state of programs and interventions, as well as challenges in implementation.

APPLYING POSITIVE PSYCHOLOGY AND MINORITY STRESS THEORY

Even though the Joint Resolution stems from the minority stress theory (i.e., everyday prejudice and internalized stigma increase stress levels among minority groups), it was also influenced by the tenets of positive psychology (i.e., positive social institutions, positive subjective experiences, and recognizing character strengths; Hendricks & Testa, 2012; Meyer, 2003; Seligman & Csikszentmihalyi, 2014). The authors of the resolution are aware of how chronic discrimination in combination with general stressors can impact the mental health of GSD students (Lytle et al., 2014; Meyer, 2003). Thus, we want to emphasize that it is the responsibility of the educational system to identify

https://doi.org/10.1037/0000211-002
Supporting Gender Identity and Sexual Orientation Diversity in K–12 Schools, M. C. Lytle and R. A. Sprott (Editors)

and use interventions as well as programs that can reduce, if not eliminate, stressors that arise from prejudice against GSD individuals (APA & NASP, 2015). Indeed, the health disparities experienced by a disproportionate number of GSD individuals as the result of minority stress may decrease if schools become positive social institutions (e.g., implement affirming policies, create inclusive curricula, foster positive subjective experiences; Lytle et al., 2014).

UPDATING POLICY: THE 2014 JOINT RESOLUTION

In light of social injustices and disparities in health and education outcomes for GSD youth, the *Resolution on Gender and Sexual Orientation Diversity in Children and Adolescents in Schools* called for K–12 public institutions to be places of safety and support for all students (APA & NASP, 2015). The Joint Resolution was adopted in July 2014 by NASP and in August 2014 by APA; it was then published in 2015. This Joint Resolution was a much needed update of a policy first developed for lesbian, gay, and bisexual youth in the context of schools by NASP and APA in 1993 (APA & NASP, 1993). In 2020, the Joint Resolution was updated, incorporating the large amount of research, clinical work, and legislation concerning GSD children and youth in schools that has developed in the field since 2014. Both NASP and APA reviewed and adopted the updated and revised Joint Resolution, *Resolution on Supporting Sexual/Gender Diverse Children and Adolescents in Schools*, in March 2020 (the 2020 Joint Resolution; APA & NASP, 2020).

The educational disparities and stigma experienced by GSD children and adolescents can increase developmental risks, such as low self-esteem or internalizing problems (APA & NASP, 2015). In particular, incidences of bullying in schools are strikingly common, and most schools do not fully address the unique educational needs of GSD children and youth, let alone those who are questioning their gender and sexual identities. Many GSD children and youth experience truancy, drop out, or are pushed out of school subtly or explicitly (Greytak et al., 2009; Grossman & D'Augelli, 2006; Palmer et al., 2016; Toomey et al., 2010).

Specific language in the Joint Resolution (APA & NASP, 2015) called for the following:

- promoting safe and supportive school policies for all children and youth;
- protecting the right to privacy around gender identity, sex, and sexual orientation for children and youth in schools;
- collecting data on gender identity and sexual orientation in schools;
- developing antibullying efforts within schools;
- developing programs to increase school engagement for GSD children and youth; and
- increasing access to facilities and programs for youth and children based on their gender identity, not their gender assigned at birth.

The 2020 Joint Resolution (APA & NASP, 2020) addresses developments in the nation's schools. For instance, psychologists have investigated targeted training of mental health professionals on the impact of trauma and minority stress on GSD students (Goldbach & Gibbs, 2017; Hatzenbuehler & Pachankis, 2016), unique experiences among racially and ethnically diverse GSD students (Duran, 2019), support of GSD students in the context of rural or small towns (Ballard et al., 2017; De Pedro et al., 2018), and the importance of including questions about gender identity and sexual orientation on surveys to track the health and progress of students (Temkin et al., 2017). Because school districts often have limited resources, administrators, teachers, and staff can start implementing recommendations by exploring the free materials that are easily accessible online. For instance, some organizations provide professional development trainings, sample curriculum, model school policies, and lesson plan templates, among numerous other resources, at no cost.

LOOKING AT THE CURRENT STATE OF PROGRAMS AND INTERVENTIONS

Many of the programs and interventions developed to decrease the chronic discrimination that GSD youth face have evolved from grassroots efforts, such as teachers and parents recognizing gaps in services or activists trying to address the needs of GSD individuals in their communities. Aside from the national programs described in this section, there are online resources (e.g., Tumblr [https://www.tumblr.com/], 7 Cups [https://www.7cups.com/]), community organizations devoted to GSD individuals, and state and regional programs (e.g., Massachusetts's Safe Schools Program for Lesbian, Gay, Bisexual, Transgender, Queer and Questioning Students [http://www.doe.mass.edu/sfs/lgbtq/] and One Colorado [https://one-colorado.org/]). APA's *Respect Workshop* (see Chapter 7) and the Los Angeles Unified School District's Project 10 (see Chapter 2) are two additional resources discussed in depth later in this book. Many of these programs and interventions can be used to help schools become positive social institutions.

In 1990, GLSEN (formerly the Gay, Lesbian and Straight Education Network) was started by a group of teachers in Massachusetts who wanted to combat stigma as well as make the educational system a safer and more affirming place for GSD students (GLSEN, n.d.-a). GLSEN offers to help administrators, scholars, and educators learn about the unique experiences of GSD students through their research and advocacy work. In addition, GLSEN provides resources to help students set up or connect with gay–straight alliances (GSAs; more recently, this acronym refers to "gender and sexuality alliances" or "genders and sexualities alliances"), materials for educators, professional development resources, and information to bolster community outreach, at little to no cost. For instance, if your school is interested in a safe space kit that includes posters, stickers, and a guide, you can either purchase the kit (available in English and Spanish) or download these resources (GLSEN, n.d.-d). Similarly, educational materials, such as an elementary school tool kit, the LGBTQ [lesbian, gay, bisexual, transgender, and queer or questioning]+ History Cards flash cards, and the *School Climate Survey* can be bought or downloaded through the GLSEN website (https://www.glsen.org/). Thus, teachers and administrators can easily access basic information to make their school environments safer and more affirming.

GLSEN (n.d.-g) also provides information for students who are interested in learning about what they can do to improve their schools and communities. For instance, GSD youth can download or review materials on starting a GSA (GLSEN, n.d.-h, n.d.-i) or check out the GLSEN Gay–Straight Alliances Facebook page. In addition, students can explore these resources:

- Day of Silence (GLSEN, n.d.-c),
- Changing the Game: The GLSEN Sports Project (GLSEN, n.d.-b), and
- No Name-Calling Week (GLSEN, n.d.-e).

Many of these resources are designed for educators as well as students.

Numerous organizations have been created at the national level as well as at the community level to meet the unique needs of GSD individuals of racially and ethnically diverse backgrounds. For instance, GAPA (originally known as the Gay Asian Pacific Alliance; GAPA, n.d.) was formed in 1988 after a local support group in California decided to expand their efforts into a community resource that celebrates and advocates for Asian and Pacific Islander GSD individuals. Similarly, the Center for Black Equality (n.d.) originated after a group of Black gay men and lesbian women in Washington, DC, created the DC Black and Lesbian Gay Pride Day in 1991. By 1999, they had started the International Federation of Black Prides, which in 2012 reevaluated its mission and evolved into the Center for Black Equity. The center focuses on economic, health, and social equity. Similarly, the roots of the Latino GLBT [gay, lesbian, bisexual, and transgender] History Project (n.d.-b) stem from a collection of artifacts and stories to document the history of Latinx (i.e., a gender-neutral option aside from Latino or Latina) GSD communities that began in 1993. In 2000, the project's founder, Jose Gutierrez, put his collection on exhibit for the first time, and by 2006, a small group had laid the foundation for the Latino GLBT History Project. The group held its first meeting in 2007 (Latino GLBT History Project, n.d.-b). Aside from preserving history, this organization promotes education and acceptance of Latinx GSD individuals. These three organizations are just a few examples of resources available to GSD from diverse ethnic and racial backgrounds.

The LGBT National Help Center (n.d.-a) was founded in 1996 and offers trained peer-support to LGBTQ individuals, meaning that their volunteers identify as GSD. Among their resources are the following:

- GLBT Near Me (https://www.glbtnearme.org/),
- LGBT National Hotline (LGBT National Help Center, n.d.-b),
- LGBT National Youth Talkline (1-800-246-7743; LGBT National Help Center, n.d.-d),
- LGBT National Senior Hotline (https://www.glbthotline.org/),

- LGBT National Online Peer-Support CHAT (LGBT National Help Center, n.d.-c), and
- moderated chat rooms for GSD youth (LGBT National Help Center, n.d.-e).

Specifically, LGBT Teens is a chat room for youth between 12 and 19 years of age, Trans Teens is for transgender and gender diverse adolescents who are 12 to 19 years of age, and Trans Youth is for individuals under the age of 13. These programs and services can be used to identify local resources for GSD students. Moreover, when community organizations are too far away, GSD youth can connect with their peers in these safe and moderated online environments.

In 1998, the Genders & Sexualities Alliance Network (GSA Network, n.d.), formerly the Gay–Straight Alliance Network, was created to connect school organizations and to advocate for GSD youth. In addition to helping students develop their own GSA, the GSA Network provides leadership training to GSD youth, hosts activist camps, and organizes conferences. For example, GSD students can apply to join the National Youth Council or the California Youth Council, and through monthly activities, GSD youth develop the leadership skills they need to help make their schools and communities more safe and affirming.

The Trevor Project is the only crisis and suicide prevention organization devoted to GSD youth who are 25 years of age and younger. Before the Academy Award–winning film *TREVOR: The Trevor Project* (Rajski, 1994) aired on television for the first time in 1998, the producers created the Trevor Lifeline because no other suicide prevention resources were available for GSD youth (The Trevor Project, n.d.-a). This organization has evolved over the years, and aside from their 24/7 Trevor Lifeline (1-866-488-7386), TrevorChat, and TrevorText services (The Trevor Project, n.d.-c), they offer numerous community resources, such as TrevorSpace (i.e., a monitored social network for GSD youth) and educational resources (e.g., Lifeguard Workshop, and a model school policy). Of particular interest is the Lifeguard Workshop, a free tutorial available online to help teachers, administrators, and staff understand the unique experiences of GSD youth, identify suicide warning signs, and learn how to respond to youth in crisis (The Trevor Project, n.d.-b). Moreover, The Trevor Project also provides resources, such as posters and handouts, on request.

The Family Acceptance Project (n.d.-a) was created in 2002 by Caitlin Ryan and Rafael Dìaz to study GSD youth and families, as well as to design and disseminate resources for professionals, including school counselors and school psychologists. Educational materials, such as the *Supportive Families, Healthy Children* booklets (Family Acceptance Project, n.d.-b; available in English, Spanish, and Chinese languages as well as one that is geared toward Latter-day Saints), provide information about how family acceptance and family rejection impact GSD youth. In addition to exploring research findings, these educational materials offer personal stories and focus on how to promote the well-being of GSD youth, and the Latter-day Saints resource connects family acceptance with religious teachings. These booklets may be used to help families who are struggling after a loved one comes out as GSD or to garner support among fellow administrators, educators, and staff.

In 2010, Dan Savage and Terry Miller started the It Gets Better Project through a social media campaign to empower GSD individuals (It Gets Better Project, n.d.-a). As of 2020, more than 70,000 people have shared their stories through short videos and more than 630,000 individuals have pledged to stand up for GSD individuals (It Gets Better Project, n.d.-a). Among the It Gets Better Project videos are films about high school students and youth that may help current students who are seeking support (It Gets Better Project, n.d.-b).

Affirming programs and interventions, such as the ones discussed here, among many others, provide significant benefits to GSD students. Research suggests (e.g., Goodenow et al., 2006; Hatzenbuehler, 2011; Hatzenbuehler et al., 2014; Heck et al., 2013; Ioverno et al., 2016) that supportive school environments with GSAs, trusted adults (e.g., affirming staff), and antibullying policies or policies that specifically protect GSD youth from bullying and harassment (or both) are associated with lower prevalence of attempting suicide, being injured or threatened at school, using substances, and endorsing symptoms of depression among GSD youth. Although additional research is needed to fully understand the benefits of these programs and interventions, evidence suggests that connecting GSD youth to affirming resources may protect them against adverse outcomes (Lytle et al., 2018; Ryan et al., 2010).

Programs and interventions that support GSD youth are especially important in regions that do not protect GSD students from discrimination. For instance, a few months after marriage equality was legalized in California, Proposition 8, a voter referendum to bar same-sex marriage, was passed in November 2008. Hatzenbuehler et al. (2019) examined longitudinal data and found that bullying due to ethnicity, religion, and gender decreased in the time period leading up to the Proposition 8 vote, whereas afterward, homophobic bullying increased. Although schools with GSAs experienced similar trends, the rate of homophobic bullying was significantly lower in schools that had GSAs. Therefore, even with the existence of legalized discrimination against GSD individuals and students, these data exemplify the protective role a supportive environment may have.

CURRENT CHALLENGES IN IMPLEMENTING PROGRAMS AND INTERVENTIONS

Despite evidence that suggests GSD affirming programs and interventions may improve health outcomes and school experiences among GSD youth (Heck et al., 2013) by reducing prejudice, Meyer and Bayer (2013) reviewed how critics often cite First Amendment rights (i.e., freedom of speech and religion) in their fight against implementing affirming resources in school systems. To further complicate matters, educators within the public school system tend to have less freedom with regard to what they are allowed to say in the classroom because courts frequently defer to the school district for creating their curriculum (Dawson, 2019). Indeed, five states (Alabama, Louisiana, Mississippi, Oklahoma, and Texas) currently have "no promo homo" laws that prohibit educators from talking about homosexuality in the classrooms (GLSEN, n.d.-f; Meyer & Bayer, 2013), and two states (Alabama and Texas) require the curriculum to portray anything outside of heteronormative relationships as unacceptable (Lambda Legal, n.d.). These laws make teachers feel like they are prohibited from advocating for GSD students who report harassment and discrimination (Dawson, 2019). As a result of these no promo homo laws (also referred to as no pro homo laws), schools are creating a culture of intolerance, hostility, and bias that allows for legal discrimination against GSD individuals (Dawson, 2019).

Even within states that maintain anti-GSD laws (e.g., no promo homo laws), school officials must balance the First Amendment rights of their students with protection against violence and disruption (Dawson, 2019; Meyer & Bayer, 2013). A number of legal precedents can help teachers, administrators, and staff determine when their First Amendment rights are protected. According to Dawson (2019), based on the *Pickering v. Board of Education* (1968) and *Connick v. Myers* (1983) court cases, it is believed that public employees, such as teachers, have the freedom of speech when they are addressing a matter of public concern, such as homosexuality and the rights of GSD individuals, whereas private concerns would not be protected. If courts applied *Garcetti v. Ceballos* (2006) to the First Amendment rights of teachers, it may be determined that as public employees, they are not protected by the freedom of speech while they are on the job regardless of whether it is a matter of public concern (Dawson, 2019). Using the *Tinker v. Des Moines Independent Community School District* (1969) precedent, the belief that teaching about homosexuality and GSD individuals could cause a disturbance would not be a strong enough argument against evidence that anti-GSD laws have a negative impact on GSD students (Dawson, 2019). So, although some scholars have concluded that there are legal arguments to protect the First Amendment rights of teachers as well as implement affirming programs, other scholars have suggested that a U.S. Supreme Court ruling may be needed to formally protect the teacher's freedom of speech in terms of protecting GSD students (Dawson, 2019; Meyer & Bayer, 2013).

Even in states that do not place restrictions on school curricula, other challenges persist, such as lack of knowledge and skills to address the unique needs experienced by transgender and gender diverse youth as well as GSD students from racially and ethnically diverse backgrounds (Poteat & Scheer, 2016). All too often, the within-group differences among GSD individuals and communities are overlooked, and as a result, the unique needs and experiences of bisexual youth, racially and ethnically diverse GSD students, transgender and gender diverse individuals, as well as youth across different age groups, are not considered by educators, clinicians, and researchers. Indeed, research suggests that a large proportion of GSA advisors identify as cisgender, heterosexual, White women with limited training about GSD youth in general, let alone a feeling that they are not prepared to address the complexities associated with intersecting identities (Graybill et al., 2015; Poteat & Scheer, 2016). Despite gaps in knowledge and services, GSA advisors and educators can always seek out additional training, identify local resources, and create a more inclusive atmosphere for GSD youth across cultures. For instance, larger cities across the country often host Black pride (Center for Black Equity, n.d.) and Latinx pride (Latino GLBT History Project, n.d.-a) festivals as do community organizations that are devoted to racially and ethnically diverse GSD individuals.

It is not surprising that some teachers, administrators, staff, and students believe that improving the educational environment for GSD youth feels like an uphill battle. There may be legal issues, concerns about self-efficacy, and limited supports. However, experts across the country have come together to describe their experience with making schools safer and more affirming.

CONCLUSION

The 2014 Joint Resolution (APA & NASP, 2015) and the 2020 *Resolution on Supporting Sexual/Gender Diverse Children and Adolescents in Schools* (APA & NASP, 2020) provided updates to a 1993 policy (APA & NASP, 1993) that called for K–12 public schools to be safe and supportive for all students. Specifically, these updates not only explored the adverse outcomes and needs among lesbian, gay, and bisexual students, but they more broadly reflected on the risks and protective factors of students with diverse sexual orientations and gender identities. To help counselors, psychologists, teachers, administrators, and school staff implement the recommendations outlined in the 2014 Joint Resolution, APA created a series of fact sheets that are available for download:

- *How Educators Can Support Families With Gender Diverse and Sexual Minority Youth: Promoting Resiliency for Gender Diverse and Sexual Minority Students in Schools* (APA, 2015a)

- *Supporting Transgender and Gender Diverse Students in Schools: Key Recommendations for School Health Personnel* (APA, 2015e)

- *Supporting Transgender and Gender Diverse Students in Schools: Key Recommendations for School Administrators* (APA, 2015d)

- *School-Based Risk and Protective Factors for Gender Diverse and Sexual Minority Children and Youth: Improving School Climate* (APA, 2015c)

- *Key Terms and Concepts in Understanding Gender Diversity and Sexual Orientation Among Students* (APA, 2015b)

Since the ratification of the 2014 Joint Resolution (APA & NASP, 2015), there have been significant advances in research, laws and policies have been updated, and interventions have evolved. Other chapters in this book, along with the revised Joint Resolution (APA & NASP, 2020), will guide administrators, educators, and school personnel to the information and resources needed to make a difference in the lives of GSD youth.

TAKEAWAYS AND OPPORTUNITIES

- APA and NASP are devoted to helping school administrators, teachers, and staff create safe and affirming learning environments for GSD students.

- Resources are available to help administrators, teachers, and staff implement guidelines and recommendations, such as those from APA and NASP. Yet, numerous gaps in GSD youth-affirming services and educational materials remain.

- Do any local organizations in your area have resources specifically for GSD youth? If so, what are their areas of focus (e.g., inclusive language, safe spaces, intersecting identities)?

- What, if any, GSD youth-affirming issues is your local school board, city council, or county board of supervisors considering now? How might you best share information about it or get involved?

REFERENCES

American Psychological Association. (2015a). *How educators can support families with gender diverse and sexual minority youth: Promoting resiliency for gender diverse and sexual minority students in schools* [Fact sheet]. https://www.apa.org/pi/lgbt/programs/safe-supportive/lgbt/educators-families.pdf

American Psychological Association. (2015b). *Key terms and concepts in understanding gender diversity and sexual orientation among students* [Fact sheet] https://www.apa.org/pi/lgbt/programs/safe-supportive/lgbt/key-terms.pdf

American Psychological Association. (2015c). *School-based risk and protective factors for gender diverse and sexual minority children and youth: Improving school climate* [Fact sheet]. https://www.apa.org/pi/lgbt/programs/safe-supportive/lgbt/risk-factors.pdf

American Psychological Association. (2015d). *Supporting transgender and gender diverse students in schools: Key recommendations for school administrators* [Fact sheet]. https://www.apa.org/pi/lgbt/programs/safe-supportive/lgbt/school-administrators.pdf

American Psychological Association. (2015e). *Supporting transgender and gender diverse students in schools: Key recommendations for school health personnel* [Fact sheet]. https://www.apa.org/pi/lgbt/programs/safe-supportive/lgbt/health-personnel.pdf

American Psychological Association & National Association of School Psychologists. (1993). *Resolution on lesbian, gay, and bisexual youth in schools*. Available at https://www.nasp.online

American Psychological Association & National Association of School Psychologists. (2015). *Resolution on gender and sexual orientation diversity in children and adolescents in schools*. http://www.apa.org/about/policy/orientation-diversity.aspx

American Psychological Association & National Association of School Psychologists. (2020). *Resolution on supporting sexual/gender diverse children and adolescents in schools.* https://www.apa.org/pi/lgbt/resources/policy/gender-diverse-children

Ballard, M. E., Jameson, J. P., & Martz, D. M. (2017). Sexual identity and risk behaviors among adolescents in rural Appalachia. *Rural Mental Health, 41*(1), 17–29. https://doi.org/10.1037/rmh0000068

Center for Black Equality. (n.d.). *History: The Black pride movement and the Center for Black Equity.* https://centerforblackequity.org/about-us/history/

Center for Black Equity. (n.d.). *Black LGBTQ+PRIDES.* https://centerforblackequity.org/black-prides

Connick v. Myers, 461 U.S. 138 (1983).

Dawson, K. (2019). Teaching to the test: Determining the appropriate test for First Amendment challenges to "no promo homo" education policies. *Tennessee Journal of Law and Policy, 13*(2), Article 2.

De Pedro, K. T., Lynch, R. J., & Esqueda, M. C. (2018). Understanding safety, victimization and school climate among rural lesbian, gay, bisexual, transgender, and questioning (LGBTQ) youth. *Journal of LGBT Youth, 15*(4), 265–279. https://doi.org/10.1080/19361653.2018.1472050

Duran, A. (2019). "Outsiders in a niche group": Using intersectionality to examine resilience for queer students of color. *Journal of Diversity in Higher Education.* Advance online publication. https://doi.org/10.1037/dhe0000144

Family Acceptance Project. (n.d.-a). *Overview.* https://familyproject.sfsu.edu/overview

Family Acceptance Project. (n.d.-b). *Publications.* https://familyproject.sfsu.edu/publications

GAPA. (n.d.). *About us.* https://www.gapa.org/about-us#historyandpeople

Garcetti v. Ceballos, 547 U.S. 410 (2006).

Genders & Sexualities Alliance Network. (n.d.). *Mission, vision, & history.* https://gsanetwork.org/mission-vision-history/

GLSEN. (n.d.-a). *About us.* https://www.glsen.org/about-us#snt—1

GLSEN. (n.d.-b). *Changing the game: The GLSEN sports project.* https://www.glsen.org/programs/changing-game

GLSEN. (n.d.-c). *Day of silence.* https://www.glsen.org/day-of-silence

GLSEN. (n.d.-d). *GLSEN safe space kit.* https://www.glsen.org/activity/glsen-safe-space-kit-be-ally-lgbtq-youth

GLSEN. (n.d.-e). *No name-calling week.* https://www.glsen.org/no-name-calling-week

GLSEN. (n.d.-f). *"No promo homo" laws.* https://www.glsen.org/learn/policy/issues/nopromohomo

GLSEN. (n.d.-g). *Student and GSA resources.* https://www.glsen.org/resources/student-and-gsa-resources

GLSEN. (n.d.-h). *Support for student-led clubs.* http://live-glsen-website.pantheonsite.io/support-student-gsas

GLSEN. (n.d.-i). *10 steps to start your GSA.* https://www.glsen.org/sites/default/files/2019-11/GLSEN-10-Steps-To-Start-Your-GSA.pdf

Goldbach, J. T., & Gibbs, J. J. (2017). A developmentally informed adaptation of minority stress for sexual minority adolescents. *Journal of Adolescence, 55,* 36–50. https://doi.org/10.1016/j.adolescence.2016.12.007

Goodenow, C., Szalacha, L., & Westheimer, K. (2006). School support groups, other school factors, and the safety of sexual minority adolescents. *Psychology in the Schools, 43*(5), 573–589. https://doi.org/10.1002/pits.20173

Graybill, E. C., Varjas, K., Meyers, J., Dever, B. V., Greenberg, D., Roach, A. T., & Morillas, C. (2015). Demographic trends and advocacy experiences of gay–straight alliance advisors. *Journal of LGBT Youth, 12*(4), 436–461. https://doi.org/10.1080/19361653.2015.1077770

Greytak, E. A., Kosciw, J. G., & Diaz, E. M. (2009). *Harsh realities: The experiences of transgender youth in our nation's schools: Gay, Lesbian and Straight Education Network*. GLSEN. http://www.imatyfa.org/assets/harsh-realities.pdf

Grossman, A. H., & D'Augelli, A. R. (2006). Transgender youth: Invisible and vulnerable. *Journal of Homosexuality, 51*(1), 111–128. https://doi.org/10.1300/J082v51n01_06

Hatzenbuehler, M. L. (2011). The social environment and suicide attempts in lesbian, gay, and bisexual youth. *Pediatrics, 127*(5), 896–903. https://doi.org/10.1542/peds.2010-3020

Hatzenbuehler, M. L., Birkett, M., Van Wagenen, A., & Meyer, I. H. (2014). Protective school climates and reduced risk for suicide ideation in sexual minority youths. *American Journal of Public Health, 104*(2), 279–286. https://doi.org/10.2105/AJPH.2013.301508

Hatzenbuehler, M. L., & Pachankis, J. E. (2016). Stigma and minority stress as social determinants of health among lesbian, gay, bisexual, and transgender youth: Research evidence and clinical implications. *Pediatric Clinics, 63*(6), 985–997.

Hatzenbuehler, M. L., Shen, Y., Vandewater, E. A., & Russell, S. T. (2019). Proposition 8 and homophobic bullying in California. *Pediatrics, 143*(6), Article e20182116. https://doi.org/10.1542/peds.2018-2116

Heck, N. C., Flentje, A., & Cochran, B. N. (2013). Offsetting risks: High school gay–straight alliances and lesbian, gay, bisexual, and transgender (LGBT) youth. *Psychology of Sexual Orientation and Gender Diversity, 1*(S), 81–90. https://doi.org/10.1037/2329-0382.1.S.81

Hendricks, M. L., & Testa, R. J. (2012). A conceptual framework for clinical work with transgender and gender nonconforming clients: An adaptation of the minority stress model. *Professional Psychology, Research and Practice, 43*(5), 460–467. https://doi.org/10.1037/a0029597

Ioverno, S., Belser, A. B., Baiocco, R., Grossman, A. H., & Russell, S. T. (2016). The protective role of gay–straight alliances for lesbian, gay, bisexual, and questioning students: A prospective analysis. *Psychology of Sexual Orientation and Gender Diversity, 3*(4), 397–406. https://doi.org/10.1037/sgd0000193

It Gets Better Project. (n.d.-a). *About our global movement*. https://itgetsbetter.org/about/

It Gets Better Project. (n.d.-b). *Stories*. https://itgetsbetter.org/stories/

Lambda Legal. (n.d.). *#DontEraseUs: FAQ about anti-LGBT curriculum laws*. https://www.lambdalegal.org/dont-erase-us/faq

Latino GLBT History Project. (n.d.-a). *Latinx pride*. https://www.latinoglbthistory.org/latinx-pride

Latino GLBT History Project. (n.d.-b). *Our story*. https://www.latinoglbthistory.org/our-story

LGBT National Help Center. (n.d.-a). *About us*. https://www.glbthotline.org/about.html

LGBT National Help Center. (n.d.-b). *LGBT national hotline 888-843-4564*. https://www.glbthotline.org/national-hotline.html

LGBT National Help Center. (n.d.-c). *LGBT national online peer-support CHAT*. https://www.glbthotline.org/peer-chat.html

LGBT National Help Center. (n.d.-d). *LGBT national youth talkline 800-246-7743*. https://www.glbthotline.org/youth-talkline.html

LGBT National Help Center. (n.d.-e). *Youth CHAT ROOM lounge*. https://www.glbthotline.org/youthchatrooms.html

Lytle, M. C., Silenzio, V. M. B., Homan, C. M., Schneider, P., & Caine, E. D. (2018). Suicidal and help-seeking behaviors among youth in an online lesbian, gay, bisexual, transgender, queer, and questioning social network. *Journal of Homosexuality, 65*(13), 1916–1933. https://doi.org/10.1080/00918369.2017.1391552

Lytle, M. C., Vaughan, M. D., Rodriguez, E. M., & Shmerler, D. L. (2014). Working with LGBT individuals: Incorporating positive psychology into training and practice.

Psychology of Sexual Orientation and Gender Diversity, 1(4), 335–347. https://doi.org/10.1037/sgd0000064

Meyer, I. H. (2003). Prejudice, social stress, and mental health in lesbian, gay, and bisexual populations: Conceptual issues and research evidence. *Psychological Bulletin, 129*(5), 674–697. https://doi.org/10.1037/0033-2909.129.5.674

Meyer, I. H., & Bayer, R. (2013). School-based gay-affirmative interventions: First amendment and ethical concerns. *American Journal of Public Health, 103*(10), 1764–1771. https://doi.org/10.2105/AJPH.2013.301385

Palmer, N. A., Greytak, E. A., & Kosciw, J. (2016). *Educational exclusion: Drop out, push out, and the school-to-prison pipeline among LGBTQ youth.* GLSEN.

Pickering v. Board of Education, 391. U.S. 563 (1968).

Poteat, V. P., & Scheer, J. R. (2016). GSA advisors' self-efficacy related to LGBT youth of color and transgender youth. *Journal of LGBT Youth, 13*(4), 311–325. https://doi.org/10.1080/19361653.2016.1185757

Rajski, P. (Director). (1994). *TREVOR: The Trevor Project* [Film]. Randy Stone and Peggy Rajski.

Ryan, C., Russell, S. T., Huebner, D., Diaz, R., & Sanchez, J. (2010). Family acceptance in adolescence and the health of LGBT young adults. *Journal of Child and Adolescent Psychiatric Nursing, 23*(4), 205–213. https://doi.org/10.1111/j.1744-6171.2010.00246.x

Seligman, M. E., & Csikszentmihalyi, M. (2014). Positive psychology: An introduction. In *Flow and the foundations of positive psychology* (pp. 279–298). Springer.

Temkin, D., Belford, J., McDaniel, T., Stratford, B., & Parris, D. (2017, June). *Improving measurement of sexual orientation and gender identity among middle and high school students* (Publication No. 2017-22). Child Trends.

Tinker v. Des Moines Independent Community School District, 393 U.S. 503 (1969).

Toomey, R. B., Ryan, C., Diaz, R. M., Card, N. A., & Russell, S. T. (2010). Gender-nonconforming lesbian, gay, bisexual, and transgender youth: School victimization and young adult psychosocial adjustment. *Developmental Psychology, 46*(6), 1580–1589. https://doi.org/10.1037/a0020705

The Trevor Project. (n.d.-a). *About the Trevor Project.* https://www.thetrevorproject.org/about/

The Trevor Project. (n.d.-b). *Education.* https://www.thetrevorproject.org/education/

The Trevor Project. (n.d.-c). *Get help now.* https://www.thetrevorproject.org/get-help-now/

2

Advancing Gender and Sexually Diverse Students' Civil Rights

Leadership Efforts by Los Angeles Unified School District

Judy Chiasson

There has been a steady stream of shifting public sentiments in the United States toward gender and sexually diverse (GSD) individuals. "Homosexuality" was listed in the first edition of the *Diagnostic and Statistical Manual of Mental Disorders* (*DSM*; American Psychiatric Association, Committee on Nomenclature and Statistics, 1952) as a sociopathic personality disturbance, and 21 years later, this diagnosis was replaced with the less stigmatizing "ego-dystonic homosexuality" (Drescher, 2015; Lev, 2013). In the 1980 edition (third ed. [*DSM–III*]; American Psychiatric Association, 1980), "ego-dystonic homosexuality" was removed, and "gender identity disorder" was added to describe what was then called "transsexualism" (Koh, 2012). During the 2013 revision (fifth ed. [*DSM–5*]; American Psychiatric Association, 2013), "gender identity disorder" was renamed "gender dysphoria." The decision to maintain a diagnosis related to distress over gender identity was, in part, made to ensure that transgender and gender diverse individuals would maintain access to medically necessary treatment (Lev, 2013).

Social stigma has also decreased in conjunction with increases in legal rights for GSD individuals. In the 2003 landmark case of *Lawrence v. Texas*, the U.S. Supreme Court ruled that state laws banning consensual sexual activity between same-sex adults were unconstitutional because they violated the right to privacy. Since then, a number of statutes and constitutional decisions (e.g., the Matthew Shepard and James Byrd, Jr. Hate Crimes Prevention Act, 2009, expanding hate crimes to include gender, sexual orientation, gender

https://doi.org/10.1037/0000211-003
Supporting Gender Identity and Sexual Orientation Diversity in K–12 Schools, M. C. Lytle and R. A. Sprott (Editors)

25

identity, and disability; the *Obergefell v. Hodges* U.S. Supreme Court ruling in 2015 striking down state laws that banned same-sex marriage) have been enacted to protect GSD individuals. Despite impediments along the way, the parallel tracks of civil rights and social acceptance continue to advance in reciprocity with lessening stigma toward GSD communities.

Alongside the health care and legal systems, schools often serve as the flashpoint for many social movements. Thus, this chapter profiles significant court cases in achieving equity for GSD students. It also traces the challenges, successes, and strategies at one urban school district to create and sustain learning and working environments that are affirming of GSD identities and expressions of its students, staff, and families. The chapter ends with a discussion of emerging issues and opportunities for continued growth in schools' ability to promote civil rights.

HISTORIC COURT CASES IN K–12 EDUCATION

A series of court cases has prioritized students' rights over public sentiment. The seminal cases that gave students of color better access to education ultimately set precedents that paved the way for GSD students. *Mendez v. Westminster School District of Orange County* (1947) and *Brown v. Board of Education* (1954) told the country that separate was not equal and that all children had the right to be educated with their neighbors and without regard to skin color. In parts of the country, such as Little Rock, Arkansas, the court-ordered racial integration was met with such resistance that the National Guard was called to escort Black students to their classes (Mai, 2007).

Then in 1962, the U.S. Supreme Court affirmed students' rights over community norms again in *Engel v. Vitale* (1962),[1] holding that it was unconstitutional for schools to impose religion on the students. Similarly, in *Tinker v. Des Moines Independent Community School District* (1969),[2] the courts again held in favor of students' rights, in the often-quoted statement that students do not "shed their constitutional rights to freedom of speech or expression at the schoolhouse gate" (*Tinker v. Des Moines Independent Community School District*, 1969, pp. 733, 746). The Tinker case weighed schools' obligations to protect students' First Amendment rights against the schools' interest to prevent disruption. These opinions were instrumental in prioritizing students' rights and identities. The courts set a high bar that must be met to justify limitations of student expression.

---

[1]The opinion held that use of the prayer in schools violated the Establishment Clause of the First Amendment by breaching the constitutional wall of separation between church and state.
[2]The opinion held that "even a legitimate interest in school discipline does not outweigh a student's right to peacefully express his views in an appropriate time, place, and manner" (*Tinker v. Des Moines Independent Community School District*, 1969, p. 388).

One of the first GSD-related education cases that came into the national spotlight was that of Aaron Fricke. In 1980, Fricke wanted to bring his same-sex date to his high school prom. The school principal denied Fricke's request on the grounds of "real and present threat of physical harm to you, your male escort and to others . . ." (*Fricke v. Lynch*, 1980, p. 389). In the ensuing case, *Fricke v. Lynch* (1980), the District Court of Rhode Island held that the First Amendment mandated that Fricke had a free expression right in bringing his same-sex date to the prom. The school must not only allow Fricke and his male date to attend prom but also ensure their safety.

Despite the Fricke ruling, additional support was needed to protect GSD youth. Jamie Nabozny of Wisconsin was brutally and chronically victimized by his classmates throughout his middle and high school years. The schools reportedly took no disciplinary actions against the offenders and made no effort to ensure Nabozny's safety. One of the attacks was so vicious that he required surgery to correct his injuries. Ultimately, in 1996, the U.S. Court of Appeals for the Seventh Circuit held that the school district and the school officials had infringed on Nabozny's equal protection rights as guaranteed by the Fourteenth Amendment (*Nabozny v. Podlesny*, 1996) by not protecting him from the harassment and by limiting his access to education by changing his schedule.

Similar to Jamie Nabozny, Dylan Theno was subjected to chronic antigay harassment and assaults by his peers throughout his middle and high school years in Kansas. In 2005, the jury found that the Tonganoxie Unified School District had been deliberately indifferent to the abuse (*Theno v. Tonganoxie Unified School District No. 464*, 2005). However, unlike Nabozny, Theno's school had taken action against the offenders—just not at a level that effectively deterred repeat offenses. It is noteworthy that Theno identified as heterosexual. Thus, this ruling underscores the onus of schools for ensuring student safety and that the nature of the offense (e.g., homophobic in nature), not the identity of the target, is the determinant of bias.

Each of these rulings prioritized the rights of students over the prevailing attitudes at their schools. Federal acts, such as the Education for All Handicapped Children Act of 1975, the Every Student Succeeds Act (2015), its predecessor, No Child Left Behind Act of 2001, and a plethora of state and federal acts consistently compel schools to mitigate the barriers that prevent vulnerable and disenfranchised students from accessing the education to which they are entitled.

GSD-AFFIRMING POLICIES AND LEGISLATION

Two pieces of legislation catapulted Los Angeles Unified School District's (LAUSD's) GSD-affirming practices into the national spotlight. First, the California Senate Bill 48 of 2011, commonly known as the FAIR Education Act, called for *f*air, *a*ccurate, *i*nclusive, and *r*espectful inclusion of historical

GSD figures, such as Harvey Milk, Audre Lorde, Frida Kahlo, and Alan Turing, in history and social studies classes (FAIR Education Act, 2011). Because of its size and history of inclusive practices, leaders from LAUSD were invited to testify before the California Senate in support of the bill. In response, the school district received a barrage of calls and emails (mostly from out of state) from people who were concerned that teachers would be having sexually explicit conversations with young children. The callers were educated about the difference between identity and behavior and assured that schools have been teaching about historical figures since the 1800s without any mention of sexual activity.

Second, California Assembly Bill 1266 of 2013 was passed the next year. Known as the School Success and Opportunity Act, it requires that all students shall be permitted to participate in sex-segregated school activities and use facilities consistent with their affirmed gender identity without regard to their gender assigned at birth (School Success and Opportunity Act, 2013). The response was a tsunami of media attention and negative reactions from people (again mostly from out of state) who feared that cisgender female students would be preyed on by girls who had been assigned male at birth or by cisgender boys pretending to be transgender girls. Having had transgender-affirming policies since 2005, LAUSD was perfectly positioned to quell fears and offer evidence of success.

These cases are excellent illustrations that fear cannot be allowed to drive decisions when it comes to the dignity of students and that the voice of experience is vital in addressing resistance. Fostering diversity and inclusion is in the best interest of all children. Advocates must not be complacent because as the power pendulum will continue to swing, and hard-won gains for GSD individuals can quickly erode under less progressive leadership. For example, as of 2020, conversion therapy for minors, a discredited practice that seeks to change same-sex sexual orientation, is banned in 20 states (Human Rights Campaign, n.d.; Movement Advancement Project, n.d.). However, in September 2019, New York City repealed its ban on conversion therapy as a protective measure out of concern that the Supreme Court would hear the case and overturn all bans on conversion therapy (Mays, 2019).

LOS ANGELES UNIFIED SCHOOL DISTRICT: A LEADER IN GSD ADVOCACY

LAUSD is the second largest school district in the country. Its 1,300 schools educate more than 600,000 students who bring 102 different home languages from an area of 710 square miles. Ninety percent of the students identify as people of color, and 80% of the families are considered low income (*Los Angeles Unified Fingertip Facts, 2019–2020*, n.d.). LAUSD has a long history of advocating for GSD students, staff, and families. In the earliest days of advocacy, educational institutions and activist communities conceived of their work as addressing gay and lesbian concerns. Over the decades, the scope has expanded to recognize a wider breadth of sexual and gender diversities in addition to intersectionality with other identities. The many individual steps that the school district has taken are admirable, but their impact is that each step institutionalized a standard of a commitment amongst all stakeholders. This section highlights LAUSD's policies, procedures, and grassroots initiatives that have paved the way for school districts across the country to become safer and more affirming.

Making GSD Students Visible

There is no question that schools should take proactive efforts to support their GSD students. However, finding the students can be challenging. Sexual orientation and gender are self-declared identities that are confidential, and only a few states allow students to identify as non-binary. Such data are collected from parents when they complete a student enrollment form before their child begins school. The parents' representation of their child's sexual orientation and gender identity may not accurately reflect how the child actually does (or will later) identify. In 2019, LAUSD revised the student enrollment forms to ask parents or guardians about their child's sex and gender, and included intersex and non-binary as additional options.

The coming out process begins with an emerging awareness, followed by ever expanding circles of openness, so asking the student to self-identify has its own shortcomings. There can be incongruity between students' affinities, behaviors, and labels. A youth may be having exclusively same-sex romantic or sexual relationships, or both, but continues to identify as mostly hetero-sexual (Guittar, 2014; Savin-Williams, 2017; Thompson & Morgan, 2008). Surveys are just a snapshot in time; thus, school questionnaires must ask the right questions at the right time for students to feel comfortable enough to disclose their identities.

The U.S. Department of Education's Office of Civil Rights also requires school districts to collect data on identity-based bullying and discrimination. Discrimination is widely considered to be underreported, and school-based discrimination data related to sexual orientation and gender identity are especially elusive. Schools tend to code incidents as generic bullying or sexual harassment unless the incident is blatantly homophobic *and* the target is an openly GSD student. Schools are cautious about outing or stigmatizing targeted students as well as hesitant to add the enhancement of "bias-motivated" unless they are certain that the hostility was motivated solely by prejudice. To capture information on students' identity group affiliation, which may change over their course of their school career, LAUSD found it helpful to solicit feedback directly from the families served by the schools and to do so multiple times. LAUSD (n.d.-b) gives its *School Experience Survey* annually to parents, teachers, and students Grades 4 through 12. Respondents are queried about academics; school climate; bullying; school safety; social emotional learning; and at the secondary level, sexual and gender identities.

The 2018 *School Experience Survey* (LAUSD, n.d.-a) showed that 8.3% of high school students and 5.6% of middle school students identified as "lesbian, gay, bisexual, transgender and/or queer." National data consistently cite that GSD students feel disproportionately unsafe at school (Berlan et al., 2010; Parent et al., 2020; Shramko et al., 2019). Yet, a surprising finding on LAUSD's (n.d.-a) *School Experience Survey* was the slight differences in ratings of feeling safe at school between GSD and heterosexual students. Approximately 59% of GSD and 64% of heterosexual high school students said that they feel safe at school. At the middle school level, that safe rating was given by 64% of GSD and 67% of heterosexual students. Additional research is being conducted to isolate the protective factors (e.g., "I feel close to people at this school"; "Adults at this school treat people with respect") that are particularly meaningful to GSD students.

Using the Youth Risk Behavior Survey

The *Youth Risk Behavior Survey* (YRBS) is among the few federal surveys that measure the health conditions of GSD students. This survey, conducted by the Centers for Disease Control and Prevention (CDC), monitors health-related behaviors that contribute to the leading causes of death and disability among youth. Their findings report that in all focus areas of the study—high-risk substance use, violence victimization, mental health, and suicide—lesbian, gay, bisexual, and questioning students (i.e., endorsed a sexual orientation of gay, lesbian, bisexual, or not sure) had significantly higher risk rates than their heterosexual classmates in the decade between 2007 and 2017 (CDC, Division of Adolescent and School Health, n.d.). Unfortunately, the data have not changed over time as much as one would expect. An analysis of the YRBS data between 2005 and 2017 found a notable decrease in the prevalence of nonsuicidal self-injury among heterosexual youth but only a slight decrease in the same behavior among sexually diverse youth (Liu, 2019).

In 2017, LAUSD was among the first districts to pilot the YRBS with newly added questions on transgender identity (Johns et al., 2019). Compared with cisgender males and cisgender females, transgender students were more likely to report multiple risk factors. Almost 24% had been forced to have sexual intercourse, and 26.4% had experienced dating violence. The rates of suicide risk, use of drugs and alcohol, number of sexual partners, age of first sexual encounter, and lack of safer sex practices among transgender youth were significantly higher than those of their cisgender peers (Johns et al., 2019). Moreover, 66% of the GSD high school students reported being so sad that they stopped doing their usual activities (Romero, 2018). Although researchers and scholars across the country often use aggregated YRBS data to learn about the experiences of youth, LAUSD has used the YRBS data from its district to improve its school system. The school district has developed a number of actionable items, such as GSD competency trainings for educators and mental health practitioners, visibility campaigns, and more all-user restrooms to promote more affirming learning environments.

Instituting Initiatives to Promote Protective Factors Among GSD Youth

Data on the risk factors of GSD youth make compelling headlines and trigger passionate responses but often fail to inform best practices. It is infinitely more productive to focus on solutions than merely pointing out the short-comings. Not to discount those who are suffering, but in the long run, most GSD youth are—or will be—just fine. There is a growing body of research examining the protective factors for GSD youth that can lead the work of change agents. Indeed, supportive families (Ryan et al., 2010), the presence of a genders and sexualities alliance (GSA), an acronym that has referred to "gay–straight alliance" but more recently refers to "gender and sexuality alliance" or "genders and sexualities alliance" (Toomey et al., 2011), openly affirming staff (Kosciw et al., 2018), support groups on campus (Goodenow et al., 2006), enumerated policies (Russell et al., 2016), GSD-inclusive curriculum (Russell et al., 2006), having a romantic partner (Baams et al., 2014), and having a peer group (Snapp et al., 2015) are all associated with more positive outcomes for GSD students. With the exception of romantic partners, schools can reasonably institute these affirming initiatives. Schools can facilitate support groups for parents and for students, ensure that their curricula and policies are inclusive of GSD-persons and issues, be vocal advocates of GSD-students and concerns, and encourage the formation of GSAs. The recommended protective factors are all within the wheelhouse of education.

Schools can never rest on their laurels. Every advancement toward affirming GSD identities has been achieved by dedicated visionaries who pressed forward through reluctance, resistance, and opposition. Their commendable accomplishments serve as stepping-stones on the path for continued growth. Educational institutions must prepare students to flourish in a pluralistic society and master skills for a future that can barely be imagined. New programs and initiatives must navigate and reconfigure organizational structures. These unchartered territories have inherent challenges and missteps. School leaders may feel like the world is changing so quickly that they are building their planes in the air, as evidenced by the LAUSD-sponsored examples listed that follow.

Project 10

Project 10 provided education and support services for GSD students by establishing confidential support groups at schools and assisting school staff to implement policies that positively impact queer students. Project 10 was born in 1984 at Fairfax High School in Los Angeles, where a student confided in his teacher, Virginia Uribe, that he had been kicked out of his house for being gay. This was his fourth high school, and he was considering dropping out because of the intolerable harassment from his classmates and lack of support by school administrators. Uribe thought that was unconscionable and stepped up to support the student. More and more GSD students gravitated to her classroom, seeing Uribe as oasis of acceptance in an inhospitable campus. Many already knew and trusted her as the faculty sponsor for the Black Student

Union. The group coalesced and became the country's first formal support group for lesbian and gay students. They named themselves Project 10 in recognition of the popular statistic from the Kinsey (1948) study that 10% of the population was gay (Uribe, 1993; V. Uribe, personal communication, February 8, 2019).

Uribe's consistently clear and uncontestable message resonated with every educator. Interviewed for this chapter shortly before her death, she shared the guiding light of her work:

> Every young person has a right to a sense of self-respect and dignity. In public education, we serve the needs of all our students. Some are gay and lesbian, and we need to serve them, too. We're supposed to be teaching them to live in an increasingly diverse society. This shouldn't be a place where prejudice is fostered; it's where discrimination should be fought. (V. Uribe, personal communication, February 8, 2019)

Models of Pride

Uribe's vision continued to grow. In 1993, she collaborated with LAUSD's Gay and Lesbian Commission to offer the first Models of Pride, a full-day conference for GSD youth. Initially, the youth would slip out of their homes with a fabricated story about where they were going. Over time, the teachers started to accompany their students, and then parents started arriving. By 2000, teachers and parents had their own strands of workshops. Models of Pride continues under the leadership of the Los Angeles LGBT Center (Los Angeles LGBT [Lesbian, Gay, Bisexual, and Transgender] Center, n.d.). It is advertised as the world's largest free conference for GSD youth and allies. In 2019, 1,438 youth and 507 parents and professionals were offered a selection of 156 different workshops over 1 full day (D. Perez, Los Angeles LGBT Center, personal communication, October 27, 2019). The Youth Track offered workshops on such topics as meditation, yoga, community and political activism, gender fluidity, and bisexuality. The Parent and Professional Institute offered workshops in Spanish and English on faith, parenting of GSD youth, substance abuse, affirming classrooms, and more. Most of the youth attendees are in high school, but the number of middle school students attending has steadily increased such that the organizers are designing special workshops for that age group.

Gay Prom

Uribe believed that her students should enjoy the same high school celebrations as anyone else. Friends of Project 10 (the nonprofit arm of LAUSD's Project 10) held its first gay prom in 1994. The event came under harsh attack by Lou Sheldon of the Traditional Values Coalition. "Project 10 is clearly a recruitment program," Sheldon said. "It advocates for young people the homosexual life style. Why should taxpayers' dollars support only one life style?" (Quintanilla, 1989, para. 33). Sheldon and others picketed the prom and pressured the California State Assembly Education Committee to withhold funds from LAUSD if they did not disband Project 10. However, Uribe had already secured the trust of the Los Angeles Unified School Board. The board held firm in its support of Project 10, and the threatened sanctions never materialized (Friends of Project 10, n.d.).

IMPACT

Project 10 eventually became institutionalized in LAUSD and was expanded to high schools throughout the school district. Teachers were trained to facilitate themed therapeutic support groups for students who were disengaged because of a variety of stressors, such as grief, substance abuse, and emerging sexual and gender identities. The Project 10 curriculum focused on resiliency, self-esteem, healthy relationships, and self-advocacy for GSD students. The program dissipated when funding was lost in 2010 but is currently under consideration for reinstatement.

ENTRY POINTS FOR CREATING SUPPORTIVE SCHOOLS AND ENVIRONMENTS

Schools are well-positioned to address the disproportionalities that plague GSD youth. For some youth, school may be their only oasis of safety and acceptance. Many of the lessons learned from LAUSD over the years can be summed up this way: A healthy school environment for GSD youth requires that staff members be equipped to support students and families in their journeys.

Staff need to have nuanced conversations with GSD youth that bolster them against the toxins of bias while not inadvertently promoting shame or justifying that bias. Staff also need to watch for elevated risk factors without pathologizing the GSD populations. In addition, before doling out harsh punishments to students who perpetuate antigay harassment, schools should pause to consider whether that student's offensive act may be a manifestation of their struggle with their own gender or sexual identity. It's complicated.

Schools reside inside the larger macrocosm of the student's world; the education system is not the only component of children's welfare. Families are children's first teachers; therefore, the influence of families cannot be minimized. When GSD youth have strong and affirming family relations, the elevated risk factors associated with GSD youth can be dramatically minimized, and they can enjoy physical and mental well-being (Ryan et al., 2010; Snapp et al., 2015; Travers et al., 2012). Indeed, Caitlyn Ryan's landmark Family Acceptance Project compared the health outcomes of LGBT youth with accepting families to those with rejecting families. Ryan identified family rejection as the significant determinant in a host of risk factors, including low self-esteem, risky sexual behavior, substance abuse, and suicidal ideations and attempts (Ryan et al., 2009).

The parents' journeys should not be overlooked in this narrative. Coming out is a major landmark in a person's journey toward authenticity. A young person's assertion catapults their family into their own journey. The family must recalibrate their image of their child and their future. Some families turn into fierce allies; for others, the path is more challenging. There can be friction when family members progress at different paces. While parents are navigating their own processes, they also worry about their child who is now identified with a stigmatized minority that has among the highest rates of being targeted with bullying, engaging in risky behavior, and struggling with suicide ideation as well as suicide attempts. Therefore, school staff are often called on to not only support GSD youth but their families as well.

Thus far, this chapter has outlined laws, policies, and procedures that help make schools more affirming and safer environments. The long-abiding advocacy work of LAUSD exemplifies how school districts can respond to the educational disparities experienced by GSD youth. The next sections provide details about how your school district can take action—specifically, what types of changes to focus on and relational strategies for carrying out change.

Recommended Targets for Change

Inclusive policies, forms, and curriculum represent powerful targets for change because they benefit not only GSD students and families but the entire school community. School districts should ensure that all their policies that somehow address orientation or identity are inclusive. LAUSD, for example, has 22 policies and hundreds of forms that bear some reference to sexual orientation or gender identity. Enrollment forms, dress code policies, student identification cards, homecoming and prom events, and overnight field trips are just a few of the many opportunities for inclusion and affirmation.

Policies

Policies communicate the philosophy of an organization. They translate case law, regulations and legislation, and education code into a language that is familiar to its members. Policies are the guiding principles in the trifecta of policy, practice, and accountability through which all actions must be evaluated. Policies should be enumerated and cite specific protocol that recognizes diverse genders and sexualities. Districts must then ensure that the policies are followed with fidelity by all relevant stakeholders.

Policy writers must engage in a continual feedback loop with critical stakeholders to ensure that the policies accurately represent the needs of the schools and comply with state and federal regulations. Before launching its Sexual Orientation Gender Identity/Expression Affirming Schools Project, LAUSD solicited input from stakeholders by hosting listening sessions with students, staff, families, community agencies, and academics. The listening sessions provided a valuable opportunity for stakeholders to lend their voices to the direction of the district.

A synergistic approach is imperative to lead and sustain affirming campuses. School district leaders wishing to support affirming learning and working environments can ensure that all relevant policies are enumerated to include sexual orientation and gender identity and expression. By specifically naming the protected categories of actual or perceived sexual orientation, gender, and gender identity along with sex, race, ethnicity, ancestry, nationality, national origin, religion, color, ability status, age, and immigration status, people are prompted to think broadly about supporting bias-free environments. The following are some specific policies to address the needs of GSD students along with suggestions for useful approaches.

Non-Binary Students

Several states allow people to officially identify as non-binary. Essentially, schools are expected to treat transgender and gender diverse students like any other youth without regard to their gender assigned at birth. Non-binary identities challenge current gender binary practices. School districts must revisit their restroom, locker room, and athletic policies to ensure that they accommodate gender diverse students. Gender diversity is unexplored territory in K–12 education, and all too often, educators seek guidance from outside arenas—guidance that may provide solutions that do not translate well to children and teens.

The world of athletics is wrestling with how to recognize transgender and gender diverse athletes. For example, Caster Semenya is a two-time Olympic champion who identifies as a cisgender woman. Yet, because of her exceptional athleticism and physical appearance, Semenya has faced brutal scrutiny and been forced to undergo gender verification tests. In 2019, the Swiss Supreme Court ruled that to compete in certain events of the 2020 Olympics, Semenya must take hormone suppressants to counter her naturally high levels of testosterone and "preserve the integrity of women's sports" (Longman, 2019). In addition, some athletes are encouraging athletic institutions at all levels to rethink their guidelines and to become more inclusive of non-binary and gender diverse individuals. Lauren Lubin was not only the first non-binary individual to compete in the New York City Marathon, but they started the We Exist movement (https://www.facebook.com/WeExistMovement/; *About*, n.d.) and produced the *We Exist: Beyond the Binary* film (Seger, 2018) to advocate for more inclusiveness in sports. Similarly, G Ryan is a genderqueer college athlete who has successfully helped their university become more inclusive by adding all-gender restrooms and using gender-neutral language. For instance, G Ryan's swim squad was referred to as "Team 43" instead of "the women's team" (Dockray, 2018).

Dress Codes

Schools' dress code policies often disproportionately regulate feminine and urban expression and violate federal guidelines of nondiscrimination (Jones, 2018). Dress code policies should hold the standard of gender neutrality by regulating the clothing, regardless of wearer. Students cannot be prohibited from wearing what may be considered traditionally female or male attire based on the gender they were assigned at birth.

Affirmed Name and Gender

Policies should clearly state that all staff are required to model affirming language and use students' affirmed names and pronouns. Student identification cards, diplomas, and graduation ceremonies should recognize students by their affirmed names and pronouns regardless of what is used on official enrollment records or transcripts.

Access to Facilities and Activities

Restroom, locker room, and athletics policies should specify that students have access to facilities and activities according to their affirmed gender identity. Accommodations must be made for anyone who desires a more private setting for changing or toileting. Most importantly, transgender and gender diverse students cannot be forced to use single-user restrooms or gendered facilities that do not align with their gender identity. Accommodations can also be made in locker rooms, such as privacy curtains for dressing as well as thoughtful selection of the location of the student's locker and the students with adjacent lockers. Coaches do not need to be inside the dressing area in the locker room, but they do need to remain in close enough proximity that they can quickly respond if something goes awry.

Restroom access is one of the most common concerns of gender diverse youth. They vacillate between feeling uncomfortable in one restroom (typically the girls') and feeling unsafe in the other (typically the boys') but do not want to be stigmatized by using the nurses' bathroom. Many prefer private or all-user facilities. State building codes establish a ratio of sex-segregated toilets that must be allotted per student and per adult based on the size of the campus and the number of users. If a school exceeds the baseline number of toilets, they may convert excess multiple-user restrooms to all-gender. Any staff member may provide supervision in an all-user restroom because adults must be able to access the child in the event of a critical situation.

Forms and Instructional Materials

The materials must use language that recognizes GSD among students, staff, and families. Materials also must guard against using exclusively cisnormative and heteronormative representations in vignettes that are used as teaching tools for instruction and for bullying, sexual harassment, or child abuse trainings. All parent forms should recognize diversity by allowing caregivers to select among several options that best represent them, such as mother, father, parent, guardian, or caregiver. If salutations are offered, include the non-gendered title *Mx.*

Many children are vocal about their gender diversity from a young age. Student enrollment forms should inquire as to the child's affirmed name and pronoun. Schools should not only provide information to parents on how the school supports gender diverse children but provide training to teachers, staff, and administrators about how to create an affirming environment for students of all ages. Gender Spectrum (http://www.genderspectrum.org) and Human

Rights Campaign's *Schools in Transition* (Human Rights Campaign, n.d.) are excellent resources on creating gender-affirming schools.

Curriculum

The curriculum must reflect the population it serves. Youth find it empowering to see themselves and their stories embedded in the curriculum (de los Ríos et al., 2015). Years ago, there was a paucity of books about GSD identities. In 2005, LAUSD could not find a health book that was affirming of both sexual and gender diversity; therefore, the school district worked with Holt, Rinehart and Winston publishing company to write a chapter on sexual and gender identities ourselves, and we scrubbed the book for cisheterosexism. LAUSD felt it was important that the book spoke to our GSD students of color so the personal stories and images reflected our students' lived experiences (Chiasson, 2005).

Since then, the California Healthy Youth Act (2016), enacted in January 2016, requires comprehensive sexual health education for all secondary students that is medically accurate and promotes healthy attitudes concerning sexual orientation and gender identity. Today, GSD-inclusive books number in the thousands. The selections have expanded with themes and stories that include multiple ethnic, racial, religious, and linguistic identities and family structures. It is important to remember that diversity education benefits all students—not just the target group. Even if there are no known GSD-identified students in a teacher's particular class, it is guaranteed that children will interact with GSD people in school, in the community, in the workplace, and even in their own families. It is important that students develop cultural competencies to create affirming spaces for themselves and their peers.

LAUSD also hosts an annual OUT for Safe Schools campaign. Each year brings a new theme to targeted stakeholders. The inaugural 2013 launch was the creation and distribution of thousands of OUT for Safe Schools badges for staff to represent themselves as allies. The badges have since been adopted by school districts across the country. Subsequent years have included other OUT for Safe Schools branded materials, such as whistles for coaches in Blow The Whistle on Hate campaign; Read the Stories bookmarks with reading lists as well as posters for librarians; calendars with GSD-related events in the Know Your History campaign; pronoun buttons in the My Pronouns Are campaign; and a showcase of student artists' representation of GSD diversity in the 20/20 Vision for 2020 campaign. Among the pieces from the 2020 campaign are *Colors Are for Everyone*, which is an impressive mural of rainbow-hued butterflies painted by a kindergarten class. A middle school student drew a poignant self-portrait of themselves looking in a mirror. One rendering is visibly female; the reflection is visibly male. They titled the piece *No One Knows Who I Really Am*.

Recommended Strategies for Change-Making

There are several approaches to building collaborative relationships with teachers and school officials. Ethics guide staff on what they *should* do, mandates guide staff on what they *must* do, and practical applications show the *how*. Awareness is just one leg of a three-legged stool. People are more receptive to messages that align with their personal and professional standards. Always begin with the shared commitment to the ethics that guide our practice. Teachers have a front-row seat to witness how affirming practices can enhance a child's self-esteem and school connectedness. Personal stories often touch teachers' hearts. Knowledge of legal and policy mandates empowers administrators to both direct their staff and justify their actions.

Become a Resource

K–12 educators must take the initiative to learn about the populations they serve. Teachers are professional lifelong learners. They should seek out opportunities to learn about GSD history, symptoms of minority stress and stigma management, and strategies to build resiliency among vulnerable students and families.

Be a Champion

Critics are typically quite vocal and purport to represent the entire school community. Schools rarely receive complimentary phone calls and emails. Thus, school personnel need to know that other parents applaud the teachers' and school's efforts to be GSD inclusive and affirming. Acknowledge the school's achievements and offer to help them enhance their success.

School board members are elected officials who are accountable to the constituents they serve. School boards can be influential in promoting positive and affirming attitudes. The same recommendations given regarding working with school staff apply to working with board members. Above all, the school officials need to be assured that GSD-affirming practices solve problems rather than create them.

Most important, school and district leaders must be vocal advocates for GSD students, staff, and families. Many GSD students and families do not ask for help because they anticipate rejection. It is incumbent on the school leaders to ensure that the schools' commitment to affirming campuses and classrooms is known to all stakeholders. Visibly out GSD staff can be invaluable role models, offsetting some students' fears that they are all alone.

Set the Tone

School districts have a multitude of stakeholders with vested interests in supporting the inclusion of GSD topics and influencing the experiences of GSD students, staff, and families. Students and staff may hesitate to advocate at their sites, waiting for a signal from school leadership that their efforts will be welcomed. Conversely, school administrators may perceive silence as a lack of interest. Systemic change is optimized when all parties take the initiative to use a multiprong approach that targets multiple entry points. Too many schools are stymied when the leadership and the stakeholders wait on each other to make the first move.

There are undoubtedly schools in which biased attitudes and behaviors proliferate. There are also many schools that espouse affirming attitudes.

Unfortunately, most students do not report incidents of GSD-biased bullying or harassment to their school officials. They may be embarrassed, fear retaliation, fear being outed, or doubt if staff would be willing or able to resolve the issue (Kosciw et al., 2018). Either way, that silence can mislead the school officials into believing that all is copacetic. Schools are obligated to take definitive actions when they have a reasonable suspicion that a student has been targeted with bias, bullying, or harassment. It is also critical that schools build climates of trust and systems of communication so all parties can realize the school they imagine.

Creating affirming schools is the task of all members of the community. The school should actively work with staff and students to prominently place GSD identity in the school's actions and initiatives. GSD-related events should be included on the district calendar along with other commemorative dates. For example, November is American Indian/Alaska Native Heritage Month *and* Transgender Day of Remembrance; October is Latino Heritage Month *and* LGBT History Month; May recognizes Asian American and Pacific Islander Heritage *and* Harvey Milk Day. These events should be displayed prominently on the schools' bulletin boards, in newsletters, on the marquee, and on the website home page.

Work With School Staff

Virginia Uribe, mentioned earlier, was a maverick and champion of GSD students. Much of her success resulted from her uncanny ability to frame the message in manner that was obvious and indisputable, for example, that public schools are obligated to educate all students and cannot discriminate. She secured the support of her school and district administrators in advance of any pushback and helped them become heroes for youth. Advocates should garner support from administration by advising them of both developing issues and viable responses.

Teachers are more likely to address GSD topics with students if they feel confident in their skills and are supported by their colleagues (Bryk et al., 2015). Build staff members' capacity by teaching strategies on how to respond to delicate situations. For example, the principal or teacher may need to respond to an assertion that GSD-inclusive content is offensive. One response may be to open dialogue with the person to assuage their concerns. Another response may be to present the education code and district policies that call for the curriculum. Yet another option may be to talk about the importance that all children see themselves and their families in the curriculum and that the school wants to offset insensitive remarks made by classmates. Each strategy has its merit, and the options capacitate the staff member's confidence in responding to an incident.

Start a Genders and Sexualities Alliance

Students who desire to start a GSA should follow the same protocols as any other club on campus. Some GSAs are social in nature, whereas others take on more of an activist or support lens. The school environment can be an oasis of safety or a sentence in purgatory. As stated previously, GSAs have long been a litmus for a number of protective factors. Students in schools with a GSA represent their schools as being safer and more affirming; as providing more buffers against negative experiences; and as having higher student attendance and academic achievement than do students in schools without a GSA (Baams et al., 2018; Kosciw et al., 2018; Poteat et al., 2016). The presence of a GSA ripples throughout the campus and empowers all students to stand up to bias they may encounter (Lapointe, 2015). The benefits of participating in a GSA continue into adulthood (Toomey et al., 2011). But a GSA cannot bear the full burden of school change; it must be an integral component of a larger comprehensive system of support and advocacy (Griffin & Ouellett, 2002).

GSAs are protected under federal guidelines. Nevertheless, there can be hurdles and misconceptions. Some school administrators try to skirt the federal protections afforded to student groups by imposing onerous and discriminatory requirements on GSAs. For instance, in November 2018, Leo Junior/Senior High School in Indiana prohibited its GSA from using the word "gay" in their name or announcements, wanted a list of all members, and censored its announcements and activities. The parties ultimately settled, and the group was allowed to call itself "Leo GSA" (*Leo Pride Alliance v. East Allen County Schools*, 2019).

CONCLUSION

Complex problems need complex solutions. In an ideal world, all schools and all families are affirming, and GSD-diverse students can enjoy an educational experience that is no different from any other with the typical discoveries, challenges, and ups and downs in their journeys to adulthood. Schools have changed dramatically for GSD students. Twenty years ago, few would have imagined having openly queer principals, teachers, and board members; homecoming courts with transfeminine and transmasculine students; and GSD couples being voted the cutest couple on campus. Many communities have discontinued their gay proms because their queer students are perfectly comfortable at their home school's prom. However, there is still work to be done.

As discussed previously, despite having supportive families, friends, and schools, many of our GSD students still struggle (Aragon et al., 2014). In our current gendered society, non-binary, gender-expansive, agender, and transgender students may feel anxious navigating gendered social or physical spaces. Schools must support students in gaining confidence, managing anxiety, and navigating the social hiccups that inevitably arrive.

Increased awareness of microaggressions, implicit bias, cultural humility, and political as well as emotional correctness has lowered the social acceptability of offenses that would have been tolerated in the past. This awareness is good in the sense that there is an increased social value to be sensitive and caring. At the same time, it is unreasonable to expect that everyone can master the nuances of language and norms for a group to which they do not belong. The vocabulary for sexual and gender diversity is in constant revision. A term that was affirming yesterday may be offensive tomorrow. Missteps and awkward moments will occur. Progress will require that we all embrace our roles as kind teachers and eager learners and help each other be our best in an increasingly diverse society.

As with most social trends, there are divides. Generally speaking, older and more conservative people lean toward perceiving sexual orientation as a behavior, whereas younger and more liberal people perceive it as an identity (Hart-Brinson, 2018). The differences in perception often correlate with levels of acceptance and may influence the approach you take to create an affirming educational environment. The more people view sexual orientation and gender identity as innate, the more likely they are to have accepting attitudes (Rachmilovitz, 2017). Pew Research Center (2019) found that Americans' attitudes toward same-sex marriage have steadily improved since 2002 across all generational, racial, religious, and political groups.

As a country, we continue to evolve and redefine how to be global citizens. The goal of education is to support lifelong learning and prepare students for a future we cannot imagine. Our teachers and students need the skills to ask questions, learn from each other, and exemplify cultural competencies as they create the world they envision.

TAKEAWAYS AND OPPORTUNITIES

- Remember that courts prioritize student rights over public sentiment. Schools have an ethical obligation to prepare students to be thriving and contributing members of an increasingly diverse world. Ultimately, schools can be oases of safety for GSD youth and beacons for the future.

- Policy, practice, and accountability are the trinity through which all actions must be evaluated.

- Which staff members in your district are known to exemplify GSD-affirming schools and classrooms? What are their promising practices in supporting students? Do leaders acknowledge their efforts?

- What GSD-affirming (or nonaffirming) policies, practices, and accountability measures are in place in your school district now? Are you aware of current efforts to update any of them?

REFERENCES

About. (n.d.). Lauren Lubin. http://www.laurenlubin.com/about/

American Psychiatric Association. (1980). *Diagnostic and statistical manual of mental disorders* (3rd ed.). American Psychiatric Press.

American Psychiatric Association. (2013). *Diagnostic and statistical manual of mental disorders* (5th ed.). American Psychiatric Publishing.

American Psychiatric Association, Committee on Nomenclature and Statistics. (1952). *Diagnostic and statistical manual: Mental disorders.* American Psychiatric Association Mental Hospital Service.

Aragon, S. R., Poteat, V. P., Espelage, D. L., & Koenig, B. W. (2014). The influence of peer victimization on educational outcomes for LGBTQ and non-LGBTQ high school students. *Journal of LGBT Youth, 11*(1), 1–19. https://doi.org/10.1080/19361653.2014.840761

Baams, L., Bos, H. M. W., & Jonas, K. J. (2014). How a romantic relationship can protect same-sex attracted youth and young adults from the impact of expected rejection. *Journal of Adolescence, 37*(8), 1293–1302. https://doi.org/10.1016/j.adolescence.2014.09.006

Baams, L., Pollitt, A. M., Laub, C., & Russell, S. T. (2018). Characteristics of schools with and without gay–straight alliances. *Applied Developmental Science,* 1–6. https://doi.org/10.1080/10888691.2018.1510778

Berlan, E. D., Corliss, H. L., Field, A. E., Goodman, E., & Austin, S. B. (2010). Sexual orientation and bullying among adolescents in the growing up today study. *Journal of Adolescent Health, 46*(4), 366–371. https://doi.org/10.1016/j.jadohealth.2009.10.015

Brown v. Board of Education, 347 U.S. 483, 74 S. Ct. 686, 98 L. Ed. 873 (1954). https://www.courtlistener.com/opinion/105221/brown-v-board-of-education/

Bryk, A. S., Gomez, L. M., Grunow, A., & LeMahieu, P. G. (2015). *Learning to improve: How America's schools can get better at getting better.* Harvard Education Press.

California Healthy Youth Act, Cal. Educ. Code §§ 51930–51939 (2016).

Centers for Disease Control and Prevention, Division of Adolescent and School Health. (n.d.). *Youth Risk Behavior Survey: Data summary & trends report, 2007–2017.* https://www.cdc.gov/healthyyouth/data/yrbs/pdf/trendsreport.pdf

Chiasson, J. (2005). The diversity of relationships. In D. Neiman, R. Cole, J. Chiasson, R. Loya, M. Fischer, B. Brownell, E. McPeak Gilsan, L. Gaul, J. Altobelli, & K. Young (Contributors), *Sexuality and society* (pp. 92–99). Holt, Rinehart and Winston.

de los Ríos, C. V., López, J., & Morrell, E. (2015). Toward a critical pedagogy of race: Ethnic studies and literacies of power in high school classrooms. *Race and Social Problems, 7*(1), 84–96. https://doi.org/10.1007/s12552-014-9142-1

Dockray, H. (2018, March 26). *How the Olympics can embrace non-binary athletes for the future.* Mashable. https://mashable.com/2018/02/26/olympics-non-binary-genderqueer-athletes/

Drescher, J. (2015). Queer diagnoses revisited: The past and future of homosexuality and gender diagnoses in *DSM* and ICD. *International Review of Psychiatry, 27*(5), 386–395. https://doi.org/10.3109/09540261.2015.1053847

Education for All Handicapped Children Act of 1975, Pub. L. No. 94–142 (1975). Renamed the Individuals With Disabilities Education Improvement Act, codified at 20 U.S.C. §§ 1400–1482.

Engel v. Vitale, 370 U.S. 421, 82 S. Ct. 1261, 8 L. Ed. 601 (1962). https://www.courtlistener.com/opinion/106443/engel-v-vitale/

Every Student Succeeds Act, 20 U.S.C § 6301 (2015). https://www.congress.gov/114/plaws/publ95/PLAW-114publ95.pdf

Fair Education Act, Cal. Educ. Code §§ 51204.5, 51500, 51501, 60040, and 60044 (2011).

Fricke v. Lynch, 491 F. Supp. 381, 385 (D.R.I. 1980). https://law.justia.com/cases/federal/district-courts/FSupp/491/381/1799237/

Friends of Project 10. (n.d.). *Welcome to friends of Project 10 Inc.!* http://friendsofproject10.org/history.html

Goodenow, C., Szalacha, L., & Westheimer, K. (2006). School support groups, other school factors, and the safety of sexual minority adolescents. *Psychology in the Schools, 43*(5), 573–589. https://doi.org/10.1002/pits.20173

Griffin, P., & Ouellett, M. (2002, March). Going beyond gay–straight alliances to make schools safe for lesbian, gay, bisexual, and transgender students. *Angles: Policy Journal of The Institute for Gay and Lesbian Strategic Studies, 6*(1), 1–8.

Guittar, N. A. (2014). "At first I just said 'I Like Girls'": Coming out with an affinity, not an identity. *Journal of LGBT Youth, 11*(4), 388–407. https://doi.org/10.1080/19361653.2014.910486

Hart-Brinson, P. (2018). *The gay marriage generation: How the LGBTQ movement transformed American culture*. NYU Press. https://doi.org/10.18574/nyu/9781479800513.001.0001

Human Rights Campaign. (n.d.). *The lies and dangers of efforts to change sexual orientation or gender identity*. https://www.hrc.org/resources/the-lies-and-dangers-of-reparative-therapy

Johns, M. M., Lowry, R., Andrzejewski, J., Barrios, L. C., Demissie, Z., McManus, T., Rasberry, C. N., Robin, L., & Underwood, J. M. (2019). Transgender identity and experiences of violence victimization, substance use, suicide risk, and sexual risk behaviors among high school students—19 states and large urban school districts, 2017. *Morbidity and Mortality Weekly Report, 68*(3), 67–71. https://doi.org/10.15585/mmwr.mm6803a3

Jones, S. (2018, August 31). Do school dress codes discriminate against girls? *Education Week*. https://www.edweek.org/ew/articles/2018/09/05/do-school-dress-codes-discrimate-against-girls.html

Kinsey, A. (1948). *Sexual behaviour in the human male*. W. B. Saunders.

Koh, J. (2012). The history of the concept of gender identity disorder. *Seishin Shinkeigaku Zasshi* = Psychiatria Et Neurologia Japonica, *114*(6), 673–680.

Kosciw, J. G., Greytak, E. A., Zongrone, A. D., Clark, C. M., & Truong, N. L. (2018). *The 2017 National School Climate Survey: The experiences of lesbian, gay, bisexual, transgender, and queer youth in our nation's schools*. GLSEN. https://www.glsen.org/research/2017-national-school-climate-survey-0

Lapointe, A. (2015, April 3). Standing "straight" up to homophobia: Straight allies' involvement in GSAs. *Journal of LGBT Youth, 12*(2), 144–169. https://doi.org/10.1080/19361653.2014.969867

Lawrence v. Texas, 539 U.S. 558, 123 S. Ct. 2472, 156 L. Ed.2d 508 (2003). https://www.courtlistener.com/opinion/130160/lawrence-v-texas/

Leo Pride Alliance v. East Allen County Schools, Case. No. 1:18-cv–00396-TLS-SLC (N. D. Ind.) (2019).

Lev, A. I. (2013). Gender dysphoria: Two steps forward, one step back. *Clinical Social Work Journal, 41*(3), 288–296. https://doi.org/10.1007/s10615-013-0447-0

Liu, R. T. (2019). Temporal trends in the prevalence of nonsuicidal self-injury among sexual minority and heterosexual youth from 2005 through 2017. *JAMA Pediatrics, 173*(8), 790–791. https://doi.org/10.1001/jamapediatrics.2019.1433

Longman, J. (2019, July 30). Caster Semenya barred from 800 meters at world championships. *The New York Times*. https://www.nytimes.com/2019/07/30/sports/caster-semenya-world-championships.html

Los Angeles LGBT Center. (n.d.). *Info.* https://modelsofpride.org/info

Los Angeles Unified Fingertip Facts, 2019–2020. (n.d.). https://achieve.lausd.net/site/handlers/filedownload.ashx?moduleinstanceid=52741&dataid=89340&FileName=Fingertip%20Facts%202019-2020.pdfF.pdf

Los Angeles Unified School District. (n.d.-a). *LAUSD School Experience Survey results 2018–19*. https://achieve.lausd.net/Page/15606

Los Angeles Unified School District. (n.d.-b). *School Experience Survey (SES)*. https://achieve.lausd.net/Page/8397

Mai, L. (2007, September). "I had a right to be at Central": Remembering Little Rock's integration battle. *TIME*. https://time.com/4948704/little-rock-nine-anniversary/

Matthew Shepard and James Byrd, Jr. Hate Crimes Prevention Act, 18 U.S.C. § 249 (2009).

Mays, J. (2019, September 13). *New York City is ending a ban on gay conversion therapy. Here's why.* https://www.nytimes.com/2019/09/12/nyregion/conversion-therapy-ban-nyc.html

Mendez v. Westminster School District of Orange County, 64 F. Supp. 544 (S.D. Cal. 1946), *aff'd,* 161 F.2d 774 (9th Cir. 1947).

Movement Advancement Project. (n.d.). *Conversion therapy laws.* https://www.lgbtmap.org/equality-maps/conversion_therapy

Nabozny v. Podlesny, 92 F.3d 446 (7th Cir. 1996).

No Child Left Behind Act of 2001, Pub. L. 107–110, 20 U.S.C. §§ 6301–8962 (2001).

Obergefell v. Hodges, ___ U.S. ___, 135 S. Ct. 2584, 192 L. Ed. 2d 609 (2015).

Parent, M. C., Johnson, K. E., Russell, S., & Gobble, T. (2020). Homophobic bullying and suicidal behavior among US heterosexual youth. *Journal of the American Academy of Child and Adolescent Psychiatry, 59*(2), Article e1, 205–208. https://doi.org/10.1016/j.jaac.2019.08.473

Pew Research Center. (2019, May 14). *Attitudes on same-sex marriage.* https://www.pewforum.org/fact-sheet/changing-attitudes-on-gay-marriage/

Poteat, V. P., Calzo, J. P., & Yoshikawa, H. (2016). Promoting youth agency through dimensions of gay–straight alliance involvement and conditions that maximize associations. *Journal of Youth and Adolescence, 45*(7), 1438–1451. https://doi.org/10.1007/s10964-016-0421-6

Quintanilla, M. (1989, December 7). Haven for gay teens: Education: Some people call Project 10 a bad idea, but the counseling program gives some homosexual students in L.A. the courage to stay in school. *Los Angeles Times.* https://www.latimes.com/archives/la-xpm-1989-12-07-vw-404-story.html

Rachmilovitz, O. (2017). No queer child left behind. *University of San Francisco Law Review, 51*(2), 203–270.

Romero, E. (2018). Los Angeles schools accelerate support for LGBTQ students as data show more than half have been bullied in high school. *LA School Report.* http://laschoolreport.com/los-angeles-schools-accelerate-support-for-lgbtq-students-as-data-show-more-than-half-have-been-bullied-in-high-school/

Russell, S., Kostrowski, O., McGuire, J. K., Laub, C., & Manke, E. (2006). LGBT issues in the curriculum promotes school safety. *California Safe Schools Coalition Research Brief, 4.*

Russell, S. T., Day, J. K., Ioverno, S., & Toomey, R. B. (2016). Are school policies focused on sexual orientation and gender identity associated with less bullying? Teachers' perspectives. *Journal of School Psychology, 54*, 29–38. https://doi.org/10.1016/j.jsp.2015.10.005

Ryan, C., Huebner, D., Diaz, R. M., & Sanchez, J. (2009). Family rejection as a predictor of negative health outcomes in White and Latino lesbian, gay, and bisexual young adults. *Pediatrics, 123*(1), 346–352. https://doi.org/10.1542/peds.2007-3524

Ryan, C., Russell, S. T., Huebner, D., Diaz, R., & Sanchez, J. (2010). Family acceptance in adolescence and the health of LGBT young adults. *Journal of Child and Adolescent Psychiatric Nursing, 23*(4), 205–213. https://doi.org/10.1111/j.1744-6171.2010.00246.x

Savin-Williams, R. C. (2017). *Mostly straight: Sexual fluidity among men.* Harvard University Press. https://doi.org/10.4159/9780674981034

School Success and Opportunity Act, Cal. Educ. Code § 221.5 (2013).

Seger, A. (Director). (2018). *We exist: Beyond the binary* [Documentary film]. Flannel Projects.

Shramko, M., Gower, A. L., McMorris, B. J., Eisenberg, M. E., & Rider, G. N. (2019). Intersections between multiple forms of bias-based bullying among lesbian, gay, bisexual, and queer youth. *International Journal of Bullying Prevention.* https://doi.org/10.1007/s42380-019-00045-3

Snapp, S. D., Watson, R. J., Russell, S. T., Diaz, R. M., & Ryan, C. (2015). Social support networks for LGBT young adults: Low cost strategies for positive adjustment. *Family Relations, 64*(3), 420–430. https://doi.org/10.1111/fare.12124

Theno v. Tonganoxie Unified School District No. 464, 377 F. Supp. 2d 952 (D. Kan. 2005). https://www.courtlistener.com/opinion/2384008/theno-v-tonganoxie-unified-school-dist-no-464/

Thompson, E. M., & Morgan, E. M. (2008). "Mostly straight" young women: Variations in sexual behavior and identity development. *Developmental Psychology, 44*(1), 15–21. https://doi.org/10.1037/0012-1649.44.1.15

Tinker v. Des Moines Independent Community School District, 393 U.S. 503, 89 S. Ct. 733, 21 L. Ed. 2d 731 (1969). https://www.law.cornell.edu/supremecourt/text/393/503

Toomey, R. B., Ryan, C., Diaz, R. M., & Russell, S. T. (2011). High school gay–straight alliances (GSAs) and young adult well-being: An examination of GSA presence, participation, and perceived effectiveness. *Applied Developmental Science, 15*(4), 175–185. https://doi.org/10.1080/10888691.2011.607378

Travers, R., Bauer, G., Pyne, J., Bradley, K., Gale, L., & Popadimitriou, M. (2012). *Impacts of strong parental support for trans youth*. Trans PULSE Project.

Uribe, V. (1993). Project 10: A school-based outreach to gay and lesbian youth. *High School Journal, 77*(1–2), 108–112.

3

Supporting Gender and Sexually Diverse Students in Socially Conservative School Communities

Emily S. Meadows and Jeremy D. Shain

Rural Georgia, downtown Kuwait City, and religious schools in Hong Kong have in common certain social constraints when it comes to implementing safeguards for gender and sexually diverse (GSD) students. Take it from us: We have been there. Literally, we—the authors of this chapter—have worked as school counselors in each of these settings. I (Meadows) hung a safe space poster—in Arabic—on my office door in the Middle East. My coauthor (Shain) started a student support group for GSD students in the small-town American South. However, we did not take these steps without careful consideration and evaluation of our relative contexts. Because we were familiar with the social structures in our schools and the roles we held within them, our initiatives were received without great contest. Cultivating a climate of safety and inclusion for GSD students is particularly challenging when the culture in which you are embedded is resistant to these efforts. I have even coined the term *context paralysis* to describe a reluctance to engage with issues when the cultural context may make doing so difficult (Meadows, 2019). However, it is possible for school counselors to support GSD youth in socially conservative places, and this chapter tells you how.

Lesbian, gay, bisexual, transgender, and queer or questioning (LGBTQ) kids attend schools around the world (United Nations Educational, Scientific and Cultural Organization, 2016), likely including yours. There is growing acknowledgment in educational communities that this erasure of students with diverse gender identities and sexual orientations is both harmful to the children themselves and antithetical to the mission of schools to cultivate

https://doi.org/10.1037/0000211-004
Supporting Gender Identity and Sexual Orientation Diversity in K–12 Schools, M. C. Lytle and R. A. Sprott (Editors)

growth, development, and learning. That said, although we may be less likely to run into stakeholders expressing open biases against GSD folks today, heteronormativity and cisnormativity are still the widespread cultural default in schools (Vega et al., 2012). And, in many districts, it is not uncommon for GSD children to face discrimination, violence, and exclusion at school. As this chapter outlines, significant data show this is the case, and a robust body of research demonstrates the negative impact this stigma presses onto gender and sexual minority (GSM) students. Inclusive schools are simply better for kids.

The trouble is that most of us grew up drinking and swimming in heterosexual, cisgender waters, and our counseling training programs did not give much attention—if any—to GSD issues. Although the majority (90%) of school counselors have experience working with lesbian, gay, bisexual, and questioning students, only a fraction (less than 20%) feel prepared to do so (Hall et al., 2013). More than three quarters (76%) of school mental health practitioners reported receiving little or no training in competencies with GSD youth (Kull et al., 2019). Furthermore, a 2017 study revealed school counselors' low self-perception of their level of competency in working with GSD youth (Shi & Doud, 2017). Even graduate students studying to be school psychologists who reported positive attitudes toward social justice generally lack sympathetic attitudes and knowledge of issues faced by GSD youth, and they reported similar inadequacies among their school colleagues (McCabe & Rubinson, 2008). Therefore, we, and those working alongside us, are usually ill equipped to support this demographic. Good intentions are a start, but they are not enough to lift us out from the heterosexual, cisgender flood, if you will. And, given that gender and sexuality are such loaded and taboo subjects, we may feel hesitant to broach them at all, much less in our professional setting, lest we step on toes or put a foot in our mouth.

What follows is a practical how-to guide for school counselors and educational professionals on how to be a leader in cultivating greater inclusion of GSD students in schools. We emphasize strategies and interventions that have high positive impact for GSD children without setting off a tidal wave of backlash in conservative communities. We start with an overview of the academic literature demonstrating why schools are important settings to promote GSD equity. That is the section to get you inspired and provide a bit of fuel for your fire. Next, we follow with a list of five concrete suggestions to implement in your workplace. Each one is bite sized to read but family sized in benefits for your students. And all of them are relatively feasible, even if your director does not yet see through rainbow-colored lenses.

We gear our suggestions toward mental health professionals in schools, but we encourage you to pass the information along to administrators, teachers, school nurses, policymakers, team leaders, influencers, and any other stakeholders who can help make schools safer and more welcoming for GSD students. Share it with colleagues who do not know where to start or those who could simply use a bit of encouragement in their advocacy. We have dug through the research to make sense of what really works. Backed with these basic recommendations, schools can be powerful supporters of GSM children.

SCHOOLS AS POINTS OF INTERVENTION

The years of K–12 education can be difficult for any child. Not only are students expected to acquire academic skills to prepare for entry into the world of work, they are also learning to navigate relationships with peers and adults other than their parents. For GSD students, however, these years may be particularly challenging. Adelman and Woods (2006) noted that "schools can be hostile places where heterosexism and homophobia . . . flourish unnoticed or without intervention" (p. 6). More than a decade later, these students continue to endure discrimination during their years of public education (Craig et al., 2018; Roe, 2015). These issues are amplified for GSD students who live in more socially conservative locations. Students in conservative communities report feeling less safe in school and less comfortable talking with school staff about issues related to sexual orientation or gender identity than their GSD counterparts in urban and suburban locations (Cooper et al., 2014). A study exploring the experiences of GSD students in rural and small-town schools noted that 81% of these students reported feeling unsafe at school during the previous academic year (Palmer et al., 2012). Cooper et al. (2014) stated that circumstances for GSD students in conservative communities "would conceivably be improved through the development of school-based allies" (p. 356).

Individuals we have worked with in K–12 education often cite their love of children as a primary reason for seeking employment in the school system. Emotional investment alone should provide ample reason for working to improve the conditions for GSD students in conservative communities. However, the ethical codes of numerous educational associations also address a commitment to the welfare of GSD students, including code of ethics of the National Education Association (2010), National Association of School Psychologists (2010), National Association of Social Workers (2017), National Association of School Nurses (2016), and the American School Counselor Association (2016). Caring for GSM students is both a professional and ethical responsibility.

During a single school year, full-time students spend more waking hours in the classroom and with their peer group than they do with their family members. When one accounts for work schedules and other commitments, a student may well see more of their teacher and other adults in the school building than they do of their own parents. The proportion of time spent in this environment serves to partially explain the tremendous power that schools hold regarding the identity and self-esteem of any student. What, then, is the experience of GSD students who do not receive the supports they so desperately need at school?

Roe (2015) interviewed students about their experiences of harassment in school. Some of the study's participants reported vicious verbal attacks by their peers that were left unaddressed by school personnel. Their reports serve as reminders to adults, who may be insulated in the world of work, that acts of bigotry may go unchecked within the school system. Likewise, information from a major survey, as reported by Heck et al. (2013), provides a startling glimpse into the daily lives of these students: 86% of GSD students reported verbal harassment, 44% reported physical harassment, and 22% reported a physical assault within the previous academic year. Transgender students appear to be at particular risk with 96% reporting physical harassment and 83% reporting verbal harassment at school (Toomey et al., 2013).

As disturbing as reports such as these are, schools also provide an opportunity for adults to intervene on behalf of GSD students—to model acceptable behaviors, inclusion, and acceptance. The potential impact of teachers, policies, and allies to improve conditions for these students is powerful and inspiring. Craig et al. (2018) noted that the presence of "safe" adults in a school setting can have a profound impact on GSD youth, including in the area of academic engagement. Improving conditions for GSD students may be as simple as having teachers serve as advocates by intervening when they overhear derogatory language (toward any student) or by teaching basic vocabulary related to GSD-issues. Even in the most conservative of areas, steps can be taken to strengthen and support GSD children at school.

RISKS FOR GSD CHILDREN IN SOCIALLY CONSERVATIVE COMMUNITIES

So, you work in a school that is less than supportive of your GSD students. And, yes, conditions are tough. But aren't they for all kids? Some would tell you that "adversity builds character," and these same people may hesitate to intervene. But multiple outcome measures paint a dark portrait for students who suffer daily in their schools. The difficulties that GSM youth face in schools are real and insidious, and have profound effects on their physical and mental health. Understanding the risks associated with at-school victimization is imperative.

Physical Health

To improve social and academic outcomes for GSD, school counselors should not neglect the connection between physical and mental health. Challenges to physical health have been linked to poorer outcome in the areas of social, emotional, and educational success (Michael et al., 2015). A host of physical health disparities affect GSD youth, including smoking patterns, unplanned pregnancy among lesbian and bisexual teenage girls, and increased risk for HIV and other sexually transmitted infections (STIs). One study on the smoking behaviors of sexual minority youth found that more than 19% self-identified as current smokers, whereas, for heterosexual youth, the number of active smokers was about half that rate (Kann et al., 2016). Researchers further noted that the vast majority of adult cigarette smokers began smoking before adulthood, many of them continuing on to be lifetime smokers, further elucidating the importance of early intervention (Kann et al., 2016). The risks associated with cigarette smoking have been well established through countless medical studies and include lung and throat cancer, emphysema, and chronic obstructive pulmonary disease (Centers for Disease Control and Prevention [CDC], 2017). Specific to adolescent girls who identify as lesbian, the rate of cigarette smokers was nearly triple that of their heterosexual peers (Dai, 2017).

A phenomenon that may seem puzzling on the surface is pregnancy among self-identified lesbian and bisexual adolescent females. Charlton et al. (2018) reported that lesbian and bisexual adolescents were approximately twice as likely as their heterosexual peers to experience a pregnancy during their teenage years. From the same study, bullying and childhood maltreatment were noted as significant risk factors. Furthermore, Saewyc et al. (2008) noted that lesbian and bisexual girls were more likely than their heterosexual counterparts to engage in survival sex or to be coerced into sexual encounters, and, in such situations, birth control was rarely used. Another possible explanation has to do with self-protection. It has been hypothesized that some of these sexual minority females may be allowing themselves to become pregnant as a means of concealing their true sexual orientation (Saewyc et al., 2008). In a heterosexist or homophobic school environment, it may be that some lesbian or bisexual adolescent girls would choose to become pregnant to avoid being a target of serious harassment.

There is information to support the assertion that GSD adolescents engage in increased levels of sexual risk-taking, thus increasing their odds for infection with HIV and other STIs. In 2017, the CDC published a study comparing the rates of risk-taking behaviors of GSM youth with their cisgender, heterosexual (cishet) peers. Results of that study pointed to increased levels of risk-taking behaviors of GSD youth over a 1-year period (see Figure 3.1). On all measures of sexual risk-taking behaviors included in this CDC study, GSD participants showed higher levels of risk-taking, placing them at an increased risk for HIV and other STIs. Smoking behaviors, teenage pregnancy, and increased risk for HIV are just some examples of the physical health disparities that face GSD youth.

Mental Health

In addition to complications with physical health, there is the issue of mental health to consider. In-school harassment has been reported as one of the factors associated with poorer mental health for GSD students (Heck et al., 2013; Toomey et al., 2013). Survey data provided by the CDC (2017) are indicative of disproportionately high negative mental health outcomes (see Figure 3.2).

Given these risks, taking steps toward building a more supportive environment for GSD students is a critical matter. Research indicates that a supportive environment that addresses concerns of homophobia and transphobia can help to mitigate the risk for GSD adolescents and reduce the disparity in suicide (Ream, 2019).

FIGURE 3.1. Risk Behavior Comparison of Gender and Sexual Minority Youth

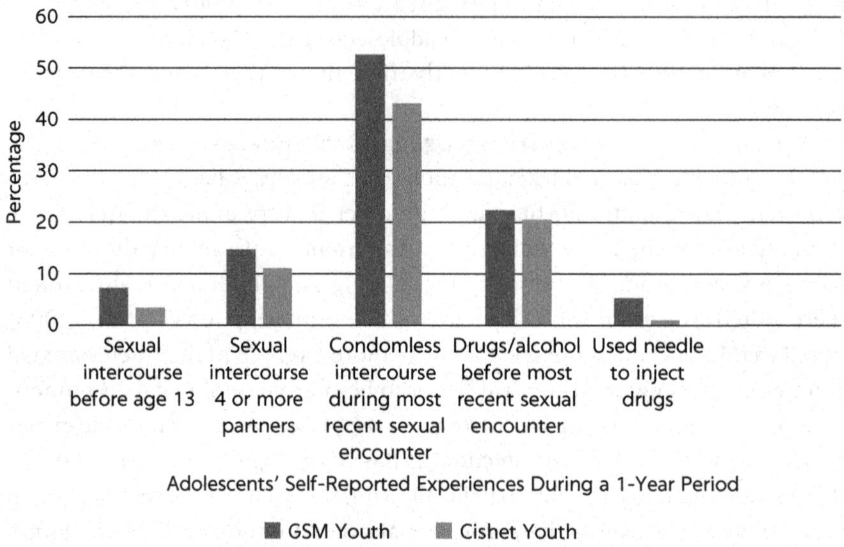

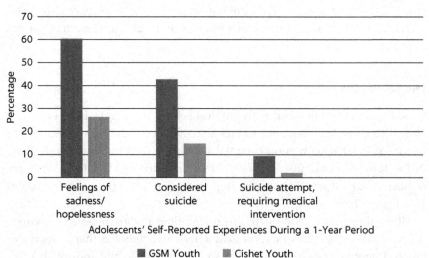

Note. GSM = gender and sexual minority; Cishet = cisgender, heterosexual. Data from Centers for Disease Control and Prevention (2017).

Identification of Allies

When seeking to build a more supportive school environment for GSD students in a conservative community, one initial step can be identifying potential allies. While an individual school staff can certainly provide supports for GSD students on an informal basis, a network of allies within a school or school

FIGURE 3.2. Mental Health Disparities of Gender and Sexual Minority Youth

Note. GSM = gender and sexual minority; Cishet = cisgender, heterosexual. Data from Centers for Disease Control and Prevention (2017).

system is better positioned to advocate for changes to policies and procedures to benefit these students (Cooper et al., 2014). Cooper et al. (2014) proposed that such allies can be developed among individuals who have a broad interest in social justice but may lack knowledge or experience with GSD individuals in particular.

Building allies for GSD students involves identifying individuals who show a commitment to social justice, offering them educational opportunities to learn about the GSD communities, identifying concrete steps that can be taken to improve conditions within the school building, and providing ongoing emotional support (Cooper et al., 2014). Such intervention is not a quick fix, and a complete transformation of the culture of a school cannot be expected to occur within the space of an academic year. However, it is likely that some allies already exist even within schools in the most conservative communities; indeed, students may have already identified these individuals.

As part of *The 2017 National School Climate Survey* (Kosciw et al., 2018), GSD students were asked to rate their comfort level in speaking one-on-one with various members of school personnel about issues related to sexual orientation and gender identity. Encouragingly for us as professional counselors, the category that rated the highest was school-based mental health professionals (i.e., school counselors, psychologists, and school social workers). Teachers, librarians, and school nurses were also identified as points of faculty support for GSD students (Kosciw et al., 2018). When seeking to build a team of allies, these individuals may provide a good place to start. School counselors are well positioned to advocate for the needs of GSD students, are ethically bound to do so, and may be charged with providing training on cultural diversity to other staff members.

In addition, in this nationwide survey (Kosciw et al., 2018), 43.7% of students noted that they could identify at least one "out" member of GSD communities who worked in their school. It should be noted that although these individuals may be personally vested in advocating for their GSD students, they may also be hesitant to engage in such work out of a sense of fear. These individuals are a potential resource for students, but in conservative communities, they may be in a vulnerable position themselves, and their willingness to participate in efforts to change the culture of a school should not be automatically assumed. School counselors, however, by nature of their job description and responsibility to school climate, are well positioned to advocate on behalf of students, particularly when empowered with research on how to do so effectively.

Research on What Works

School safety has been known to be a protective factor against suicidal ideation among sexual minority students (Eisenberg & Resnick, 2006). Hatzenbuehler et al. (2014) provided a resource for school counselors seeking data-driven guidance on how to support GSD students, particularly in conservative contexts. The Hatzenbuehler et al. study, which serves as a point of reference throughout this chapter, is particularly pertinent for this topic because it measures the impact of GSD supports in schools regardless of the social and political context. The team of researchers analyzed data from a range of districts across the United States, accumulating a sample size of more than 55,000 student participants. They compared the results of these student responses to questions about suicidality with indicators of school climate to determine whether GSD students' levels of suicidal thoughts and behaviors were linked to GSD supports and protections (so-called protective factors) offered by their school. The results of the study suggested that, not only were certain school-based initiatives to support GSD students beneficial and impactful, but this was the case regardless of the cultural climate where the school was located. That is to say that the protective factors identified by Mark Hatzenbuehler and his coauthors are effective from San Francisco to Maine. From this work, and with additional supporting evidence, we have developed our list of five protective factors for school counselors to increase support for GSD students in conservative schools.

FIVE TIPS FOR SCHOOL COUNSELORS TO INCREASE SUPPORT FOR GSD STUDENTS IN CONSERVATIVE SCHOOLS

Most of the interventions we suggest in this chapter can be done in any order you see fit. However, we start here with language because it is so basic but also is utterly critical to carry out the rest of the strategies confidently and sensitively.

Tip #1: Use Inclusive Language

How (and if) we talk about GSD issues appears simple at first glance, but it is meaningful. One study found that participating in dialogues about teachers' attitudes, feelings, and behaviors around lesbian, gay, and bisexual people significantly reduced their prejudice toward sexual minorities (Dessel, 2010). Being able to talk about—and acknowledge—our biases in schools is a starting point.

This section covers three main topics on language. First, we recommend learning and teaching vocabulary and terminology related to GSMs. Next, we introduce the concept of pronouns and how this humble part of speech is fundamental in supporting gender minorities. We conclude the section with a guide on non-binary language and use of inclusive semantics when speaking.

Terminology

It is difficult to talk about inclusivity for minorities when we do not have the words to do so. Indeed, one study indicated that a major barrier to including sexual minorities in schools is the lack of discussion on the topic (McIntyre, 2009). Already in this chapter, we have used some words that readers may find unfamiliar. LGBTQ is a relatively well-known acronym for "lesbian, gay, bisexual, transgender, and queer or questioning." In this chapter, we use the umbrella term "gender and sexually diverse" in most instances to include the same demographics spelled out in LGBTQ. We also use GSD to include those who are marginalized because of their gender, sexuality, or both, but who may not identify with any of the specific LGBTQ labels.

Learning about GSM students is consequential. Hatzenbuehler et al. (2014) found that staff trainings on creating supportive environments for LGBTQ youth is a protective factor that reduces suicidality in GSD students. While conservative communities may not yet welcome or have access to this type of training, educational professionals can begin by teaching themselves the basic vocabulary scaffolding for discussing issues around GSMs.

Begin by looking through glossaries published by reputable organizations, including the Human Rights Campaign (n.d.-a), Teaching Tolerance (n.d.), or GLSEN (originally the Gay, Lesbian and Straight Network; n.d.-a). Use these resources to get familiar with words, such as "cisgender," "transgender," "gender identity," "gender expression," and "sexual orientation." Print them out and post them in your office, share them with colleagues, and leave copies in the faculty lounge. Teach the terms in sexual health and relationship education classes if you can, or at least make sure that the sexuality education teacher has a copy (Meadows, 2018). This initiative will serve to normalize and clarify terminology and concepts colleagues may not be familiar with (Case & Meier, 2014). Indeed, I (Meadows) have found in my work in conservative contexts that educators are nervous to engage with GSD issues because of concern that they will say "the wrong thing." Getting the basic terminology down is a foot in the door on training yourself and those you work with, even if your school district does not bring training to you. Just remember that, as you learn new terms, follow others' leads on how they self-identify rather than make assumptions or label people yourself.

Pronouns

Many of us learn about gendered pronouns (or the absence thereof) when learning another language, but usually we take for granted knowing how to use pronouns in the language(s) we speak without really thinking about it. This is a privilege afforded to cisgender people who can generally count on being called by their correct pronouns (Smith et al., 2012). Using inclusive language in schools means calling people what they want to be called (Gay–Straight Alliance Network, 2004). For transgender, genderqueer, gender-fluid, gender-nonconforming, and non-binary students, their pronouns may not be the same as what is indicated in the school's records.

To ensure that you are recognizing students' identity when you speak to and about them, find out what their pronouns are rather than assume and keep in mind that they may be words you did not learn in English class, such as "ze/hir/hirs" (Kosciw et al., 2018). Try offering your pronouns when you introduce yourself along with your name: "My name is Emily Meadows; I use the pronouns 'she/her/hers.'" People may reply with their own pronouns, or you could ask as a follow-up question in your introduction. An open pronouns/gender question may also be part of your school or counseling office's intake form (Frohard-Dourlent et al., 2017; Goins & Pye, 2013).

If you aren't sure about someone's pronouns, use "they/them/their." This is correct English, and fluent Anglophones already know how to do this when speaking about somebody whose gender we do not know. It goes like this: "Someone left me a surprise gift on my desk this morning! I would like to find out who they are so that I can thank them for their generosity."

Do your best to use the right pronouns once you learn them. It is respectful and recommended practice by the American Psychological Association (2014). But, if you slip up, do not make a big fuss; apologize briefly, keep the conversation moving, and resolve to do better next time. Remember also that gender is fluid (Diamond et al., 2011), and peoples' pronouns may change over time, so let students know how they can notify you if their pronouns change. This is one fairly innocuous way to support gender minority students, but it is nonetheless a powerful statement.

Non-Binary Semantics

Non-binary semantics means opening up our language to think of gender as more than two rigid categories. Research indicates that school personnel tend to view transgender and gender-nonconforming students as "other" (Marx et al., 2017). Rather than imagining our students as fitting into one of two boxes—male or female—and relegating those who do not identify within these boxes as "others," it is helpful to recognize that gender is nuanced (Butler, 1990). Children of all genders can benefit from gender norm flexibility (Meyer, 2007), so this is a positive strategy to use in conservative contexts. For example, I advocate for replacing "ladies and gentlemen" or "boys and girls" with the more inclusive (and, frankly, more creative) "scholars," "scientists," "readers," "artists," and so on (Meadows, 2017). You could also opt for basic descriptors like "seniors," "section 3B," or "Mx. Ali's class."

Furthermore, when grouping or dividing up students, consider more inclusive and creative ways that people can be divided rather than by gender or sex (Orr et al., 2015): birthday month, favorite fruit, color of shoes they are wearing, third letter of their name, and so forth. This permits all students regardless of gender and sexuality to break away from the rigorous expectations of their socialized gender role and allows for more diversity in groupings. Language matters, and reinforcing a restrictive gender binary through the "boys and girls" call can be easily replaced with something more expansive, inclusive, and appropriate. These are strategies I (Meadows) was able to implement in a religious school in Hong Kong that was both inclusive of gender and sexual diversity, and inoffensive to the local and school community cultures.

Tip #2: Back Inclusive Nondiscrimination and Harassment Policies

Nondiscrimination and harassment policies in schools, as their names imply, generally prohibit harassment or discrimination against others. Your school may call them something else, such as antibullying policies, but the objective is similar: to create a safe learning environment and to protect minority groups from bias. The language varies from district to district, reading something along these lines: "We maintain a safe and equitable learning environment, and do not tolerate harassment or discrimination based on actual or perceived race, religion, sex, national origin, ability, ethnicity, sexual orientation, or gender identity." The policy then goes on to explain how it will be enforced, consequences for infractions, and so on. Our guiding study by Hatzenbuehler et al. (2014) identified prohibition of harassment based on sexual orientation and gender identity as a significant protective factor for GSD youth in schools.

As is documented at the beginning of this chapter, GSMs face disproportionate levels of harassment and discrimination at school as compared with their heterosexual, cisgender peers. As minority groups with a documented history of stigma and inequality (Faderman, 2015), GSD students should be recognized as a protected demographic, and this status should be explicitly included in harassment and discrimination policies. It ought not to be assumed that GSD students are implicitly covered by a general policy designed to cultivate safe schools and positive school climates; it must be unequivocally stated as such.

From a mental health perspective, a number of studies support the case for adding GSD status to protective educational policies. A large-scale report (Ryan et al., 2015) that included more than 13,000 school districts in the United States found an improvement in GSD students' reported feelings of safety based on whether their school had a GSD-inclusive antibullying policy on the books. The report's findings showed that not only did students feel safer, but they actually were safer (Ryan et al., 2015). Schools without GSD-inclusive antibullying policies see greater levels of victimization for students based on both gender expression and sexual orientation.

Building on the students' perspective is that of teachers. A recent study (Russell et al., 2016) involving more than 3,000 teacher participants showed that, from the view of the teachers, school policies that include GSD status are seen as creating safer school climates. This is hardly surprising given that teachers report offering more support for GSD students when they work in a school with policies protecting these students from bullying and harassment (Swanson & Gettinger, 2016).

Be Explicit

A meta-analysis of peer-reviewed studies found a strong correlation between improved mental health outcomes for GSD students and inclusive harassment and nondiscrimination policies at school (Black et al., 2012). Similarly, "results indicated that for those schools whose policies and programs were unclear or nonexistent, LGBT [lesbian, gay, bisexual, and transgender] youth were not as psychologically secure" (Black et al., 2012, p. 333). It must not be assumed that a generic harassment policy is sufficient to reap the benefits of policies specifically enumerating GSD status. A study of school-based policies from almost 3,000 districts found practically no difference in reported safety and victimization for GSD students when comparing between schools without any bullying policy and those with only generic antibullying policies that do not mention GSD protections (Kull et al., 2016). A generic harassment policy appears to be as useless to GSD students as no policy whatsoever. However, this same study found that GSM students in districts with GSD protections specifically included in their antibullying policies reported greater school safety, less aggression, and less victimization than schools without those protections.

Working in a conservative setting should not be prohibitive to advocating for—and enforcing—inclusive harassment and discrimination policies. Indeed, policy language can incorporate protections for students based on actual or perceived gender identity, sexual orientation, or both. Stakeholders who understand that all children will be protected from homophobic and transphobic bullying may be more willing to embrace GSD-inclusive policies. A large-scale study (Birkett et al., 2009) found that schools with lower rates of homophobic harassment had positive outcomes for the student body as a whole regardless of sexual orientation. Indeed, schools following GSD-inclusive policies saw the lowest levels of depression, suicidality, alcohol and drug use, and even truancy compared with schools that did not enforce protections for sexual minorities. These positive benefits extended to the general student population, including cisgender and heterosexual children at the school.

Enforce It

Keep in mind that it is not sufficient to simply put these inclusive policies in writing; they must be enforced. Once a policy is on the books (and before), be sure to intervene when you see harassment and discrimination play out. Prepare for a potential situation by making yourself and others familiar with the protocol for enforcing your school's policy and follow up on how the school holds itself accountable for ensuring it is applied. Reflect on how intersectional factors, such as students' race, ability, or religion, might put them at greater risk for harassment and prepare for how to address this. Students feel safer at school when such policies exist and particularly when they observe faculty reinforcing them through direct interventions (McGuire et al., 2010).

Promote It

Communicate GSD-inclusive policies to your colleagues and students so they are aware that these protective measures are in place and ensure that school community members understand the procedure for what to do when a policy is violated. The policies should extend to both students and faculty across the board. Furthermore, GSD students have reported being the targets of harassment by their teachers and other school employees (Grossman & D'Augelli,

2006; Kosciw et al., 2016), so it is critical that children understand their rights and how to report harassment or discrimination, whether directed at them by a peer or an adult.

It has been suggested that GSD-inclusive policies are also favorable from a legal perspective (Bishop & Casida, 2011; Russo, 2006). For those reluctant to embrace inclusive policies or those approaching the issue from a traditional moralistic angle, perhaps a reminder of the legal ramifications of neglecting student safety could serve as a nudge toward inclusion. The ideal situation is for educational policymakers to hold the safety of GSD students in the same regard as that of their peers who work directly with students. In the meantime, an alternative course of action—regardless of motivation—is to update school policies to specifically include protection for GSMs.

Tip #3: Make Your Support Visible

As with harassment policies that do not explicitly protect GSMs, support for GSD students is not particularly valuable unless they know it exists. Hatzenbuehler et al. (2014) identified the presence of "safe spaces" at schools as one of the key protective factors that reduces suicidality in GSD youth. These safe spaces—to function as such—should be detectable for students.

Safe Spaces

Clear indicators of your support are critical in making the safe space actually feel safe to students. Kosciw et al.'s (2018) *The 2017 National School Climate Survey* found that students were almost 3 times as likely to be able to identify supportive school faculty when safe space stickers or posters were visible, and GSD students felt significantly more comfortable talking to both teachers and school-based mental health professionals when they had seen a safe space marker within the school. When I (Meadows) worked in Kuwait at a private K–12 school, I had only two signs beside my name on my counseling office door: a safe space poster in English and one in Arabic. The signs welcomed visitors regardless of status, including race, religion, and so forth, and specifically included sexual orientation and gender identity. Posting them was an act of solidarity that I believe went unnoticed by most, but I know—because they told me—that these posters were heartening signs of support for some students.

Safe space posters are easy to acquire, and often free to print from the internet. The National Institutes of Health, Office of Equity, Diversity, and Inclusion (n.d.), offers downloadable "SafeZone" posters on their website at no charge. These are suitable to be displayed on a counseling office door or bulletin board, for example. A quick online search provides a selection of organizations that design safe space posters, including versions in many different languages. To further demonstrate your advocacy, consider choosing one from a not-for-profit organization that works to advance equity for diverse GSD people.

Rainbows and Intersectionality

Another method of showing your role as an ally is to display rainbows. This might be a rainbow flag, often associated with GSD pride, but it need not be a physical flag. You could, for example, wear your faculty identification card on a rainbow lanyard, store writing utensils in a rainbow pencil holder on your desk, or decorate your office with rainbow stickers. In the rural American South, the coauthor of this chapter (Shain) has a pride flag poster hanging on the wall in his office. Although most visitors do not seem to notice the poster, it serves as a signal to GSD students that their school counselor is a safe person for them. Consider displaying a transgender pride flag (see, e.g., *Trans Transgender Flag Pride*, n.d.) or bisexual pride flag as well (available on any internet search engine), to ensure that no communities are overlooked.

There has been a call to add additional stripes to the traditional rainbow flag to include black and brown to represent the inclusion of racial minorities (Baggs, 2019). This highlights the fact that GSMs are not a monolithic group. *Intersectionality*, the concept that our multiple social identities overlap to create distinct experiences (Crenshaw, 1989), is relevant for GSD students (Warner, 2008). Counselors should understand that a Latinx bisexual girl whose parents are undocumented immigrants will not necessarily see herself as having much in common with a White transgender boy who uses a wheelchair. Inclusive school counselors acknowledge the unique experiences of each individual student and are intentional about reflecting the diversity among GSD students (Cerezo & Bergfeld, 2013).

Whether through flags, stickers, or other decorations, trust that GSD students will recognize and appreciate your gesture of solidarity. A study in the *Journal of Adolescent Health* (Wolowic et al., 2016) found that the majority of youth participants not only noticed rainbow markers displayed by teachers and counselors but also navigated toward them for emotional and social support, describing these educators as more trustworthy than their counterparts. Similar results have been found in medical research: GSD adolescents have expressed reluctance to disclose or discus private information with clinicians unless clear indicators, such as a rainbow flag or safe space sticker, is visible in the office (Raifman, 2018). When GSD students can identify at least one supportive and protective adult at school, they experience improved mental health outcomes and even positive school outcomes, such as better attendance at school (Eisenberg & Resnick, 2006; Seelman et al., 2015). Symbols can be powerful.

Some adolescents report disappointment, in certain cases, when rainbow signs seem to be only superficial or disingenuous indicators of support (Wolowic et al., 2016). To avoid this situation, we encourage you to use the visibility strategy in coordination with other recommendations from this chapter to improve your knowledge and ability to provide effective counseling to GSD children. Consider including literature on your bookshelves that will show your status as an informed ally. These may be professional reference books or children's and young adult literature portraying GSD characters and stories in diverse, realistic, and affirming ways. This is an age-appropriate way to display support for the youngest GSD children in our schools who may not yet be familiar with safe space language and rainbow symbolism. GSD youth may not feel comfortable asking you about your position on issues of gender identity and sexual orientation diversity, so initiating the connection by visually displaying your solidarity is a conscientious way for counselors to reach GSM students.

Tip #4: Support GSD-Inclusive Support Groups

Traditionally called "gay–straight alliances," the acronym "GSAs" more recently refers to "gender and sexuality alliances" or "genders and sexualities alliances." Such a change is welcome because this new moniker is more inclusive than the previous one. GSAs comprise students who come together to support each other and provide a safe space. The benefits of an active GSA are well documented. For GSD (not to be confused with GSA) students who do not find support at home, in their places of worship, or in their communities, having access to a GSA at school could be a tremendous benefit. In addition, children of same-sex couples who may experience stigma due to the sexual orientation of their parents may find support in such groups. Researchers Heck et al. (2013) noted that students who have access to a GSA in their school may fare better than LGBT students who do not. Li et al. (2019) found that students who had access to an active GSA experienced decreased bullying, improved mental health outcomes, and increased sense of safety at school. The study further noted that the presence of an active GSA in a school had positive effects for cisgender and heterosexual students as well. This chapter's guiding research paper, Hatzenbuehler et al. (2014), found that the presence of a GSA is considered a protective factor and is partially responsible for a reduction in suicide risk for GSD students. Furthermore, Marx and Kettrey (2016) found that GSD students in schools with an active GSA experienced a statistically significant lower rate of at-school victimization (i.e., homophobic remarks and fears around safety) than GSD students who did not have access to such groups.

Starting a GSA in a socially conservative school can feel like an enormous task. However, there are steps that can be taken to make it more manageable. First, come prepared to talk with your administration. Preparation means having research to support your statements, ethical codes in hand, and a concrete plan of logistics for group meetings. Garnering support from other faculty members and influential community members can be beneficial also as you embark on this journey. If you are in an area where there has not been a GSA before, an intermediate step may be founding a "diversity group" or a "diversity support group" run by the school counselor. Although not as pertinent as a group specifically for GSD students and their allies, a group committed to respecting and celebrating diversity (e.g., ethnicity, gender identity, country of origin, race, sexual orientation, ability, immigration status, religion) can still be a positive step toward improving school climate for minority students generally and may help to lay groundwork for the formation of a GSA later.

Be prepared for resistance from other staff and members of the community. In some socially conservative communities, the commencement of such a group could cause backlash from the community. Note that in federally funded schools in which other student-led extracurricular clubs are already in existence, the federal Equal Access Act (1984) states that schools cannot discriminate against the formation of additional student-led groups provided there is no interference with academic activities (Marx & Kettrey, 2016). Remember the goal: improving conditions for GSD students. Formulate a prepared statement and be prepared to stick to it (i.e., "Research shows that groups such as these improve outcomes for all students. Protecting students is what we all want").

When you are ready to start a GSA, there is no need to reinvent the wheel. Groups such as GLSEN have ample resource materials available to help along the way, including a "Jump-Start Guide" available on their website (GLSEN, n.d.-b). Understand that students may feel hesitant to share at first; a discussion surrounding the privacy of the group (i.e., "Private information shared here, stays here") and the limits of confidentiality are important norms to set with attendees. Although this may be the most challenging tip we offer in our chapter, it can certainly be done. Within 2 years of the inception of a diversity group that one of the authors (Shain) founded in rural Georgia, students went from meeting quietly each week to sponsoring a schoolwide fundraiser benefiting a homeless shelter serving GSD people.

It is important for school counselors to note that gender identity and sexual orientation is but one part of a young person's identity. Race, ethnicity, immigration status, ableness, religious identity, and more intersect with gender identity and sexual orientation to influence an individual's life experiences. Attending to issues of privilege and oppression both within the group and in the larger system are important social justice issues for school counselors. The Association for Specialists in Group Work offers multicultural and social justice competent principles for group workers (Singh et al., 2012) that school counselors are encouraged to review and use to help shape the group experience.

Tip #5: Connect With GSD-Friendly Resources

In an ideal world, school counselors are able to create a list of GSD-friendly resources that serve the local community. Perhaps you live in a place where these resources—such as medical providers, therapists, and advocacy groups— are easily accessible or perhaps not. Where these resources are not accessible, the internet can be a valuable tool. For instance, when assisting a family in seeking a medical provider or therapist for their child, GLMA (Gay and Lesbian Medical Association; a national organization of health professionals who are advancing LGBTQ equality) provides a search engine that allows users to look for local providers who are GSD friendly and competent (GLMA, n.d.). Likewise, the Human Rights Campaign (n.d.-b) annually publishes online the *Healthcare Equality Index*. This online tool can be shared by counselors with GSD students and their families when seeking GSD-friendly and competent medical treatment. The Trevor Project (https://www.thetrevorproject.org/) is another online resource for GSD youth that provides education, resources, and a 24-hour crisis line that includes text and chat options.

For the school counselor who is committed to serving as an advocate for GSD students but is unsure where to start, all of this can feel like a daunting task. We offer some practical advice for individuals in this situation: First, seek additional training on competency in working with GSD students. The American School Counselor Association (https://www.schoolcounselor.org/) is good place to begin the search for resources. State licensing boards may advertise local training opportunities as well. Second, know your limits and be informed of best practice. If you do not know, ask. Third, a mentor can prove to be an invaluable resource. Make some calls; perhaps a school in a neighboring county started a GSA 3 years ago or the nearby college offers a course in GSD Studies. Fourth, familiarize yourself with the concept of intersectionality (Crenshaw, 1989). No two communities are the same, so knowing the demographics of the community where you work—and taking advantage of resources dedicated to your area—will help you to offer the best support tailored to the students that you work with. Keep in mind that the work you are undertaking is to build a supportive school climate that will benefit your students. One of the protective factors identified in Hatzenbuehler et al.'s (2014) guiding study is for schools to "facilitate access to providers off school property that provide health and other services specifically targeted to LGBTQ youths" (p. 280). As you will remember from the findings of this chapter's guiding study, these protections literally save lives.

SAFETY

We would be remiss to ignore the importance of safety in a chapter such as this. Demonstrating support for a marginalized group such as GSMs, whether or not you identify as a member of the group, could open you up to discrimination, harassment, or violence. No advocacy situation is risk free, and we advise you to be aware of the potential for negative personal or professional outcomes and to realistically assess your level of risk and your comfort with these possible outcomes. Having a firm understanding of your position and security within the school as well as in the broader community is critical in conducting an informed risk assessment.

Above all, we advise that advocates for GSD students maintain students' safety as top priority. Take care not to push GSD students outside of their personal boundaries or to encourage them to put themselves in vulnerable positions. Your role as a counselor may be to assist GSD students to under-stand the unique risks associated with some of their decisions and to support them in forming a plan to stay safe as they make choices. Ultimately, your students will make their own choices based on their personal comfort level, but you should be aware of how you can help to effectively plan and prepare for risks and to support them in staying as safe as possible.

CONCLUSION

Advocacy work can be awfully difficult. It may at times feel overwhelming, hopeless, or exhausting. It could make you unpopular among some. However, we hope that this chapter has given you ample reason to persevere despite the challenges and to feel empowered by the impact your efforts will have. Most important, our goal is to provide you with some solid tools to effectively support GSMs in schools and have the confidence to use them, knowing they are backed by research.

Remember that you are not alone. While loneliness can accompany GSD advocacy, it need not be the case. Once you put out signs of support, you may find that allies in the community make themselves known to you; there may even already be movements to join that you are simply not yet aware of. If you are forging what feels like a solitary path, take heart: "Considering school counselors' interaction with all school stakeholders and their ethical responsibility to advocate for all students, counselors are best suited to inter-vene on behalf of LGBTQ students" (Abreu et al., 2016, p. 339). Your work is valuable precisely because you are positioned to be in the lead.

TAKEAWAYS AND OPPORTUNITIES

- When stakeholders present concerns about GSD inclusion, listen and assume best intentions. Perhaps they are uninformed about the facts, or maybe they are speaking from a place of fear. Remind critics that your job as an educational professional is to support children. Reassure them that these strategies are backed by academic studies and give them the chance to show that they can be supportive of all students. Refocus the conver-sation on a common objective: protections and rights for the children in your care.

- Rather than writing these voices off as intolerable (and intolerant), think about how you might address their concerns. In what forums might you be able to share relevant research with them? How might you recruit them to be collaborators? How present are you, in general, in working together on projects and achieving results?

- Avoid the temptation to become complacent. This is not an all-or-nothing game, and progress toward inclusion—however minor—is still better than stagnancy. A conservative community does not constitute a valid reason for schools to neglect their responsibilities toward students.

- How can you acknowledge small steps toward more complete GSD inclusion? Where can you turn for affirmation and personal renewal so you can persist in your efforts?

REFERENCES

Abreu, R. L., Black, W. W., Mosley, D. V., & Fedewa, A. L. (2016). LGBTQ youth bullying experiences in schools: The role of school counselors within a system of oppression. *Journal of Creativity in Mental Health, 11*(3–4), 325–342. https://doi.org/10.1080/15401383.2016.1214092

Adelman, M., & Woods, K. (2006). Identification without intervention: Transforming the anti-LGBTQ school climate. *Journal of Poverty, 10*(2), 5–26. https://doi.org/10.1300/J134v10n02_02

American Psychological Association. (2014). *Transgender people, gender identity and gender expression.* https://www.apa.org/topics/lgbt/transgender

American School Counselor Association. (2016). *Code of ethics.* https://www.schoolcounselor.org/asca/media/asca/Ethics/EthicalStandards2016.pdf

Baggs, M. (2019, January 14). *Manchester pride: Does the rainbow flag need black and brown stripes?* BBC News. https://www.bbc.com/news/newsbeat-46860693

Birkett, M., Espelage, D. L., & Koenig, B. (2009). LGB and questioning students in schools: The moderating effects of homophobic bullying and school climate on negative outcomes. *Journal of Youth and Adolescence, 38*(7), 989–1000. https://doi.org/10.1007/s10964-008-9389-1

Bishop, H. N., & Casida, H. (2011). Preventing bullying and harassment of sexual minority students in schools. *The Clearing House: A Journal of Educational Strategies, Issues and Ideas, 84*(4), 134–138. https://doi.org/10.1080/00098655.2011.564975

Black, W. W., Fedewa, A. L., & Gonzalez, K. A. (2012). Effects of "safe school" programs and policies on the social climate for sexual-minority youth: A review of the literature. *Journal of LGBT Youth, 9*(4), 321–339. https://doi.org/10.1080/19361653.2012.714343

Butler, J. (1990). *Gender trouble: Feminism and the subversion of identity.* Routledge.

Case, K. A., & Meier, S. C. (2014). Developing allies to transgender and gender non-conforming youth: Training for counselors and educators. *Journal of LGBT Youth, 11*(1), 62–82. https://doi.org/10.1080/19361653.2014.840764

Centers for Disease Control and Prevention. (2017). *YRBSS results.* https://www.cdc.gov/healthyyouth/data/yrbs/results.htm

Cerezo, A., & Bergfeld, J. (2013). Meaningful LGBTQ inclusion in schools: The importance of diversity representation and counterspaces. *Journal of LGBT Issues in Counseling, 7*(4), 355–371. https://doi.org/10.1080/15538605.2013.839341

Charlton, B. M., Roberts, A. L., Rosario, M., Katz-Wise, S. L., Calzo, J. P., Spiegelman, D., & Austin, D. (2018). Teen pregnancy risk factors among young women of diverse sexual orientations. *Pediatrics, 141*(4), Article e20172278. https://doi.org/10.1542/peds.2017-2278

Cooper, J. M., Dollarhide, C. T., Radliff, K. M., & Gibbs, T. A. (2014). No lone wolf: A multidisciplinary approach to creating safe schools for LGBTQ youth through the development of allies. *Journal of LGBT Issues in Counseling, 8*(4), 344–360. https://doi.org/10.1080/15538605.2014.960128

Craig, S. L., McInroy, L. B., & Austin, A. (2018). "Someone to have my back": Exploring the needs of racially and ethnically diverse lesbian, gay, bisexual, and transgender high school students. *Children & Schools, 40*(4), 231–239. https://doi.org/10.1093/cs/cdy016

Crenshaw, K. (1989). Demarginalizing the intersection of race and sex: A Black feminist critique of antidiscrimination doctrine, feminist theory and antiracist politics. *University of Chicago Legal Forum, 1*(8), 139–167.

Dai, H. (2017). Tobacco product use among lesbian, gay, and bisexual adolescents. *Pediatrics, 139*(4), Article e20163276. https://doi.org/10.1542/peds.2016-3276

Dessel, A. B. (2010). Effects of intergroup dialogue: Public school teachers and sexual orientation prejudice. *Small Group Research, 41*(5), 556–592. https://doi.org/10.1177/1046496410369560

Diamond, L. M., Pardo, S. T., & Butterworth, M. R. (2011). Transgender experience and identity. In S. J. Schwartz, K. Luyckx, & V. L. Vignoles (Eds.), *Handbook of identity theory and research* (pp. 629–647). SpringerLink Books. https://doi.org/10.1007/978-1-4419-7988-9_26

Eisenberg, M. E., & Resnick, M. D. (2006). Suicidality among gay, lesbian and bisexual youth: The role of protective factors. *Journal of Adolescent Health, 39*(5), 662–668. https://doi.org/10.1016/j.jadohealth.2006.04.024

Equal Access Act, 20 U.S.C. § 4071 (1984).

Faderman, L. (2015). *The gay revolution: The story of the struggle.* Simon & Schuster.

Frohard-Dourlent, H., Dobson, S., Clark, B. A., Doull, M., & Saewyc, E. M. (2017). "I would have preferred more options": Accounting for non-binary youth in health research. *Nursing Inquiry, 24*(1), Article e12150. https://doi.org/10.1111/nin.12150

Gay–Straight Alliance Network. (2004). *Beyond the binary: A toolkit for gender identity activism in schools.* https://transgenderlawcenter.org/resources/youth/beyond-the-binary

GLMA. (n.d.). *GLMA provider directory.* https://glmaimpak.networkats.com/members_online_new/members/dir_provider.asp

GLSEN. (n.d.-a). *Key concepts and terms.* https://www.glsen.org/sites/default/files/GLSEN%20Terms%20and%20Concepts%20Thematic.pdf

GLSEN. (n.d.-b). *Student and GSA resources.* https://www.glsen.org/resources/student-and-gsa-resources

Goins, E. S., & Pye, D. (2013). Check the box that best describes you: Reflexively managing theory and praxis in LGBTQ health communication research. *Health Communication, 28*(4), 397–407. https://doi.org/10.1080/10410236.2012.690505

Grossman, A. H., & D'Augelli, A. R. (2006). Transgender youth: Invisible and vulnerable. *Journal of Homosexuality, 51*(1), 111–128. https://doi.org/10.1300/J082v51n01_06

Hall, W. J., McDougald, A. M., & Kresica, A. M. (2013). School counselors' education and training, competency, and supportive behaviors concerning gay, lesbian, and bisexual students. *Professional School Counseling, 17*(1), 130–141. https://doi.org/10.1177/2156759X0001700108

Hatzenbuehler, M. L., Birkett, M., Van Wagenen, A., & Meyer, I. H. (2014). Protective school climates and reduced risk for suicide ideation in sexual minority youths. *American Journal of Public Health, 104*(2), 279–286.

Heck, N. C., Flentje, A., & Cochran, B. N. (2013). Offsetting risks: High school gay–straight alliances and lesbian, gay, bisexual, and transgender (LGBT) youth. *Psychology of Sexual Orientation and Gender Diversity, 1*(S), 81–90.

Human Rights Campaign. (n.d.-a). *Glossary of terms.* https://www.hrc.org/resources/glossary-of-terms

Human Rights Campaign. (n.d.-b). *Healthcare Equality Index.* https://www.hrc.org/hei

Kann, L., Olsen, E. O., McManus, T., Harris, W. A., Shanklin, S. L., Flint, K. H., Queen, B., Lowry, R., Chyen, D., Whittle, L., Thornton, J., Lim, C., Yamakawa, Y., Brener, N., & Zaza, S. (2016). Sexual identity, sex of sexual contacts, and health-related behaviors among students in grades 9–12—United States and selected sites, 2015. *Morbidity and Mortality Weekly Report Surveillance Summary, 65*(9), 1–202.

Kosciw, J. G., Greytak, E. A., Giga, N. M., Villenas, C., & Danischewski, D. J. (2016). *The 2015 National School Climate Survey: The experiences of lesbian, gay, bisexual, transgender, and queer youth in our nation's schools.* GLSEN.

Kosciw, J. G., Greytak, E. A., Zongrone, A. D., Clark, C. M., & Truong, N. L. (2018). *The 2017 National School Climate Survey: The experiences of lesbian, gay, bisexual, and transgender youth in our nation's schools.* GSLEN. https://www.glsen.org/research/2017-national-school-climate-survey-0

Kull, R. M., Greytak, E. A., & Kosciw, J. G. (2019). *Supporting safe and healthy schools for lesbian, gay, bisexual, and queer students: A national survey of school counselors, social workers, and psychologists.* GLSEN. https://www.glsen.org/sites/default/files/2019-11/Supporting_Safe_and_Healthy_Schools_%20Mental_Health_Professionals_2019.pdf

Kull, R. M., Greytak, E. A., Kosciw, J. G., & Villenas, C. (2016). Effectiveness of school district antibullying policies in improving LGBT youths' school climate. *Psychology of Sexual Orientation and Gender Diversity, 3*(4), 407–415. https://doi.org/10.1037/sgd0000196

Li, G., Wu, A. D., Marshall, S. K., Watson, R. J., Adjei, J. K., Park, M., & Saewyc, E. M. (2019). Investigating site-level longitudinal effects of population health interventions: Gay–straight alliances and school safety. *SSM-Population Health, 7*, Article 100350. https://doi.org/10.1016/j.ssmph.2019.100350

Marx, R. A., & Kettrey, H. H. (2016). Gay–straight alliances are associated with lower levels of school-based victimization of LGBTQ+ youth: A systematic review and meta-analysis. *Journal of Youth and Adolescence, 45*(7), 1269–1282. https://doi.org/10.1007/s10964-016-0501-7

Marx, R. A., Roberts, L. M., & Nixon, C. T. (2017). When care and concern are not enough: School personnel's development as allies for trans and gender non-conforming students. *Social Sciences, 6*(1), Article 11. https://doi.org/10.3390/socsci6010011

McCabe, P. C., & Rubinson, F. (2008). Committing to social justice: The behavioral intention of school psychology and education trainees to advocate for lesbian, gay, bisexual, and transgendered youth. *School Psychology Review, 37*(4), 469–486.

McGuire, J. K., Anderson, C. R., Toomey, R. B., & Russell, S. T. (2010). School climate for transgender youth: A mixed method investigation of student experiences and school responses. *Journal of Youth and Adolescence, 39*(10), 1175–1188. https://doi.org/10.1007/s10964-010-9540-7

McIntyre, E. (2009). Teacher discourse on lesbian, gay and bisexual pupils in Scottish schools. *Educational Psychology in Practice, 25*(4), 301–314. https://doi.org/10.1080/02667360903315115

Meadows, E. (2017, September 21). Intersex students [blog post]. *Teaching Your Way Around the World.* http://blog.tieonline.com/intersex-students/

Meadows, E. (2018). Sexual health equity in schools: Inclusive sexuality and relationship education for gender and sexual minority students. *American Journal of Sexuality Education, 13*(3), 297–309. https://doi.org/10.1080/15546128.2018.1431988

Meadows, E. (2019). "That would never work here": Overcoming "context paralysis" on behalf of gender and sexual minority students worldwide. In A. W. Wiseman (Ed.), *Annual Review of Comparative and International Education 2018* (Vol. 37, pp. 287–305). Emerald Publishing. https://doi.org/10.1108/S1479-367920190000037021

Meyer, E. (2007). "But I'm not gay": What straight teachers need to know about queer theory. In N. M. Rodriguez & W. Pinar (Eds.), *Queering straight teachers: Discourse and identity in education* (pp. 15–29). Peter Lang.

Michael, S. L., Merlo, C. L., Basch, C. E., Wentzel, K. R., & Wechsler, H. (2015). Critical connections: Health and academics. *Journal of School Health, 85*(11), 740–758. https://doi.org/10.1111/josh.12309

National Association of School Nurses. (2016, June 28). *Code of ethics.* https://www.nasn.org/nasn-resources/professional-topics/codeofethics

National Association of School Psychologists. (2010). *Principles for professional ethics.* https://www.nasponline.org/assets/Documents/Standards%20and%20Certification/Standards/1_%20Ethical%20Principles.pdf

National Association of Social Workers. (2017). *Code of ethics.* https://www.socialworkers.org/About/Ethics/Code-of-Ethics/Code-of-Ethics-English

National Education Association. (2010). *Code of ethics.* http://www.nea.org/home/30442.htm

National Institutes of Health, Office of Equity, Diversity, and Inclusion. (n.d.). *Sexual & gender minority: SafeZone posters.* https://www.edi.nih.gov/people/sep/lgbti/resources/safe-zone-posters

Orr, A., Baum, J., Brown, J., Gill, E., Kahn, E., & Salem, A. (2015). *Schools in transition: A guide for supporting transgender students in K–12 schools.* Human Rights Campaign. https://www.hrc.org/resources/schools-in-transition-a-guide-for-supporting-transgender-students-in-k-12-s

Palmer, N. A., Kosciw, J. G., & Bartkiewicz, M. J. (2012). *Strengths and silences: The experiences of lesbian, gay, bisexual and transgender students in rural and small town schools.* GLSEN. https://www.glsen.org/sites/default/files/Strengths%20%26%20Silences.pdf

Raifman, J. (2018). Primary care for LGBT adolescents: Patient and provider perspectives. *Journal of Adolescent Health, 62*(2), Article S43. https://doi.org/10.1016/j.jadohealth.2017.11.085

Ream, G. L. (2019). What's unique about lesbian, gay, bisexual, and transgender (LGBT) youth and young adult suicides? Findings from the National Violent Death Reporting System. *Journal of Adolescent Health, 64*(5), 602–607. https://doi.org/10.1016/j.jadohealth.2018.10.303

Roe, S. L. (2015). Examining the role of peer relationships in the lives of gay and bisexual adolescents. *Children & Schools, 37*(2), 117–124. https://doi.org/10.1093/cs/cdv001

Russell, S. T., Day, J. K., Ioverno, S., & Toomey, R. B. (2016). Are school policies focused on sexual orientation and gender identity associated with less bullying? Teachers' perspectives. *Journal of School Psychology, 54*, 29–38. https://doi.org/10.1016/j.jsp.2015.10.005

Russo, R. G. (2006). The extent of public education nondiscrimination policy protections for lesbian, gay, bisexual, and transgender students: A national study. *Urban Education, 41*(2), 115–150. https://doi.org/10.1177/0042085905284957

Ryan, M. K., Kosciw, J. G., & Greytak, E. A. (2015). *From statehouse to schoolhouse: Anti-bullying policy efforts in U.S. states and school districts.* GLSEN.

Saewyc, E. M., Poon, C. S., Homma, Y., & Skay, C. L. (2008). Stigma management? The links between enacted stigma and teen pregnancy trends among gay, lesbian, and bisexual students in British Columbia. *Canadian Journal of Human Sexuality, 17*(3), 123–139.

Seelman, K. L., Forge, N., Walls, N. E., & Bridges, N. (2015). School engagement among LGBTQ high school students: The roles of safe adults and gay–straight alliance characteristics. *Children and Youth Services Review, 57*, 19–29. https://doi.org/10.1016/j.childyouth.2015.07.021

Shi, Q., & Doud, S. (2017). An examination of school counselors' competency working with lesbian, gay and bisexual and transgender (LGBT) students. *Journal of LGBT Issues in Counseling, 11*(1), 2–17. https://doi.org/10.1080/15538605.2017.1273165

Singh, A. A., Merchant, N., Skudrzyk, B., & Ingene, D. (2012). Association for Specialists in Group Work: Multicultural and social justice competence principles for group workers. *Journal for Specialists in Group Work, 37*(4), 312–325. https://doi.org/10.1080/01933922.2012.721482

Smith, L. C., Shin, R. Q., & Officer, L. M. (2012). Moving counseling forward on LGB and transgender issues: Speaking queerly on discourses and microaggressions. *Counseling Psychologist, 40*(3), 385–408. https://doi.org/10.1177/0011000011403165

Swanson, K., & Gettinger, M. (2016). Teachers' knowledge, attitudes, and supportive behaviors toward LGBT students: Relationship to gay–straight alliances, antibullying policy, and teacher training. *Journal of LGBT Youth, 13*(4), 326–351. https://doi.org/10.1080/19361653.2016.1185765

Teaching Tolerance. (n.d.). *A gender spectrum glossary.* https://www.tolerance.org/print/86569/print

Toomey, R. B., Ryan, C., Diaz, R. M., Card, N. A., & Russell, S. T. (2013). Gender non-conforming lesbian, gay, bisexual, and transgender youth: School victimization and young adult psychosocial adjustment. *Psychology of Sexual Orientation and Gender Diversity, 1*(S), 71–80. https://doi.org/10.1037/2329-0382.1.S.71

Trans transgender flag pride [Image by katlove]. (n.d.). Pixabay. Retrieved May 26, 2020, from https://pixabay.com/illustrations/trans-transgender-flag-pride-1792756/

United Nations Educational, Scientific and Cultural Organization. (2016). *Out in the open: Education sector responses to violence based on sexual orientation and gender identity/expression.* https://unesdoc.unesco.org/ark:/48223/pf0000244652

Vega, S., Crawford, H. G., & Van Pelt, J. (2012). Safe schools for LGBTQI students: How do teachers view their role in promoting safe schools? *Equity & Excellence in Education, 45*(2), 250–260. https://doi.org/10.1080/10665684.2012.671095

Warner, L. R. (2008). A best practice guide to intersectional approaches in psychological research. *Sex Roles, 59*(5–6), 454–463. https://doi.org/10.1007/s11199-008-9504-5

Wolowic, J. M., Heston, L., Saewyc, E., Porta, C., & Eisenberg, M. (2016). Embracing the rainbow: LGBTQ youth navigating "safe" spaces and belonging in North America. *The Journal of Adolescent Health, 58*(2), S1–S19. https://doi.org/10.1016/j.jadohealth.2015.10.018

4

Evolving Strategies to Counter School Bullying of Gender and Sexually Diverse Students

Peter S. Theodore and Judy Chiasson

Gender and sexually diverse (GSD) youths' experiences at school hold considerable importance amidst a political climate that has grown increasingly adversarial to lesbian, gay, bisexual, transgender, and queer or questioning (LGBTQ) communities and grown indifferent to the needs of GSD youth. Efforts to ban transgender individuals from serving in the military (*Karnoski v. Trump*, 2018), sanction discriminatory business practices (*Masterpiece Cakeshop v. Colorado Civil Rights Comm'n*, 2018), and withhold health care on the basis of religious beliefs send the message that GSD persons are undeserving of equal rights and protections under the law. In education, there are also controversies over allowing transgender students access to facilities and activities in alignment with their affirmed gender. For instance, on March 30, 2020, the governor of the State of Idaho signed "House Bill 500," the *Fairness in Women's Sports Act*, which requires high school and college athletes to participate in sports that align with their gender assigned at birth. As of 2020, five states (Alabama, Louisiana, Mississippi, Oklahoma, and Texas) explicitly ban schools from teaching GSD-affirming material or having enumerated antibullying policies. These laws are commonly referred to as "no pro homo" laws because they disallow protection for GSD identities in schools. Far from being agnostic, these laws do not restrict *negative* depictions of GSD identities; in fact, some states require them, thus fostering an increasingly hostile school climate for GSD students (Movement Advancement Project, 2019).

https://doi.org/10.1037/0000211-005
Supporting Gender Identity and Sexual Orientation Diversity in K–12 Schools, M. C. Lytle and R. A. Sprott (Editors)

Moreover, heterosexism is embedded within select political, legal, religious, and cultural institutions. This is particularly pronounced in more conservative and fundamentalist communities, where cisgender and heterosexual individuals experience privileges that are not afforded to GSD persons. These discrepancies fuel negative attitudes and beliefs about GSD persons as well as establish a permissive tone for the passage of the aforementioned anti-GSD laws and educational policies. Laws and policies that reinforce heterosexism, homophobia, and transphobia within academic environments perpetuate high rates of bullying, harassment, and violence against GSD students (Kosciw et al., 2018; Orue & Calvete, 2018).

LOOKING AT GSD-RELATED BULLYING FROM A SOCIAL–ECOLOGICAL PERSPECTIVE

Bullying is unwanted, aggressive behavior among school-age children that involves a real or perceived physical or social power imbalance. The behavior is repeated, or has the potential to be repeated, over time. Both the students who are bullied and those who bully others may have serious, lasting consequences from bullying (U.S. Department of Health and Human Services, 2019). The experiences of bullying range from verbal harassment (e.g., being teased and ridiculed) and threats to physical harassment (e.g., being pushed or kicked), violence/assault (e.g., being hit or threatened with a weapon), or relational aggression (e.g., being the subject of rumors or rejection).

The 2017 National School Climate Survey of 23,001 students revealed continued alarming rates of GSD-related bullying (Kosciw et al., 2018). Specifically, 70% of students frequently or often heard homophobic remarks in their schools, and almost 57% overheard such remarks from their school staff. Similarly, 62% of students frequently or often heard transphobic remarks at school, and 71% overheard them from their school staff. Beyond verbal harassment, 29% of youth had been physically harassed, and 12% had experienced violence or were assaulted based on their sexual orientation. Among transgender youth, 24% had been physically harassed, and 11% reported violence/assault based on gender expression. Cyberbullying was also reported by nearly 50% of GSD students. Consequently, 60% of students perceived their school as unsafe due to their sexual orientation, and 45% felt unsafe due to their gender expression. As a result, approximately 40% of students reported avoidance of gender-segregated spaces, such as bathrooms, and nearly 75% reported avoidance of school-wide events and extracurricular activities due to feeling unsafe.

Notably, for all students, GSD and heterosexual students alike, those who perceive experiences of bullying as homophobic or transphobic consistently report more severe outcomes relative to those experiencing bullying in general (Poteat, 2017; Russell et al., 2012; Swearer et al., 2008). High rates of GSD-related bullying have been associated with heightened psychological distress (e.g., depression, anxiety, and trauma), lower self-esteem, increased suicide ideation and attempts, substance use, as well as higher rates of risky sexual behavior, sexually transmitted infections, and pregnancy (Espelage et al., 2008; Kosciw et al., 2018; Poteat, Rivers, & Scheer, 2015; Saewyc & Homma, 2017). These outcomes likely mediate the variety of academic concerns associated with GSD-related bullying, including less school engagement, higher rates of disciplinary problems, truancy, attrition, poorer academic achievement, and lower likelihood to pursue college or postsecondary education (Aragon et al., 2014; Espelage et al., 2008; Kosciw et al., 2013).

Prior to examining the various strategies designed to reduce GSD-related bullying and enhance GSD students' learning and well-being, we must understand the multifaceted nature of bullying. The socio-ecological theory (Centers for Disease Control, 2020; Poteat et al., 2019) explains bullying as a product of reciprocal influences at the individual level (i.e., the instigator, target, bystander) and the various systems within which they exist (i.e., family, society, community, school and classroom; Espelage & Hong, 2019; Poteat et al., 2019). Based on a systems framework, bullying operates within the context of multiple overlapping and intersecting systems; therefore, strategies to address bullying most effectively should be multipronged, occur concurrently at multiple levels, and involve constituents across the various systems of influence.

STRENGTHS AND WEAKNESSES OF INDIVIDUAL-LEVEL INTERVENTIONS

Historically, bullying prevention focused on educating students and staff about the major types of bullying, the participants in a bullying incident, and examples of bullying that illustrate the harm to the victim. Experts have delineated distinct roles in the bullying triad—the individual who perpetrates or commits the act of aggression, the target who experiences the act of bullying, and the bystander who either passively witnesses the bullying or intervenes in some way to stop the bullying and defend the target (Hymel et al., 2015; Polanin et al., 2012; Poteat, 2017; Poteat, Rivers, & Vecho, 2015). Trainings that present bullying as a dyad between an aggressive perpetrator and an innocent victim can increase anxiety and cause the unintended consequence of *increasing* bullying (Jeong & Lee, 2013). An analysis of awareness-only approaches easily reveals the foundational design challenges; thus, current thought in the field of bullying prevention now includes recognition of reciprocal influences and overlap in these roles.

Target-Based Approaches

Early approaches to address bullying focused on working with the targets of bullying themselves. One premise underlying this approach was that, although it is the adults' responsibility to maintain the safety of the classroom and school campus, most bullying occurs outside the watchful eyes of adults. Therefore, school staff relied upon students to bring incidents to their attention so they can be addressed. Anticipated benefits of direct reporting by targets include enabling school staff to identify trends (e.g., unsafe places on campus where bullying may occur regularly, chronic offenders or targets, escalation of bullying behavior). By identifying trends, school staff can intercede in the bullying before it escalates into serious consequences for the target and for the offender.

Several challenges limit the benefits achieved by a target-oriented approach. First, positioning the teacher as students' only recourse can have the unintended outcome of implying that students are helpless to deal with the situation independently. This can thereby increase perceptions of vulnerability among targets, offenders, and bystanders. It also ignores the many reasons targets of bullying do not report. Kosciw and colleagues (2018) found that fewer than half the incidents of GSD-related bullying and victimization are reported to school staff, due to students' anticipation of ineffective intervention and/or fear of retaliation should remediation occur. These concerns appear valid given that 60% of those who reported incidents of GSD-related bullying and victimization experienced either no response from staff members or an unsatisfactory one (Kosciw et al., 2018). Non-GSD students are not much more likely to report bullying, due to a combination of lack of confidence in the adults, not wanting to exacerbate the situation, to maintain their independence, pride and dignity, and a desire to not violate youths' code of silence. Unfortunately, underreporting blinds adults to the depth and breadth of bullying that is occurring on the campus, thus limiting intervention.

Anonymous reporting is not recommended, because reports rarely include sufficient information for the school to conduct a valid investigation. Anonymous reporting hinders the staff's ability to obtain critical clarifications that may be needed to investigate the allegation. The school, therefore, becomes unable to adequately respond, leading the target to interpret the school's inaction as evidence that they do not care. This may generate or increase feelings of helplessness and distrust.

Another target-based approach based on building a supportive peer network has been found to bolster resilience against the harmful effects of bullying, and it insulates against being bullied in the first place. One is more vulnerable to bullying as an isolated individual. Students also learn how to negotiate relationships and resolve conflicts in the context of friendships, developing skills that reduce the likelihood of being targeted with bullying (Boulton et al., 1999; Kendrick et al., 2012). Given that targets of bullying often present as introverted, shy, socially awkward, or highly anxious, this strategy relies upon providing effective social skills and conflict management training.

Unfortunately, the utility of these target-based approaches partly depends upon the target's relative set of already-developed strengths and sources of resilience (Kosciw et al., 2014; Mustanski et al., 2011). It is important to consider the target's level of openness and comfort about their sexuality and/or gender identity as well as their subsequent developmental needs. Those who are completely open, although more visible and vulnerable to experiencing GSD-related bullying, are often more resilient following such bullying (Feinstein et al., 2019; Kosciw et al., 2013; Poteat et al., 2009). Indeed, resilient students who experience GSD-related bullying may be unfazed by their experiences and feel no need to respond or they have the confidence, strength, and resources to take action. However, those who lack resilience often feel despondent, helpless, and even hopeless. Without proper guidance, efforts amongst students (targets, instigators, and bystanders) to negotiate conflict runs the risk of escalating conflict, promoting anxiety and divisiveness, and increasing the potential for violence and further victimization.

The target-based approaches also ignore the unique needs of specific student groups. Youth may attribute their experiences of being bullied to multiple perceived and claimed social identities. National data that look at race alone suggest that White students are the most likely to be targeted with bullying, while Black and Asian students have the lowest prevalence of being targeted (Spriggs et al., 2007). Among GSD youth of color who report being bullied, their numbers vary as to whether being GSD or race was the dominant reason for being targeted (Diaz & Kosciw, 2009). Within that, it is unclear the extent to which race-based bullying occurs among peers of that shared identity (U.S. Department of Health and Human Services, 2019).

Indeed, GSD students of color represent a group for whom responses to GSD-related bullying vary and interventions require careful tailoring to address the reality of intersecting marginalized identities (Balsam et al., 2011; Poteat et al., 2009; Toomey et al., 2017; Wallace & Santacruz, 2017). GSD students of color often experience heightened conflict among their identities (e.g., ethnicity, gender, religious community, sexuality), creating significant distress around reporting experiences of GSD-related bullying for fear of outing oneself to their family. Some scholars have also suggested that GSD students of color, who have learned how to cope with multiple forms of stigma and oppression, may apply strategies for coping with oppression in a manner that lessens the impact of GSD-related bullying (Consolacion et al., 2004).

Bisexual students and students questioning their sexuality or gender identity are inarguably the most vulnerable for GSD-related bullying. Bisexual students have been found to have greater health disparities, including experiencing higher rates of GSD-related bullying and worse outcomes relative to their lesbian, gay, and heterosexual peers (Feinstein et al., 2019; Russell & Fish, 2016). This is partly due to their having to contend with a unique form of bias and harassment from both GSD and heterosexual peers. Additionally, students who are questioning their sexuality or gender identity report the highest rates of psychological distress and behavioral risk (i.e., substance use and sexual risk) compared with lesbian, gay, and bisexual (LGB) and heterosexual students (Carver et al., 2004; Herek, 1986); yet they are unlikely to report incidents of GSD-related bullying for fear of confirming rumors or others' perceptions about their identity.

Youth struggling with same-sex attractions who experience GSD-related bullying require a deeper level of intervention than relying on themselves or their peers to resolve complex emotions activated by the bullying. Such emotions, if left unresolved, can become projected outward onto others in the form of bullying. Those in the most conflict and/or in denial about any same-sex feelings may refuse help altogether, creating potential for a cycle of violence propagated by perceived threat. This is particularly true for males who report discrepancies between learned gender-role norms and their own perceptions about how they adhere to expectations of masculinity. Males who perceive themselves as inadequate in terms of their own masculinity, consciously or unconsciously, are more likely to interpret an act of GSD-related bullying as threatening their sense of heterosexual masculinity and to react defensively (Herek, 1986; Pascoe, 2007; Theodore & Basow, 2000).

Instigator-Based Interventions

Early student-based approaches to addressing bullying relied upon attempts to identify and punish the instigators—the corollary of encouraging targets to report incidents of bullying. Many schools have punitive antibullying policies that train teachers and staff to reprimand perpetrators. The strengths of punitive measures are that targets feel vindicated and school staff feels good about taking action. Harsh punishments also serve as a deterrent to those who consider perpetrating acts of aggression. An abundance of research profiles disproportionality in school discipline, where LGB individuals (Himmelstein & Brückner, 2011), as well as youth of color (Gregory & Roberts, 2017; Monroe, 2005) have higher levels of school and criminal justice sanctions. The data do not disaggregate for racial patterns of discipline related to bullying.

However, the entire premise of punishing the instigator negates the cycle of violence in which experiencing and perpetrating bullying are bidirectional—instigators often have been bullied themselves, if not by the target, then by another person within or outside the school system. Irrespective of the directionality of the alleged act, punitive responses to bullying fail to address the underlying motivators for the behavior. The bulk of bullying research has focused on the plight of the target with minimal sensitivity to psychosocial needs of the instigator. Research affirms that the reasons why a child may be an instigator of bullying are varied and complex (Rivara et al., 2016). High-status perpetrators tend to possess attributes that are valued by the peer group, such as being attractive, athletic, well-liked, and socially skilled (de Bruyn et al., 2010). In a study of adolescents who had been hospitalized for suicidal behavior, those who had been classified as bullying perpetrators had significantly higher levels of suicidal ideation, substance abuse, and psychosocial impairments than the nonbullying patients (King et al., 2013).

As professionals, we must consider the cost of labeling someone a "bully," which is inherent in delivering punishment. Labeling a student, even if they perpetrated an aggressive act, stigmatizes and deprives the child of the opportunity to learn more socially appropriate ways to manage intra- and interpersonal conflict. Bullying is a learned behavior that often occurs in conjunction with other life challenges (Davis et al., 2018; Fanti & Georgiou, 2013). Rather than being isolated and vilified, students who engage in bullying need support and guidance. Left unchecked, bullying behaviors could escalate into more serious behaviors (Espelage, Basile, et al., 2018; Espelage, Van Ryzin, et al., 2018).

Therapeutic interventions, social–emotional learning, and restorative practices delivered on larger scales are showing promise (Espelage, Valido, et al., 2018; Morrison, 2006; Thornberg & Wänström, 2018). Working to foster prosocial values and behaviors among perpetrators has been favored. Embedded within programs designed to engender prosocial dynamics amongst all students, efforts focus on socioemotional learning, increasing empathy, and compassion within bullies.

Bystander Intervention

Current practices often focus on bystander intervention (Frisén et al., 2012; Hymel et al., 2015; Polanin et al., 2012; Poteat, 2008; Poteat, Rivers, & Vecho, 2015). Utilizing the same socioemotional learning strategies, in this case with bystanders instead of perpetrators, the same aims include building empathy, problem-solving, improving emotion regulation, and assertive communication skills. These aims are intended to mobilize peer support and advocacy on behalf of the target, thereby fostering a greater sense of school belonging, community, connectedness, affirmation, and validation for the target (Thornberg & Wänström, 2018). However, a major challenge to bystander intervention lies in the fact that those who bully are trying to secure or maintain social status, whereas those being bullied are deemed tools to achieve that goal. The social dynamics of youth—desire to be liked and accepted by those who have status and to distance oneself from those of lower status—dissuades many bystanders from intervening. The key to overcome this challenge lies in creating a school climate defined by empathy and kindness, not by intimidation and bullying.

Bystanders play an important role in bullying. Their silence can serve as tacit endorsement of the bullying behavior. In the shifting tides of social dominance in the schoolyard, upstanders can gain status by interceding on behalf of targets or speaking out against the bullying. The intended targets become less anxious, less depressed, and have improved self-esteem–protective traits against being bullied in the future (Lindstrom Johnson et al., 2013; Polanin et al., 2012; Sainio et al., 2011). Targets of bullying tend to be White, female, and younger than nontargets. Upstanders to bullying also tend to be young, White females. They are the most likely to confront the instigator of the bullying or secure assistance of an adult. Males and minority students are more likely to use an aggressive response, such as bullying the person back, hitting or kicking them, or securing friends to act on their behalf (Trach et al., 2010). Research has not explored the convergence or divergence of cultural identities of those inside a bullying triad—the person instigating the bullying, the target, and the upstander. It is possible that social status can transcend cultural identity. Indeed, every peer group sets its own rules regarding the norms of behavior and expected responses in relation to the parties' positions in the food chain (Ferráns & Selman, 2014). One group of adolescent males endorsed GSD-based bullying but only against those who were presumed to be cisgender heterosexual males. It would be rude, they explained, to call a gay guy a homophobic epithet (Pascoe, 2007).

NEW PERSPECTIVES IN BULLYING EDUCATION

Schools are starting to change their approaches to bullying in dramatic ways. For instance, the words bullying and victim are being replaced with less stigmatizing terms, such as instigator and target. Although students and their parents can *allege* that they have been bullied, the actual determination of bullying can only be made by the school official who investigates the allegation. Since most individuals will highlight their innocence, investigators are encouraged to focus on what happened *before* the event escalated. In addition, bullying narratives tend to overlook age-normative, socially inappropriate behaviors. Although it is developmentally normative for a 4-year-old to push a peer in pursuit of a toy, there is an unrealistic expectation that children will discern the norms of socially appropriate behavior and possess the insight to understand how their words and actions may impact others. Children are often held to standards that even adults cannot meet, when ignorance or poor judgment may explain an act perceived by the other as a microaggression. Thus, the investigator must assess if the behavior was reasonably objectionable given the ages and relationship of the parties involved.

The current recommended strategies for bullying prevention flip the narrative to one of being prosocial, understanding, and focus on increasing compassion, resiliency, and empowerment. The point is to help facilitate communication to better understand intent. Current strategies try to help all parties involved understand that not everything is bullying, and that all relationships are marked by missteps, faux pas, and conflicts. That said, in restorative practices, students who cause harm to others strive to empathize, take responsibility for their actions, and make the appropriate amends (Morrison, 2006). Social–emotional learning helps students build resiliency and negotiation skills to repair relationships and preserve self-esteem. For example, emotionally insightful students will respond empathetically when they see a classmate engaging in negative attention seeking. Additionally, emotional intelligence helps students have a tiered response to unpleasant interactions and to seek adult assistance if the situation exceeds their own conflict resolution skills. Finally, flipping the narrative means rather than teaching students to be vigilant for bullying, it is teaching them to watch for and celebrate each other for acts of kindness. Bullies often want to be recognized or lack the ability to deal with challenging situations, such as the feeling of being socially inept with classmates who are gender diverse. Caring and kindness campaigns are infinitely more effective than previous strategies in switching the narratives on campus.

TEACHER-BASED STRATEGIES

Returning to the notion of bullying as a multifaceted, systemic issue that requires a multipronged approach to intervention, teachers play a critical role as leaders in the classroom (Logis & Rodkin, 2015; Mulcahy et al., 2016; Neal et al., 2011; Palmer et al., 2017; Pennell, 2016a, 2017; Poteat et al., 2019). First and foremost, GSD youth benefit considerably when their own teachers serve as allies and mentors. Depending on age and grade level, students navigate a variety of developmental challenges including exploration of their identities; seeking a sense of belonging and acceptance by their peers; and negotiating struggles between conformity, individuality, rejection, and fear of isolation. Such challenges are particularly complex for GSD youth given the frequency and magnitude of bullying they face. In the absence of adequate peer support, teachers must play a significant role in helping their GSD students feel safe and welcomed.

Teachers as Allies and Mentors

Qualitative findings reveal that formal and informal mentorship of GSD students in high school and college by teachers and staff confers many benefits to those students, including self-acceptance, identity integration, self-awareness, sense of safety, belonging at school, decreased loneliness, academic engagement, and motivation to pursue college (Mulcahy et al., 2016). The greater sense of self-awareness gained through GSD-affirming mentorship appears to facilitate additional benefits, including the development of more authentic peer relationships, greater involvement in school activities, and the pursuit of school leadership roles.

The work of Mulcahy and colleagues (2016) further identified various strategies used and characteristics sought by students searching for GSD-affirming mentorship. Many GSD students described a process of gradual disclosure to potential allies of personal information relevant to their LGBTQ identity. Specifically, students may begin by sharing impersonal information such as thoughts about social justice issues, followed by sharing general ideas about GSD-specific topics, and eventually sharing personal anecdotes or artwork reflecting their LGBTQ identity. Over time, GSD students gauge the potential ally's receptivity and evaluate their listening skills, openness to ideas challenging social convention, and heteronormativity. Students shared that this strategy provides an opportunity for them to evaluate the potential mentor's level of self-confidence and comfort expressing unconventional aspects of themselves. Notably, the qualitative findings revealed the initial inter-action between a student and potential mentor as critically important toward establishing trust and connectedness.

Mulcahy and colleagues (2016) also uncovered many signs, cues, and interpersonal qualities important to GSD students who are seeking allies and potential mentors. Although students certainly consider whether the poten-tial ally identifies as GSD, they weight greater importance on indicators of GSD affirmation. Teachers and staff wishing to create GSD-supportive class-rooms should display GSD symbols in their classrooms or offices, demarcating those areas that welcome discussion of sexuality and gender diversity. Sponsor-ship of, as well as active involvement in, GSD-related clubs and diversity initiatives on school campuses will also convey ability and interest to serve as allies and mentors to GSD students. Students reported that they monitor and evaluate potential mentors' level of open-mindedness and support of diversity (e.g., race, gender, ability status, political views) through their interactions with potential mentors and by listening to teachers' conversations with one another and other students. Teachers and staff should be aware that GSD students screen adult conversations for indications of endorsement or dis-approval of stereotypical gender roles, hegemony, or heterosexist humor. Other factors important to GSD students include teachers' expressing concern, recog-nizing accomplishments of GSD students, and demonstrating interest in the future of GSD students. Teachers and staff can also support GSD students by opening their classrooms and offices during noninstructional time (i.e., lunch, recess, after school) for students who want a place to talk.

Teachers as Role Models and Leaders

Social rankings start young. From even the primary grades, some aggressive children are considered to be popular by their peers (Perren & Alsaker, 2006; Rodkin et al., 2006). Teachers of all grade levels can reduce bullying by modeling prosocial behaviors that instigators of bullying can adopt to achieve the social status they desire (Juvonen & Graham, 2014; Logis & Rodkin, 2015; Rodkin et al., 2015; Serdiouk et al., 2015). Research suggests that teachers' attunement to social dynamics corresponds to a more prosocial classroom climate—classrooms that are less accepting of aggression, more community-minded, and in which students actively create a climate that is unsupportive of bullying (Hammer et al., 2003; Neal et al., 2011). Accordingly, K–12 teachers should attune themselves to the social hierarchies and cliques in the classroom while teaching, monitor patterns of participation amongst students with the intention of increasing engagement of more passive students, and model reciprocal interactions for the more assertive students. Teachers can also alter the social dynamics of the classroom by creating opportunities for healthy, positive, and meaningful interactions among less familiar peers. Developing lesson plans with group activities that encourage collaborative thinking and cooperation help shape leadership skills that counter bullying.

It is critical that teachers of all grade levels have GSD-affirming curricula. A simple opening day activity of inviting children to share their chosen names and affirmed pronouns sets a standard of inclusion and affirmation. There are students in virtually every classroom who themselves or a family member identify as (or ultimately will identify as) GSD. Inclusive curricula, visible representations of GSD families, enumerated bullying policies, and open allies benefit all students by adding to overall experience of safety on campus (Russell et al., 2006; Russell et al., 2016). Parents of young GSD children are understandably anxious about the school's willingness to support their child. Collaborative meetings with the family can assuage fears and guide schools in methods to support all students (Slesaransky-Poe et al., 2013).

Specific to GSD-related bullying, teachers should be mindful about responding effectively to GSD-related microaggressions. Against the backdrop of minority stress theory (Meyer, 1995, 2003), microaggressions represent chronic and cumulative acts rooted in stigma. Although the intent to denigrate or harm may, in some cases, be absent, the negative impact is based on the recipient's subjective experience of the interaction. Therefore, teachers should challenge these cisnormative, as well as heteronormative, biases by minimizing the use of gendered language, challenging homophobic or transphobic language, and using affirming pronouns as well as affirming terminology. When teachers intervene in response to hearing their students use biased language in the classroom, they model genuine concern and respect for GSD students, thereby increasing rates of peer-to-peer bystander intervention (Poteat et al., 2019; Wernick et al., 2013).

Unfortunately, research has documented marked deficiencies in rates of teacher intervention against homophobic language and GSD-related bullying (Poteat et al., 2019). Out of a sample of 283 teachers, less than 50% reported consistent intervention against homophobic language, whereas almost 50% reported failure to ever intervene. Research has also highlighted gaps in professional development on bullying prevention, noting that teachers have the least amount of preparation on how to address GSD-related bullying and harassment (Bradshaw et al., 2011). Given the urgency of this issue, Poteat and colleagues (2019) found that perceived norms amongst colleagues in favor of intervening and belief in one's ability to intervene predicted greater consistency of intervention when hearing homophobic comments. These findings suggest the power of shared values and peer norms in motivating teachers to intervene against GSD-related bullying in the classroom and the benefit of validating one another's efforts as teachers to challenge GSD-related bullying. Collaborative support may engender more widespread intervention amongst teachers, and teachers should be encouraged to collectively problem solve, learn from each other's attempts, generate new strategies for intervention against GSD-related bullying, and foster GSD-inclusive discussions in their school and classrooms.

INSTITUTIONAL CHANGE AND SYSTEMS-LEVEL INTERVENTIONS

Systemic change requires a multifaceted, multidirectional approach. Researchers looking at school reform frame sexual orientation and gender identity as equity issues and advise educators to participate in personal journeys to examine deeply held assumptions about GSD communities, to assess institutional practices that may promote or impede cultural proficiency, and to build alliances and advocacy (Beck, 2017; Gonzalez, 2017; Lindsey et al., 2013). The remainder of the chapter offers theoretical and practical approaches across multiple settings within a school district that aid specifically in enhancing the school climate, perceived safety, and inclusivity among GSD students. Every strategy has its strengths and weaknesses and must be evaluated in the context of the student and situation being addressed.

Olweus Bullying Prevention Program

The Olweus Bullying Prevention Program (OBPP) is system-based program designed to prevent bullying and suicide by fostering school connectedness, sense of community within classrooms and schools, and building affirming relationships (Limber et al., 2014). The program is delivered across four levels (i.e., individual, classroom, school, community) and relies heavily upon training and ongoing consultation from OBPP consultants to (a) implement the program within a specific school setting and (b) build collaborative alliances with parents and community members. One of the primary mechanisms for achieving systemic change occurs through the creation of a Bullying Prevention Coordinating Committee (BPCC) inclusive of constituents across all levels. The BPCC then functions to (a) develop school-specific plans for program implementation; (b) explain the plan to school personnel; (c) monitor program activity at the teacher, classroom, and schoolwide levels; and (d) respond to feedback from community members. Although implementation plans vary across schools, the OBPP components universally include the adoption and posting of school policies addressing bullying and promoting prosocial behaviors.

Various successful adaptations of the OBPP have been developed with ongoing parent and teacher trainings, classroom management, adherence to school-wide antibullying policies, and social–emotional learning strategies included as mechanisms of change (Espelage, Valido, et al., 2018). School-wide programs such as "Steps to Respect" and "Peaceful Schools Project" teach cognitive and social–emotional skills, such as empathy, understanding others' perspectives, and emotion regulation skills. In addition to preventing bullying, these programs are designed to enhance resilience, foster prosocial behaviors (e.g., altruism, collaborative problem-solving), and build safe and inclusive school environments. Responsibility for reducing bullying and creating a positive school climate is shared across institutional levels by all school staff (e.g., teachers, administrators, school counselors, nurses, custodians).

Group-Based Interventions

GSD students may be harmed by both the actions and the inactions of their teachers and peers. Schools should create spaces for GSD youth that are explicitly helpful, affirming, safe, supportive, empowering, and therapeutic. These include genders and sexualities alliances (GSAs), counseling, participating in school leadership, support groups, and identifying adult allies. Educating for the *other* includes educating all students in a manner that challenges heteronormativity and cisnormativity (Kumashiro, 2000).

Revisiting the socio-ecological framework, GSD-related bias, bullying, and harassment operate both interpersonally and systemically at multiple levels (Centers for Disease Control and Prevention, 2020). Interventions to address GSD-related bullying must seek to effect change at the individual level as well as the group level. Within the school system, fostering GSD-affirming clubs, student groups, and curriculum have all proven beneficial toward cultivating a safer and more accepting school climate for GSD students.

Genders and Sexualities Alliances

Formerly known as "gay–straight alliances," GSAs are student clubs sponsored by a faculty advisor that provide forums for students to engage in discussion of and advocacy for GSD issues, as well as other intersecting forms of oppression (Chong et al., 2019; Palmer et al., 2017; Poteat, Calzo, Yoshikawa, et al., 2018; Poteat et al., 2017). An abundance of research reflects that when GSD students at schools that host GSAs are compared with those at schools without a GSA, there are lower rates of victimization and homophobic slurs, greater acceptance by peers, increased comfort speaking to teachers, higher rates of school attendance, engagement and connectedness, and experiences of safety at school when GSAs are hosted (Goodenow et al., 2006; Griffin & Ouellett, 2002; Kosciw et al., 2018; Lapointe, 2015; Palmer et al., 2017).

Recent research involving high school students from 33 GSAs found that GSA involvement conferred empowerment and sense of agency through a variety of mechanisms (Chong et al., 2019; Poteat, Calzo, & Yoshikawa, 2018; Poteat et al., 2017). Chong and colleagues (2019) found that greater attendance at meetings, adoption of leadership roles, and assumption of responsibilities on projects helped predict members' self-efficacy to discuss and address issues of diversity. In other words, critical discussion and debate of ideas may lead to collective conscience and social action on behalf of many, including some of the most marginalized and victimized of communities, such as transgender people of color. GSA involvement is also associated with greater civic engagement and GSD-specific advocacy, with sense of agency mediating the link between GSA involvement and civic engagement across social justice issues (Poteat, Calzo, & Yoshikawa, 2018). Perhaps GSA engagement engenders shared prosocial values that promote advocacy and activism across all systems of oppression, including belief in one's ability to effect change in the direction of social equality.

Cautions and Concerns About GSAs

On campuses that host GSAs, many of the students who would likely benefit the most from their participation (i.e., those who are significantly distressed about their gender and sexual identities) avoid becoming involved for fear of being "outed" or being confronted with feelings they are not ready to process. Another concern relates to the faculty/teacher sponsors of the GSA—the position is voluntary and any teacher can serve as the sponsor on record. There are no trainings nor evaluations of a teacher's preparedness or skill to manage a GSA, although GSA Network does publish handbooks for faculty advisors and student leaders.

GSD Student Support Groups

Unlike GSA clubs, GSD support groups are narrowly focused on psychotherapeutic interventions designed to support students who are struggling with emerging sexual or gender diverse identities (Burnes et al., 2010; Palmer et al., 2017). Individual and group sessions by a skilled facilitator can be extremely effective in helping queer youth and their families to manage stressors associated with GSD identities (Burnes et al., 2010; Noll, 2017; Russell & Fish, 2016). Support groups are confidential, can establish qualifiers for participation, and are led by adults who have experience and training in facilitating such groups. Although they are far less available across the school system, such groups can be found in some schools or community agencies— often in larger, urban or metropolitan settings.

Cautions About GSD Student Support Groups

It is essential that adult facilitators thoroughly understand the stages of sexual identity development, gender identity development, the coming out process, minority stress management, intersecting identities, and students' home cultures. The goals of these groups must be on self-acceptance rather than on disclosure or identifying as GSD. Even well-intended actions have resulted in tragedy—with youth ending up assaulted or suicidal after a well-meaning clinician failed to assess the resiliency of clients or safety of their home prior to encouraging them to come out.

Inclusive Education About the Other

Otherness is a social construct that is always based on partial knowledge about a group. No story, book, or curriculum can represent the depth and breadth of the queer experience. There are two main approaches to inclusive education—inclusive and focused. GSD persons abound in history, however, their identities as LGBTQ are often omitted. Alan Turing was a brilliant mathematician and code breaker who developed the idea for the modern computer. Turing was instrumental in turning the tide in World War II. What is often omitted from textbooks is that his country turned against him and prosecuted him for gross indecency for being a gay man. In inclusive education, the person's sexual orientation or gender identity is highly relevant, but it is secondary to their professional contributions. The other approach, akin to that of ethnic studies, focuses on the experiences and perspectives of a specific group and is a learning opportunity that benefits all (Blackburn & Pennell, 2018). For example, a GSD literature course would be exclusively by or about GSD persons.

GSD Inclusive Curriculum
Curricula are largely absent of any mention of GSD history, events, notable figures, or accomplishments. This may be especially true at private and religiously affiliated schools. GSD inclusive textbooks and classroom material have increased over time, yet they remain very limited (Kosciw et al., 2014). When included, there is little oversight to ensure that the information is affirming and includes positive representations. For example, Kosciw and colleagues (2018) found that only 20% of GSD students reported that LGBTQ people were positively represented within their curricula, and 18% noted exposure to negative LGBTQ content. This is disheartening for GSD students, as seeing themselves in positive representations within the school curriculum could have a significant impact on their emotional well-being and subsequent school engagement, attendance, and academic achievement. For non-GSD students, learning about GSD history, figures and events could foster desire to serve as advocates and allies who intervene against GSD-related bullying and harassment of peers (Palmer et al., 2017).

A GSD-inclusive curriculum is typically found in social studies and health education classes. Examples of notable historical events and figures include (a) the Mattachine Society (a gay rights group founded in 1950); (b) the 1969 Stonewall riots in New York City, which marked the most widely known catalyst to the gay rights movement; (c) the "Don't Ask, Don't Tell" policy issued in 1994 and repealed in 2011; and (d) the federal legalization of same-sex marriage after the Defense of Marriage Act was ruled unconstitutional in 2015. GSD notable figures include civil rights activists Marsha P. Johnson, Sylvia Rivera, and Harvey Milk. Celebrated historical figures include Alan Turing, Oscar Wilde, Audre Lorde, James Baldwin, and Keith Haring. Celebrated athletes include Sue Bird, Megan Rapinoe, Caitlyn Jenner, Michael Sam, and Jason Collins. Additionally, celebrities who have contributed significantly include RuPaul, Lady Gaga, Laverne Cox, and Ellen DeGeneres.

Learning About GSD Individuals
Learning about GSD persons in a helpful manner involves carefully balancing education about risks and unique challenges with information about accomplishments and contributions. When done skillfully, education about GSD persons helps normalize being queer, highlights GSD strengths, identifies positive role models to empower GSD students, and reduces bias among non-GSD students. The imbalance of information has the potential to bias teachers toward viewing GSD students through a deficit lens (Pennell, 2016a, 2017)

and to bias non-GSD students toward pathologizing GSD students. Doing so also places GSD students in the position of having to become spokespersons for their group (Kumashiro, 2000).

Pennell (2016a) drew upon queer theory when asserting that teachers should view education as a bridge toward social justice and empowerment, and they should strive to become conduits for information about queer communities from a strength-based perspective. Pennell described many ways in which teachers can learn to disseminate "queer cultural capital": through discussion of positive GSD historical figures and current events; by creating class assignments linked to GSD-affirming books, movies and documentaries; through highlighting resilience (e.g., celebrations of pride) amidst ongoing oppression and adversity; and by highlighting leadership skills gained through protest and other forms of activism.

Education That Encourages Change and Progress

To be change agents, schools must embrace a desire for change and difference. This includes a commitment to continually seek the truth, seek out the voices of others, and to look beyond. An inquiring mind embraces having a growth mind-set and seeking continual improvement (Kumashiro, 2000). Schools and students should engage in courageous reflections as to their own structural and ideological complicity with oppression (Blackburn & Pennell, 2018; Kumashiro, 2004). One strategy would be to teach both *The Laramie Project* and *Love, Simon* and invite the students to compare the implied messages about being gay. Regarding privilege, teachers and school staff should strive to challenge cisnormativity and heteronormativity across the school. Pennell (2017) encourages teachers to conduct an inventory of their classrooms for overt forms of heterosexism through activities such as examining images on posters in their classrooms and school hallways.

POLICY AND ADVOCACY RECOMMENDATIONS FOR EDUCATORS

As discussed elsewhere in this book, schools are minutely regulated. The state sets guidelines for school districts, although school boards set visions for their districts. Elected officials propose regulations, recommendations, and policies intended to recognize or advance the needs and interests of their constituents. Advocates can work directly with their local elected officials to address emerging issues that are not covered by existing laws and regulations. States and districts can extend rights and considerations to its members beyond the minimum established at the federal level. There is tremendous variation among states in their support for sexual orientation and gender identity concerns related to education, taxes, family, employment, housing, discrimination, and health care that are not covered at the federal level.

District superintendents and their executive teams are tasked with ensuring that the vision of the school board and the state department of education regulations are being followed. The district communicates these visions and regulations via policies and communications to the schools. The executive team relies on a steady flow of information from the schools, so they can leverage resources to support schools' current or anticipated needs.

There are a number of ways that educators can help mitigate the negative effects of trauma, family and community rejection, victimization, engagement in risky behaviors, and minority stress. There are many extenuating circumstances that would favor the particulars of one strategy over another. Drawing from material throughout this chapter, the following best practices are offered for consideration.

Get Educated About GSD Concerns

Evidence suggests risk factors and victimization are disproportionately high among GSD persons. GSD youth are more likely to experience harassment or assault at school (Kosciw et al., 2018), more likely to be victimized by bullying for a prolonged period of time (Kaufman et al., 2019), and more likely to be assaulted or threatened with a weapon on school property (Kosciw et al., 2018).

Facilitate School Connectedness and a Positive, Safe School Climate

The value of a school climate that is supportive and caring of all its members cannot be sufficiently emphasized. Students who feel connected to one another and develop collaborative methods of problem-solving learn to navigate their own life challenges, to support one another, and are less likely to bully their classmates.

In addition to a broader, positive school climate, individual students also benefit from support that is targeted for their specific needs. The psychological cost of concealing one's sexual or gender identity can be crippling (Becerra-Culqui et al., 2018; Pachankis, 2007). One of the common woes among GSD youth is the feeling that they are the *only one*. As discussed in greater detail elsewhere in this chapter, it is extremely validating to commune with others of shared experiences. GSAs combat that sense of isolation and provide a haven of safety, affirmation, and connectedness that may not be available in the broader school community (Poteat, Calzo, & Yoshikawa, 2016).

Adopt a Strengths-Based Perspective

Although it is critical for educators to be alerted to the elevated risks and health disparities impacting GSD students, we must be cautious to avoid perpetuating a deficit-model approach or normalizing trauma, risky behavior, and victimization as endemic to the coming out process (Craig, 2012; Hamby et al., 2018; Hinduja & Patchin, 2017; Pennell, 2016b). For most, the coming out process is ultimately a freeing and empowering experience (Espelage, Valido, et al., 2018). It is important to balance awareness of risks with discussion of GSD strengths and positive examples of GSD leaders and scholars.

Do Not Make Assumptions

It is accurate for a teacher to assume that *most* of their students and their family members are cisgender and heterosexual; it is wholly inaccurate to assume that *all* of them are. The odds are that every classroom has at least two students who identify or will identify as LGBTQ. Sexual orientation and gender identity are self-asserted and invisible identities—until the person declares themselves as such, it is impossible to be certain. The gap between awareness of same-sex attractions and self-disclosure is an average of 10 years (Savin-Williams & Diamond, 2000). Ten years is an exceedingly long time for a young person to be a solo navigator. Thus, schools and teachers from grade school through high school should consistently use inclusive language.

Offer Quality Professional Development and Support

Staff training is the standard recommendation for any initiative. The biggest shortcoming with diversity trainings is that they rarely achieve or sustain the intended goals (Dobbin & Kalev, 2016; Gassam, 2019). Shaming, blaming, and calling people out on their implicit bias or privilege does not promote positive solutions. To the contrary, it increases divisions, as participants avoid situations where they fear saying the wrong thing.

Typical antibias trainings assume that showing examples of bias and oppression will evoke empathy, and participants will intuitively adopt behaviors that are the antithesis of those being illustrated. The unintended consequences of traditional antibias trainings are that persons who are of that target group are represented as a victimized population that should be pitied or rescued. This can be disempowering for GSD students in the early stages of coming out. Those outside the target group similarly come to see queer students as a pathologized group and see themselves positioned as the villains who are to blame. Fortunately, there are some effective strategies:

- Facilitators can build alliances across identity groups if they foster a safe place for participants to learn, to express their angsts, hesitations, and concerns.

- People were more willing to share their opinions about GSD topics with surveyors who wore clothing of a local sports team (Harrison & Michelson, 2017).

- Gathering questions at the beginning allows the facilitator to better respond to the participants' identified needs and to sidebar extrinsic topics.

- Frame the training as a *solution*, not a new task, and as a bridge to social justice.

- Teachers should be encouraged to dissect and confront their own heterosexist and binary notions of gender and sexuality.

- Include psychoeducation about the prevalence, costs, and manifestations of peer and family rejection, as well as stigma management.

- Share a story of a young GSD student in which a teacher made a difference.

- Being knowledgeable about the district's policies and how to advocate for GSD students gives the presenter credibility.

- Give activities and vignettes for small group discussions. Assist them in practicing the complementary languages of education.

- Give links to instructional resources, lesson plans, and professional articles.

Build Relationships, Seek Opportunities, Continue Learning

As the saying goes, slow and steady wins the race; but from an educator's perspective, there is no end point. Student needs are always evolving; society is always changing. Educators must respond to and anticipate those changing needs. Commit to learning and seeking new opportunities that will address gaps in your knowledge and skills. We can look to our past to celebrate our growth and look to the future to seek out new horizons.

CONCLUSION

As detailed in this chapter, behind the face of significant advancements in legislation, policies, and social attitudes that affirm diverse sexual and gender identities, there is a stronghold that is attempting to turn back those advancements. Schools have always been positioned as agents of social change and can never forget their calling to protect *all* youth who have been entrusted to their care, even in the light of social opposition. In addition to providing a rigorous education, schools are, therefore, expected to provide a safe environment where all students can benefit from that education and can flourish. Given the disproportionate rates of bias, bullying, and harassment in schools that GSD students continue to face, this chapter is written to describe the evolving trends in GSD bullying prevention and response, and to provide recommendations for best practices. Bullying prevention models have shifted from punitive and divisive positions to restorative and prosocial positions. Education to increase resiliency, social–emotional learning, and conflict resolution are becoming the preferred methods to reduce the prevalence of bullying and the peer attitudes that support/encourage bullying, as well as to empower targets to seek help or take action if they do experience such bullying.

TAKEAWAYS AND OPPORTUNITIES

- Educators must be aware of the disproportionate rates of bullying and subsequent health disparities impacting GSD youth.

- Educators should reflect on their own heterosexist and cisnormative biases, assumptions, and practices in an effort to foster safe and welcoming school climates where all students feel a sense of belonging.

- Educators should develop affirming, strengths-focused learning environments that incorporate discussion of GSD strengths and examples of GSD leaders within the curriculum.

- School administrators and boards of education must support teachers by providing GSD-affirming trainings and professional development opportunities.

- What approach does your school use to address bullying?

- What are some steps you can take to create a more affirming and inclusive environment to decrease bullying naturally?

REFERENCES

Aragon, S. R., Poteat, V. P., Espelage, D. L., & Koenig, B. W. (2014). The influence of peer victimization on educational outcomes for LGBTQ and non-LGBTQ high school students. *Journal of LGBT Youth, 11*(1), 1–19. https://doi.org/10.1080/19361653.2014.840761

Balsam, K. F., Molina, Y., Beadnell, B., Simoni, J., & Walters, K. (2011). Measuring multiple minority stress: The LGBT People of Color Microaggressions Scale. *Cultural Diversity & Ethnic Minority Psychology, 17*(2), 163–174. https://doi.org/10.1037/a0023244

Becerra-Culqui, T. A., Liu, Y., Nash, R., Cromwell, L., Flanders, W. D., Getahun, D., Giammattei, S. V., Hunkeler, E. M., Lash, T. L., Millman, A., Quinn, V. P., Robinson, B., Roblin, D., Sandberg, D. E., Silverberg, M. J., Tangpricha, V., & Goodman, M. (2018). Mental health of transgender and gender nonconforming youth compared with their peers. *Pediatrics, 141*(5), e20173845. https://doi.org/10.1542/peds.2017-3845

Beck, M. (2017). "Lead by example": A phenomenological study of school counselor-principal team experiences with LGBT students. *Professional School Counseling, 21*(1), 1–13. https://doi.org/10.1177/2156759X18793838

Blackburn, M. V., & Pennell, S. M. (2018). Teaching students to question assumptions about gender and sexuality. *Phi Delta Kappan, 100*(2), 27–31. https://doi.org/10.1177/0031721718803566

Boulton, M. J., Trueman, M., Chau, C., Whitehand, C., & Amatya, K. (1999). Concurrent and longitudinal links between friendship and peer victimization: Implications for befriending interventions. *Journal of Adolescence, 22*(4), 461–466. https://doi.org/10.1006/jado.1999.0240

Bradshaw, C. P., Waasdorp, T. E., O'Brennan, L. M., Gulemetova, M., & Henderson, R. D. (2011). *Findings from the National Education Association's nationwide study of bullying*. National Education Association. https://www.nea.org/assets/docs/2010_Survey.pdf

Burnes, T. R., Singh, A. A., Harper, A. J., Harper, B., Maxon-Kann, W., Pickering, D. L., Moundas, S., Scofield, T. R., Roan, A., Hosea, J. (2010). American Counseling Association competencies for counseling with transgender clients. *Journal of LGBT Issues in Counseling, 4*(3–4), 135–159. https://doi.org/10.1080/15538605.2010.524839

Carver, P. R., Egan, S. K., & Perry, D. G. (2004). Children who question their heterosexuality. *Developmental Psychology, 40*(1), 43–53. https://doi.org/10.1037/0012-1649.40.1.43

Centers for Disease Control and Prevention. (2020, January 28). *The social–ecological model: A framework for prevention*. National Center for Injury Prevention and Control, Division of Violence Prevention. https://www.cdc.gov/violenceprevention/publichealthissue/social-ecologicalmodel.html

Chong, E. S. K., Poteat, V. P., Yoshikawa, H., & Calzo, J. P. (2019). Fostering youth self-efficacy to address transgender and racial diversity issues: The role of gay–straight alliances. *The School Psychologist, 34*(1), 54–63. https://doi.org/10.1037/spq0000258

Consolacion, T. B., Russell, S. T., & Sue, S. (2004). Sex, race/ethnicity, and romantic attractions: Multiple minority status adolescents and mental health. *Cultural Diversity & Ethnic Minority Psychology, 10*(3), 200–214. https://doi.org/10.1037/1099-9809.10.3.200

Craig, S. L. (2012). Strengths first: An empowering case management model for multiethnic sexual minority youth. *Journal of Gay & Lesbian Social Services, 24*(3), 274–288. https://doi.org/10.1080/10538720.2012.697833

Davis, J. P., Ingram, K. M., Merrin, G. J., & Espelage, D. L. (2018). Exposure to parental and community violence and the relationship to bullying perpetration and victimization among early adolescents: A parallel process growth mixture latent transition analysis. *Scandinavian Journal of Psychology, 61*(1), 77–89. https://doi.org/10.1111/sjop.12493.

de Bruyn, E. H., Cillessen, A. H. N., & Wissink, I. B. (2010). Associations of peer acceptance and perceived popularity with bullying and victimization in early adolescence. *The Journal of Early Adolescence, 30*(4), 543–566. https://doi.org/10.1177/0272431609340517

Diaz, E. M., & Kosciw, J. G. (2009). *Shared differences: The experiences of lesbian, gay, bisexual, and transgender students of color in our nation's schools.* Gay, Lesbian and Straight Education Network. https://www.glsen.org/sites/default/files/2020-01/Shared_Differences_LGBT_Students_of_Color_2009.pdf

Dobbin, F., & Kalev, A. (2016, July 1). Why diversity programs fail. *Harvard Business Review.* https://hbr.org/2016/07/why-diversity-programs-fail

Espelage, D. L., Aragon, S. R., Birkett, M., & Koenig, B. W. (2008). Homophobic teasing, psychological outcomes and sexual orientation among high school students: What influence do parents and schools have? *School Psychology Review, 37*(2), 202–216.

Espelage, D. L., Basile, K. C., Leemis, R. W., Hipp, T. N., & Davis, J. P. (2018). Longitudinal examination of the bullying-sexual violence pathway across early to late adolescence: Implicating homophobic name-calling. *Journal of Youth and Adolescence, 47*(9), 1880–1893. https://doi.org/10.1007/s10964-018-0827-4

Espelage, D. L., & Hong, J. S. (2019). School climate, bullying, and school violence. In M. J. Mayer & S. R. Jimerson (Eds.), *School safety and violence prevention: Science, practice, policy* (pp. 45–69). https://doi.org/10.1037/0000106-003

Espelage, D. L., Valido, A., Hatchel, T., Ingram, K. M., Huang, Y., & Torgal, C. (2018). A literature review of protective factors associated with homophobic bullying and its consequences among children & adolescents. *Aggression and Violent Behavior, 45,* 98–110. https://doi.org/10.1016/j.avb.2018.07.003

Espelage, D. L., Van Ryzin, M. J., & Holt, M. K. (2018). Trajectories of bully perpetration across early adolescence: Static risk factors, dynamic covariates, and longitudinal outcomes. *Psychology of Violence, 8*(2), 141–150. https://doi.org/10.1037/vio0000095

Fairness in Women's Sports Act, Idaho Code, § 33-62 (2020).

Fanti, K. A., & Georgiou, S. N. (2013). Bullying, victimization, school performance, and mother–child relationship quality: Direct and transactional associations. *Journal of Criminology, 2013,* 1–11. https://doi.org/10.1155/2013/289689

Feinstein, B. A., Turner, B. C., Beach, L. B., Korpak, A. K., & Phillips, G., II. (2019). Racial/ethnic differences in mental health, substance use, and bullying victimization among self-identified bisexual high school-aged youth. *LGBT Health, 6*(4), 174–183. https://doi.org/10.1089/lgbt.2018.0229

Ferráns, S. D., & Selman, R. (2014). How students' perceptions of the school climate influence their choice to upstand, bystand, or join perpetrators of bullying. *Harvard Educational Review, 84*(2), 162–187. https://doi.org/10.17763/haer.84.2.h488313410l651mm

Frisén, A., Hasselblad, T., & Holmqvist, K. (2012). What actually makes bullying stop? Reports from former victims. *Journal of Adolescence, 35*(4), 981–990. https://doi.org/10.1016/j.adolescence.2012.02.001

Gassam, J. (2019, March 31). 5 Reasons why diversity programs fail. https://www. forbes.com/sites/janicegassam/2019/03/31/5-reasons-why-diversity-programs-fail/ #4cb0f8b2637d

Gonzalez, M. (2017). Advocacy for and with LGBT students: An examination of high school counselor experiences. *Professional School Counseling, 20*(1a). https://doi.org/ 10.5330/1096-2409-20.1a.38

Goodenow, C., Szalacha, L., & Westheimer, K. (2006). School support groups, other school factors, and the safety of sexual minority adolescents. *Psychology in the Schools, 43*(5), 573–589. https://doi.org/10.1002/pits.20173

Gregory, A., & Roberts, G. (2017). Teacher beliefs and the overrepresentation of Black students in classroom discipline. *Theory Into Practice, 56*(3), 187–194. https://doi.org/ 10.1080/00405841.2017.1336035

Griffin, P., & Ouellett, M. L. (2002). Going beyond gay–straight alliances to make schools safe for lesbian, gay, bisexual, and transgender students. *Angles. The Policy Journal of The Institute for Gay and Lesbian Strategic Studies, 6*(1), 1–8.

Hamby, S., Taylor, E., Jones, L., Mitchell, K. J., Turner, H. A., & Newlin, C. (2018). From poly-victimization to poly-strengths: Understanding the web of violence can transform research on youth violence and illuminate the path to prevention and resilience. *Journal of Interpersonal Violence, 33*(5), 719–739. https://doi.org/10.1177/ 0886260517744847

Hammer, M. R., Bennett, M. J., & Wiseman, R. (2003). Measuring intercultural sensitivity: The intercultural development inventory. *International Journal of Intercultural Relations, 27*(4), 421–443. https://doi.org/10.1016/S0147-1767(03)00032-4

Harrison, B., & Michelson, M. (2017). *Listen, we need to talk: How to change attitudes about LGBT rights.* Oxford University Press. https://doi.org/10.1093/acprof:oso/ 9780190654740.001.0001

Herek, G. M. (1986). On heterosexual masculinity: Some psychical consequences of the social construction of gender and sexuality. *American Behavioral Scientist, 29*(5), 563–577. https://doi.org/10.1177/000276486029005005

Himmelstein, K. E. W., & Brückner, H. (2011). Criminal-justice and school sanctions against nonheterosexual youth: A national longitudinal study. *Pediatrics, 127*(1), 49–57. https://doi.org/10.1542/peds.2009-2306

Hinduja, S., & Patchin, J. W. (2017). Cultivating youth resilience to prevent bullying and cyberbullying victimization. *Child Abuse & Neglect, 73*, 51–62. https://doi.org/ 10.1016/j.chiabu.2017.09.010

Hymel, S., McClure, R., Miller, M., Shumka, E., & Trach, J. (2015). Addressing school bullying: Insights from theories of group processes. *Journal of Applied Developmental Psychology, 37*, 16–24. https://doi.org/10.1016/j.appdev.2014.11.008

Jeong, S., & Lee, B. H. (2013). A multilevel examination of peer victimization and bullying preventions in schools. *Journal of Criminology, 2013*, 1–10. https://doi.org/ 10.1155/2013/735397

Juvonen, J., & Graham, S. (2014). Bullying in schools: The power of bullies and the plight of victims. *Annual Review of Psychology, 65*(1), 159–185. https://doi.org/ 10.1146/annurev-psych-010213-115030

Karnoski v. Trump, 2018 U.S. App. LEXIS 19912 (9th Cir. July 18, 2018).

Kaufman, T. M. L., Baams, L., & Veenstra, R. (2019). Disparities in persistent victimization and associated internalizing symptoms for heterosexual versus sexual minority youth. *Journal of Research on Adolescence, 30*(52), 516–531. https://doi.org/ 10.1111/jora.12495

Kendrick, K., Jutengren, G., & Stattin, H. (2012). The protective role of supportive friends against bullying perpetration and victimization. *Journal of Adolescence, 35*(4), 1069–1080. https://doi.org/10.1016/j.adolescence.2012.02.014

King, C. A., Horwitz, A., Berona, J., & Jiang, Q. (2013). Acutely suicidal adolescents who engage in bullying behavior: 1-year trajectories. *The Journal of Adolescent Health, 53*(1, Suppl.), S43–S50. https://doi.org/10.1016/j.jadohealth.2012.09.016

Kosciw, J. G., Greytak, E. A., Palmer, E. A., & Boesen, M. J. (2014). *The 2013 National School Climate Survey: The experiences of lesbian, gay, bisexual and transgender youth in our nation's schools.* GLSEN. http://arks.princeton.edu/ark:/88435/dsp01wd375z94x

Kosciw, J. G., Greytak, E. A., Zongrone, A. D., Clark, C. M., & Truong, N. L. (2018). *The 2017 National School Climate Survey: The experiences of lesbian, gay, bisexual, transgender, and queer youth in our nation's schools.* GLSEN.

Kosciw, J. G., Palmer, N. A., Kull, R. M., & Greytak, E. A. (2013). The effect of negative school climate on academic outcomes for LGBT youth and the role of in-school supports. *Journal of School Violence, 12*(1), 45–63. https://doi.org/10.1080/15388220.2012.732546

Kumashiro, K. (2000). Toward a theory of anti-oppressive education. *Review of Educational Research, 70*(1), 25–53. https://doi.org/10.3102/00346543070001025

Kumashiro, K. K. (2004). Uncertain beginnings: Learning to teach paradoxically. *Theory into Practice, 43*(2), 111–115. https://doi.org/10.1207/s15430421tip4302_3

Lapointe, A. A. (2015). Standing "straight" up to homophobia: Straight allies' involvement in GSAs. *Journal of LGBT Youth, 12*(2), 144–169. https://doi.org/10.1080/19361653.2014.969867

Limber, S. P., Riese, J., Snyder, M., & Olweus, D. (2014). The Olweus Bullying Prevention Program: Efforts to address risks associated with suicide and suicide-related behaviors. In P. B. Goldblum, D. L. Espelage, & J. Chu, (Eds.), *Youth suicide and bullying: Challenges and strategies for prevention and intervention* (pp. 203–215). Oxford.

Lindsey, R. B., Diaz, R., Nuri-Robins, K., Terrell, R. D., & Lindsey, D. (2013). *A culturally proficient response to LGBT communities: A guide for educators.* Corwin. https://doi.org/10.4135/9781483304281

Lindstrom Johnson, S., Waasdorp, T. E., Debnam, K., & Bradshaw, C. P. (2013). The role of bystander perceptions and school climate in influencing victims' responses to bullying: To retaliate or seek support? *Journal of Criminology, 2013,* 1–10. https://doi.org/10.1155/2013/780460

Logis, H. A., & Rodkin, P. C. (2015). Bullying, rejection, and isolation: Lessons learned from classroom peer ecology studies. In P. Goldblum, D. L. Espelage, J. Chu, & B. Bongar (Eds.), *Youth suicide and bullying: Challenges and strategies for prevention and intervention.* (pp. 191–202). Oxford University Press.

Masterpiece Cakeshop v. Colorado Civil Rights Comm'n, 584 U.S., ____ 138 S. Ct. 1719, 201 L. Ed. 2d 35 (2018).

Meyer, I. H. (1995). Minority stress and mental health in gay men. *Journal of Health and Social Behavior, 36*(1), 38–56. https://doi.org/10.2307/2137286

Meyer, I. H. (2003). Prejudice, social stress, and mental health in lesbian, gay, and bisexual populations: Conceptual issues and research evidence. *Psychological Bulletin, 129*(5), 674–697. https://doi.org/10.1037/0033-2909.129.5.674

Monroe, C. R. (2005). Why are "bad boys" always Black? Causes of disproportionality in school discipline and recommendations for change. *The Clearing House: A Journal of Educational Strategies, Issues and Ideas, 79*(1), 45–50. https://doi.org/10.3200/TCHS.79.1.45-50

Morrison, B. (2006). School bullying and restorative justice: Toward a theoretical understanding of the role of respect, pride, and shame. *Social Issues, 62*(2), 371–392.

Movement Advancement Project. (2019). Equality maps: Safe schools laws. http://www.lgbtmap.org/equality-maps/safe_school_laws

Mulcahy, M., Dalton, S., Kolbert, J., & Crothers, L. (2016). Informal mentoring for lesbian, gay, bisexual, and transgender students. *The Journal of Educational Research, 109*(4), 405–412. https://doi.org/10.1080/00220671.2014.979907

Mustanski, B., Newcomb, M., & Garofalo, R. (2011). Mental health of lesbian, gay and bisexual youth: A developmental resiliency perspective. *Journal of Gay and Lesbian Social Services, 23*(2), 204–225. https://doi.org/10.1080/10538720.2011.561474

Neal, J. W., Cappella, E., Wagner, C., & Atkins, M. S. (2011). Seeing eye to eye: Predicting teacher–student agreement on classroom social networks. *Social Development, 20*(2), 376–393. https://doi.org/10.1111/j.1467-9507.2010.00582.x

Noll, F. W. (2017). LGBTQIA students' perceptions of level of care in relation to sexual orientation & gender identity. *Counselor Education Capstone,* 36. https://digitalcommons. brockport.edu/cgi/viewcontent.cgi?article=1039&context=edc_capstone

Orue, I., & Calvete, E. (2018). Homophobic bullying in schools: The role of homophobic attitudes and exposure to homophobic aggression. *School Psychology Review, 47*(1), 95–105. https://doi.org/10.17105/SPR-2017-0063.V47-1

Pachankis, J. E. (2007). The psychological implications of concealing a stigma: A cognitive-affective-behavioral model. *Psychological Bulletin, 133*(2), 328–345. https://doi.org/10.1037/0033-2909.133.2.328

Palmer, N. A., Kosciw, J. G., Greytak, E. A., & Boesen, M. J. (2017). Disrupting hetero-gender-normativity: The complex role of LGBT affirmative supports at school. In S. T. Russell & S. S. Horn (Eds.), *Sexual orientation, gender identity, and schooling: The nexus of research, practice, and policy* (pp. 58–74). Oxford University Press.

Pascoe, C. J. (2007). *Dude you're a fag: Masculinity and sexuality in high school.* University of California Press.

Pennell, S. M. (2016a). Queer cultural capital: Implications for education. *Race, Ethnicity and Education, 19*(2), 324–338. https://doi.org/10.1080/13613324.2015.1013462

Pennell, S. M. (2016b). Transitional memoirs: Reading using a queer cultural capital model. In S. J. Miller (Ed.), *Teaching, affirming, and recognizing trans and gender creative youth: A queer literacy framework* (pp. 199–230). https://doi.org/10.1057/978-1-137-56766-6_11

Pennell, S. M. (2017). Training secondary teachers to support LGBTQ+ students: Practical applications from theory and research. *High School Journal, 101*(1), 62–72. https://doi.org/10.1353/hsj.2017.0016

Perren, S., & Alsaker, F. D. (2006). Social behavior and peer relationships of victims, bully-victims, and bullies in kindergarten. *Journal of Child Psychology and Psychiatry, and Allied Disciplines, 47*(1), 45–57. https://doi.org/10.1111/j.1469-7610.2005.01445.x

Polanin, J. R., Espelage, D. L., & Pigott, T. D. (2012). A meta-analysis of school-based bullying prevention programs' effects on bystander intervention behavior. *School Psychology Review, 41*(1), 47–65.

Poteat, V. P. (2008). Contextual and moderating effects of the peer group climate on use of homophobic epithets. *School Psychology Review, 37*(2), 188–201.

Poteat, V. P. (2017). Understanding and reducing homophobic harassment and victimization in schools. In S. T. Russell & S. S. Horn (Eds.), *Sexual orientation, gender identity, and schooling: The nexus of research, practice, and policy* (pp. 15–38). Oxford University Press.

Poteat, V. P., Aragon, S. R., Espelage, D. L., & Koenig, B. W. (2009). Psychosocial concerns of sexual minority youth: Complexity and caution in group differences. *Journal of Consulting and Clinical Psychology, 77*(1), 196–201. https://doi.org/10.1037/a0014158

Poteat, V. P., Calzo, J. P., & Yoshikawa, H. (2016). Promoting youth agency through dimensions of gay–straight alliance involvement and conditions that maximize associations. *Journal of Youth and Adolescence, 45*(7), 1438–1451. https://doi.org/10.1007/s10964-016-0421-6

Poteat, V. P., Calzo, J. P., & Yoshikawa, H. (2018). Gay–Straight Alliance involvement and youths' participation in civic engagement, advocacy, and awareness-raising. *Journal of Applied Developmental Psychology, 56,* 13–20. https://doi.org/10.1016/j.appdev.2018.01.001

Poteat, V. P., Calzo, J. P., Yoshikawa, H., Miller, S., Ceccolini, C. J., Rosenbach, S., & Mauceri, N. (2018). Discussing transgender topics within gay–straight alliances: Factors that could promote more frequent conversations. *International Journal of Transgenderism, 19*(2), 119–131. https://doi.org/10.1080/15532739.2017.1407983

Poteat, V. P., Heck, N. C., Yoshikawa, H., & Calzo, J. P. (2017). Gay–Straight Alliances as settings to discuss health topics: Individual and group factors associated with substance use, mental health, and sexual health discussions. *Health Education Research*, *32*(3), 258–268. https://doi.org/10.1093/her/cyx044

Poteat, V. P., Rivers, I., & Scheer, J. R. (2015). Mental health concerns among LGBTQ youth in schools. In M. K. Holt & A. E. Grills (Eds.), *Critical issues in school-based mental health: Evidence-based research, practice, and interventions* (pp. 105–117). Routledge.

Poteat, V. P., Rivers, I., & Vecho, O. (2015). The role of peers in predicting students' homophobic behavior: Effects of peer aggression, prejudice, and sexual orientation identity importance. *School Psychology Review*, *44*(4), 391–406. https://doi.org/10.17105/spr-15-0037.1

Poteat, V. P., Slaatten, H., & Breivik, K. (2019). Factors associated with teachers discussing and intervening against homophobic language. *Teaching and Teacher Education*, *77*, 31–42. https://doi.org/10.1016/j.tate.2018.09.006

Rivara, F., Menestrel, S. L., Committee on the Biological and Psychosocial Effects of Peer Victimization: Lessons for Bullying Prevention, Committee on Law and Justice, Board on Children, Youth, and Families, Division of Behavioral and Social Sciences and Education, Health and Medicine Division, & National Academies of Sciences, Engineering, and Medicine. (2016). *Preventing bullying through science, policy, and practice*. National Academies Press. https://doi.org/10.17226/23482

Rodkin, P. C., Espelage, D. L., & Hanish, L. D. (2015). A relational framework for understanding bullying: Developmental antecedents and outcomes. *American Psychologist*, *70*(4), 311–321. https://doi.org/10.1037/a0038658

Rodkin, P. C., Farmer, T. W., Pearl, R., & Acker, R. V. (2006). They're cool: Social status and peer group supports for aggressive boys and girls. *Social Development*, *15*(2), 175–204.

Russell, S., Kostrowski, O., McGuire, J. K., Laub, C., & Manke, E. (2006). LGBT issues in the curriculum promotes school safety. *California Safe Schools Coalition Research Brief*, *4*.

Russell, S. T., Day, J. K., Ioverno, S., & Toomey, R. B. (2016). Are school policies focused on sexual orientation and gender identity associated with less bullying? Teachers' perspectives. *Journal of School Psychology*, *54*, 29–38. https://doi.org/10.1016/j.jsp.2015.10.005

Russell, S. T., & Fish, J. N. (2016). Mental health in lesbian, gay, bisexual, and transgender (LGBT) youth. *Annual Review of Clinical Psychology*, *12*(1), 465–487. https://doi.org/10.1146/annurev-clinpsy-021815-093153

Russell, S. T., Sinclair, K. O., Poteat, V. P., & Koenig, B. W. (2012). Adolescent health and harassment based on discriminatory bias. *American Journal of Public Health*, *102*(3), 493–495. https://doi.org/10.2105/AJPH.2011.300430

Saewyc, E., & Homma, Y. (2017). School safety and connectedness matter for more than educational outcomes: The link between school connectedness and adolescent health. In S. T. Russell & S. S. Horn (Eds.), *Sexual orientation, gender identity, and schooling: The nexus of research, practice, and policy* (pp. 39–57). Oxford University Press. https://doi.org/10.1093/med:psych/9780199387656.003.0003

Sainio, M., Veenstra, R., Huitsing, G., & Salmivalli, C. (2011). Victims and their defenders: A dyadic approach. *International Journal of Behavioral Development*, *35*(2), 144–151. https://doi.org/10.1177/0165025410378068

Savin-Williams, R. C., & Diamond, L. M. (2000). Sexual identity trajectories among sexual-minority youths: Gender comparisons. *Archives of Sexual Behavior*, *29*(6), 607–627. https://doi.org/10.1023/A:1002058505138

Serdiouk, M., Rodkin, P., Madill, R., Logis, H., & Gest, S. (2015). Rejection and victimization among elementary school children: The buffering role of classroom-level predictors. *Journal of Abnormal Child Psychology*, *43*(1), 5–17. https://doi.org/10.1007/s10802-013-9826-9

Slesaransky-Poe, G., Ruzzi, L., Dimedio, C., & Stanley, J. (2013). Is this the right elementary school for my gender nonconforming child? *Journal of LGBT Youth, 10*(1–2), 29–44. https://doi.org/10.1080/19361653.2012.718521

Spriggs, A. L., Iannotti, R. J., Nansel, T. R., & Haynie, D. L. (2007). Adolescent bullying involvement and perceived family, peer and school relations: Commonalities and differences across race/ethnicity. *The Journal of Adolescent, 41*(3), 283–293. https://doi.org/10.1016/j.jadohealth.2007.04.009

Swearer, S. M., Turner, R. K., Givens, J. E., & Pollack, W. S. (2008). "You're so gay!": Do different forms of bullying matter for adolescent males? *School Psychology Review, 37*(2), 160–173.

Theodore, P. S., & Basow, S. A. (2000). Heterosexual masculinity and homophobia: A reaction to the self? *Journal of Homosexuality, 40*(2), 31–48. https://doi.org/10.1300/J082v40n02_03

Thornberg, R., & Wänström, L. (2018). Bullying and its association with altruism toward victims, blaming the victims, and classroom prevalence of bystander behaviors: A multilevel analysis. *Social Psychology of Education, 21*, 1133–1151. https://doi.org/10.1007/s11218-018-9457-7

Toomey, R. B., Huynh, V. W., Jones, S. K., Lee, S., & Revels-Macalinao, M. (2017). Sexual minority youth of color: A content analysis and critical review of the literature. *Journal of Gay & Lesbian Mental Health, 21*(1), 3–31. https://doi.org/10.1080/19359705.2016.1217499

Trach, J., Hymel, S., Waterhouse, T., & Neale, K. (2010). Bystander responses to school bullying: A cross-sectional investigation of grade and sex differences. *Canadian Journal of School Psychology, 25*(1), 114–130. https://doi.org/10.1177/0829573509357553

U.S. Department of Health and Human Services. (2019, May 30). *What is bullying?* https://www.stopbullying.gov/what-is-bullying/index.html

Wallace, B. C., & Santacruz, E. (2017). LGBT psychology and ethnic minority perspectives: Intersectionality. In R. Ruth & E. Santacruz (Eds.), *LGBT Psychology and Mental Health: Emerging Research and Advances* (pp. 87–108). ABC-CLIO.

Wernick, L. J., Kulick, A., & Inglehart, M. H. (2013). Factors predicting student intervention when witnessing anti-LGBTQ harassment: The influence of peers, teachers, and climate. *Children and Youth Services Review, 35*(2), 296–301. https://doi.org/10.1016/j.childyouth.2012.11.003

5

Providing Inclusive Strategies for Practitioners and Researchers Working With Gender and Sexually Diverse Youth Without Parental/Guardian Consent

Sarah Kiperman, Gabriel DeLong, Kris Varjas, and Joel Meyers

Gender and sexually diverse (GSD) youth are marginalized and resilient individuals whose voices need to be represented in practice and research (Mayberry, 2013). The American Psychological Association (APA) and National Association of School Psychologists (NASP; 2015) Joint Resolution on gender and sexual orientation diversity for children and adolescents enforces these ideals, calling for inclusive practice (see Chapter 1, this volume, for details). It calls for the inclusion of gender identity, gender expression, and sexual orientation in school district policies and for inclusive data collection in research. However, barriers (e.g., requiring parental consent) prevent GSD youth from participating in research or seeking mental health services, or both, that do not affect their cisgender, heterosexual peers.

Informed consent is an ethical practice that researchers and practitioners routinely use in health, mental health, and education settings (Dorn et al., 1995; Roth-Cline & Nelson, 2013). It is a voluntary agreement to participate in practice or research. Informed consent typically includes signing a form acknowledging the participant consents to and comprehends what the research or practice entails. Minors, however, are typically required to have a parent or guardian consent on their behalf because their capacity is

https://doi.org/10.1037/0000211-006
Supporting Gender Identity and Sexual Orientation Diversity in K–12 Schools, M. C. Lytle and R. A. Sprott (Editors)

perceived as not fully matured (Roth-Cline & Nelson, 2013). Although there are guidelines and ethical considerations regulating informed consent (e.g., APA, 2017, 2018; NASP, 2010), little published information exists on how to engage youth—who may not have access to parental/guardian consent—in research and practice. Even if youth have access to parental/ guardian consent, this process may not be in the best interest of the child or adolescent. For instance, GSD youth who have not disclosed their sexual orientation or gender identity, or both, to a parent/guardian for fear of rejection or lack of support (Varjas et al., 2016) may not have access to supportive parental/guardian consent. This, in turn, may explain the limited representation of GSD youth in research and their underutilization of mental health services.

In this chapter, we use a *culturally informed* framework, which refers to practitioners and researchers' demonstrating awareness of diversity, providing effective care across lines of difference, recognizing power differentials, promoting inclusivity, and adapting existing practice and research methods to meet the needs of diverse individuals (Fisher-Borne et al., 2015; Ponterotto, 2010; Sue, 2001). From this framework, informed consent may present as a barrier to GSD youth participating in research and practice (Mustanski & Fisher, 2016). Requiring informed consent from GSD youth assumes they are out to their parents, live in homes in which their identities are accepted, and are able to celebrate and advocate for their GSD identity/communities. Although some youth live in these supportive settings, many youth have parents to whom they have not disclosed, who do not accept their identity, or who (in an attempt to protect them) want them to present as mainstream and not "draw attention" to their GSD identity. Power in this instance is given to parents, and if consent to research or services is unavailable or altogether denied, it could invalidate one's self-worth or even contribute to a trauma narrative. Power is also held by cisgender, heterosexual youth who are not faced with disclosure or an unaccepted identity as an obstacle in obtaining parental consent. Researchers and practitioners who carry out consent procedures and determine whether youth can access practice and research hold power as well. Requiring consent for GSD youth enforces existing barriers and challenges their empowerment.

A culturally informed framework also highlights the need to adapt informed consent procedures to foster an inclusive, representative research sample of GSD youth and to promote their equal access to mental health and school-based services. Thus, in this chapter, we discuss what is informed consent and assent, limitations of requiring parental/guardian consent with GSD youth, available consent/assent methods sans parental consent aimed at fostering culturally inclusive practices with GSD youth, specific examples of where inclusive consent/assent practices have been carried out, consent/assent procedures worth noting when waiving parent/guardian involvement, and recommendations and future directions.

WHAT ARE INFORMED CONSENT AND ASSENT?

Informed consent gives individuals the right to decide whether or not they will participate in a service by evaluating the five components of consent in NASP Standard I.1.3: (a) the nature of services offered, (b) goals and procedures, (c) foreseeable risks, (d) costs of services, and (e) expected benefits (NASP, 2010). A main goal of informed consent includes preventing situations in which individuals would not have consented to a service had they known what would be involved before beginning that provision of therapy, research, or assessment (Bester et al., 2016). With assent, it is not mandatory to ensure comprehension of risks, benefits, and alternatives to the proposed research or practice.

Informed Consent

The NASP (2010) code of ethics defines informed consent as follows:

> The person giving consent has the legal authority to make a consent decision, a clear understanding of what it is he or she is consenting to, and that his or her consent is freely given and may be withdrawn without prejudice. (p. 3)

It is the practitioners' and researchers' responsibility to provide individuals with developmentally adequate and culturally appropriate information so they are apprised of the services in which they will engage (Beahrs & Gutheil, 2001).

The Protection of Human Subjects (2009), a policy put in place by the U.S. Department of Health & Human Services, calls for informed consent to be a signed form that comprehensively reviews the practice or research in which an individual will engage. Informed consent is documented by reporting the date it was received, reporting if it was approved by an institutional review board (IRB), and suggesting that the consenting individual understands the entirety of their commitment (APA, 2017; NASP, 2010; Protection of Human Subjects, 2009). When an individual demonstrates understanding, that indicates their participation is consensual, safe, and not coerced (Bester et al., 2016).

According to the *Belmont Report* by the National Commission for the Protection of Human Subjects of Biomedical and Behavioral Research (1979), informed consent is obtained by someone of majority age or by a parent/guardian on a minor's behalf. Minors are perceived as demonstrating limited capacity to make informed decisions and cannot typically provide informed consent for research and practice (Rossi et al., 2003). To safeguard children and their maturing cognition, children's participation in research and practice should be linked to a protective mechanism, such as parental permission, even when this requirement is waived (Miller & Nelson, 2006). Permission for minors to participate in research or practice can be attained from one parent when research either involves minimal risk or greater than minimal risk with direct benefit to the child participant. However, both parents must consent when research or practice demonstrates greater than minimal risk without direct benefit to the child (Horng & Grady, 2003).

Culturally informed practice requires knowing at what age individuals can consent for themselves in services and research because that age can differ by state and region. Table 5.1 lists information in research and practice pertaining to who provides consent with minors. It gives a list of ages from Kerwin et al. (2015) that informs when youth are able to consent without parental involvement in drug and mental health treatment. It also provides information from World Population Review (n.d.) on the age at which youth reach majority. The research column reflects the age of majority when one can consent for themselves. The mental health and drug treatment columns inform who can consent for minors and at what age.

TABLE 5.1. Legal Age of Consent: Parent and Adolescent Decision-Making Authority for Inpatient and Outpatient Drug and Mental Health Treatment and Research

States[a]	Research[a]	Mental health treatment[b]		Drug treatment[b]	
		Inpatient[b]	Outpatient[b]	Inpatient[b]	Outpatient[b]
Alabama	19	Minor (≥14)	Minor (≥14)	Minor	Minor
Alaska	18	No law	No law	No law	No law
Arizona	18	Parent	Parent	Either (≥12)	Either (≥12)
Arkansas	18	No law	No law	No law	No law
California	18	Minor (≥12)	Minor (≥12)	Either (≥12)	Either (≥12)
Colorado	18	Minor (≥15)	Minor (≥15)	Minor	Minor
Connecticut	18	Either (≥14)[a]	Minor	Either	Either
Delaware	18	Parent	Parent	Parent	Either (≥14)
District of Columbia	18	Parent	Minor	Minor	Minor
Florida	18	Parent	Minor (≥13)	Either	Minor
Georgia	18	Parent	Either (≥12)	Either (≥12)	Minor
Hawaii	18	Parent	Minor	Minor	Minor
Idaho	18	Either (≥14)	Either	Either	Either
Illinois	18	Either (≥16)	Minor (≥12)	Minor (≥12)	Minor (≥12)
Indiana	18	Minor	Minor	Minor	Minor
Iowa	18	Minor/Both	Minor	Either	Either
Kansas	18	Either (≥14)	Either (≥14)	Minor	Minor
Kentucky	18	Minor (≥16)	Minor (≥16)	Either	Minor
Louisiana	18	Minor	Minor	Minor	Minor
Maine	18	Minor	Minor	Both	Minor
Maryland	18	Either (≥16)	Either (≥16)	Either	Minor
Massachusetts	18	Either (≥16)	Either (≥16)	Minor (≥12)	Minor (≥12)
Michigan	18	Either (≥14)	Minor (≥14)	Either (≥14)	Either (≥14)
Minnesota	18	Minor (≥16)	Minor (≥16)	Minor (≥16)	Minor (≥16)
Mississippi	18	Parent	No law	Parent	Minor (≥15)
Missouri	18	Parent	Parent	Either	Either
Montana	18	Either (≥16)	Either (≥16)	Minor	Minor
Nebraska	19	Either	Either	Either	Either
Nevada	18	Parent	Parent	Minor	Minor
New Hampshire	18	Either	Either	Minor (≥12)	Minor (≥12)
New Jersey	18	Parent	Parent	Minor	Minor

TABLE 5.1. Legal Age of Consent: Parent and Adolescent Decision-Making Authority for Inpatient and Outpatient Drug and Mental Health Treatment and Research (*Continued*)

States[a]	Research[a]	Mental health treatment[b]		Drug treatment[b]	
		Inpatient[b]	Outpatient[b]	Inpatient[b]	Outpatient[b]
New Mexico	18	Minor (≥14)	Minor (≥14)	Minor (≥14)	Minor (≥14)
New York	18	Either (≥16)	Either	Either	Either
North Carolina	18	Parent	Minor	Parent	Minor
North Dakota	18	Parent	Parent	Minor (≥14)	Minor (≥14)
Ohio	18	Parent	Minor (≥14)	Minor	Minor
Oklahoma	18	Minor (≥16)	No law	Minor (≥16)	Minor
Oregon	18	Parent	Minor (≥14)	Minor	Minor (≥14)
Pennsylvania	18	Either (≥14)	Either (≥14)	Either	Either
Rhode Island	18	Both	Both	Either	Either
South Carolina	18	Minor (≥16)	Minor (≥16)	Minor (≥16)	Minor (≥16)
South Dakota	18	Both (≥16)	Both (≥16)	Either	Either
Tennessee	18	Minor (≥16)	Minor (≥16)	Either (≥16)	Either (≥16)
Texas	18	Either (≥16)	No law	Either (≥16)	Either (≥16)
Utah	18	No law	No law	Parent	Parent
Vermont	18	Minor (≥14)	Minor (≥14)	Minor (≥12)	Minor (≥12)
Virginia	18	Both (≥14)	Minor	Both (≥14)	Minor
Washington	18	Minor (≥13)	Minor (≥13)	Parent	Minor (≥13)
West Virginia	18	Both (≥12)	Both (≥12)	Minor	Minor
Wisconsin	18	Both (≥14)	Both (≥14)	Parent	Either (≥12)
Wyoming	18	No law	No law	No law	No law

Note. Parent = parental consent only required; Minor = minor consent only required; Either = either parental or minor consent; Both = both parental and minor consent required; No law = No law was found addressing that particular form of treatment. If a state specified an age at which a minor was considered mature, that age is indicated in parentheses.
[a]Data from World Population Review (n.d.). [b]From "What Can Parents Do? A Review of Tate Laws Regarding Decision Making for Adolescent Drug Abuse and Mental Health Treatment," by M. E. Kerwin, K. C. Kirby, D. Speziali, M. Duggan, C. Mellitz, B. Versek, and A. McNamara, 2015, *Journal of Child & Adolescent Substance Abuse*, *24*(3), p. 170. Copyright 2015 by Taylor & Francis. Adapted with permission.

Assent

When engaging in practice or research, minors are expected to *assent*, which refers to their "affirmative agreement to participate in psychological services or research" (NASP, 2010, p. 3). Young minors are not held to the same standards with assent as informed consent because assent serves to provide a sense of self-determination when full capacity is not met, whereas informed consent from parents/guardians indicates the permission needed for youth to engage in practice or research, according to the National Commission for the Protection of Human Subjects of Biomedical and Behavioral Research (1979). The commission states that the assenting individual should know what procedures will be performed, choose freely to participate, communicate this choice without doubt, and be aware of the option to withdraw.

Assent from adolescents looks different from assent practices for younger youth because minors older than 13 years of age demonstrate similar decision-making abilities as adults (e.g., Tait et al., 2003; Weithorn, 1983). Evaluating adolescent capacity involves assessing one's age, maturity, and psychological state (Redding, 1993; Roth-Cline & Nelson, 2013). Adolescents should demonstrate understanding of consent content similar to that of an adult figure representing them. While research indicates minors can demonstrate decreased executive function and risk awareness compared with adults, Bernhardt et al. (2003) found that asking adolescents to personalize the implications of their practice/research involvement or to share the results of their participation with others leads to their demonstrating similar risk awareness and executive function capacities as adults. Thus, a culturally informed approach with GSD youth calls for researchers to acknowledge GSD youth's developmental capacity and to enact practices that can guide their capacity to be similar to that of adults. Nevertheless, the expectation remains that minors are typically required to have adult-informed consent as a safeguard until they are of a majority age to consent for themselves.

LIMITATIONS OF REQUIRING PARENTAL/GUARDIAN CONSENT

A culturally informed framework involves identifying current practices that conflict with specific cultural groups' not having equal access to treatment in research and practice (Fisher-Borne et al., 2015; Sue, 2001). For instance, working with GSD youth typically requires informed consent and may pose challenges that prevent these youth from participating in the access to mental health services or research, or both. For example, families may not reside in a supportive environment, families themselves may be unsupportive of their GSD children, or families may be actively learning how to be supportive of their GSD child (e.g., trying to manage unsupportive actions). Family rejection could result in negative mental health outcomes for GSD youth, such as increased depression, substance use, and suicidal ideation (McConnell et al., 2016; Ryan et al., 2010). Furthermore, families of GSD youth may disapprove of mental health services in general and may encourage youth to resolve their concerns on their own, which could also limit access to services or to research participation (Richardson, 2001).

Although requiring informed consent and assent for therapy, assessment, and research may present as a safeguard to minors, this requirement may also prevent a significant portion of the population from participating (U.S. Department of Health & Human Services, 2001). Therefore, APA (2018) developed the *Resolution on Support for the Expansion of Mature Minors' Ability to Participate in Research*, which supports including GSD youth in research without requiring parent/guardian consent. The writers of the resolution called for cultural humility by seeking to eliminate harmful situations for youth by removing the requirement of having parental consent to participate. The resolution writers promoted public health and wellness agendas by calling for inclusivity of marginalized populations via alternate consent procedures. They acknowledged the existence of a federal mandate enforcing waived consent alongside the inconsistent application of this standard by IRBs (Mustanski, 2011). The writers of the resolution also highlighted the risk of not including youth without access to parental or guardian consent in research. For instance, research cannot accurately reflect the views of GSD youth when those presenting with more risk (e.g., limited access to parental or guardian consent) are not included.

The APA (2018) resolution called for (a) research to extend "mature minor laws" from practice to research, in which consent can be waived when no more than minimal risk is posed; (b) IRBs to become more knowledgeable about research protocols to allow ethical inclusion of GSD youth without access to parental/guardian consent when requiring consent could bring harm and alternative research protections are in place; and (c) research to use advocates in consent procedures when appropriate. Alternative consent methods are needed by GSD youth to promote their inclusion, foster competent practice and research, and limit harmful practice with marginalized individuals (Diamond et al., 2012). The following section informs the available practices when seeking parental consent presents as harmful or violates the ethical standard of nonmaleficence (NASP, 2010).

CONSENT/ASSENT PROCEDURES SANS PARENTAL CONSENT

After identifying practices that do not meet the needs of specific cultures via a culturally informed framework, next steps involve addressing ways to amend current practice to make it culturally inclusive (Fisher-Borne et al., 2015; Sue, 2001). There are ethically sound consent/assent procedures that permit youth to participate in research without pursing parental consent methods when it could bring them harm. Both emancipated youth and mature youth give consenting power to youth themselves. For youth who are not considered emancipated or mature by law, waived parental consent and loco parentis procedures are available. Because consent from parents is a removed practice from these alternative methods, youth must demonstrate the capacity to consent via their age, maturity, and psychological state; and they must demonstrate full comprehension of the assent or consent form (Roth-Cline & Nelson, 2013).

Emancipated Youth

Youth under the age of 18 and as young as 14 may have the right to access care and provide informed consent under legal principles, such as emancipated minor rulings. An *emancipated minor* refers to youth who become legally responsible for themselves and are able to consent to their own treatment or care. Emancipated youth may include but are not limited to those who have a court document declaring their independence from their parents/guardians, are married, are pregnant, have a child, or have served in the military (Cohen et al., 2015; English et al., 2010). Researchers and practitioners should consult state laws and regulations that determine what constitutes a youth as emancipated in their state. There are few examples of GSD-emancipated youth included in research and practice.

Mature Minors

A *mature minor* is an unemancipated minor who demonstrates the cognitive maturity to give informed consent for themselves (English et al., 2010). DeKraai and Sales (1991) discussed that medical doctors in some states are qualified to determine if a mature minor demonstrates the capacity to consent to medical procedures. Approved medical procedures include donating blood, treating substance use, addressing sexual/reproductive health (e.g., sexually transmitted infections, abortions), or emergency medical procedures (Coleman & Rosoff, 2013). To identify if researchers and practitioners are permitted to work with mature minors, DeKraai and Sales (1991) recommended consulting one's state laws regarding mature minor guidelines.

Waived Consent and in Loco Parentis Procedures

The Protection of Human Subjects (2009) indicates that for research that is no more than minimal risk the IRB may approve a request to waive some or all of the required elements of informed consent under specific circumstances. The Protection of Human Subjects policy specifies that to waive informed consent, the IRB must determine that

> (1) The research involves no more than minimal risk to subjects; (2) The waiver or alteration will not adversely affect the rights and welfare of the subjects; (3) The research could not practicably be carried out without the waiver or alteration; and (4) Whenever appropriate, the subjects will be provided with additional pertinent information after participation. (Protection of Human Subjects, 2009, p. 8)

When informed consent cannot be waived, in loco parentis is another option that addresses the need to safeguard measures when parents are unavailable as a protective measure for minors. In loco parentis procedures could include identifying an accepting adult figure independent of the enacted research or practice to support a GSD youth's participation in lieu of the minor's parent or guardian (e.g., Varjas et al., 2008). In research, various roles, as follows, are affiliated with enacting waived consent with in loco parentis procedures.

Researcher

The researcher is the individual or team conducting the research. A separate entity is needed for the in loco parentis representative to prevent a biased assessment of a youth's capacity to participate.

In Loco Parentis Representative

An *in loco parentis representative* is an adult figure who is trained to assess capacity of a minor to participate in research. The individual serving in loco parentis is unaffiliated with the research or outcomes of a study to prevent biased assessment of youth's capacity to participate (Freedman et al., 1993). They should be regarded as an accepting ally to GSD youth communities.

Crisis Management Specialist

If a minor seeks involvement or is already involved with a study, the crisis management specialist (CMS) serves to manage times when the youth reports intent to harm themselves or others. The CMS is immediately contacted at the time of identified risk to evaluate the acuteness of risk, assess if means or plans are identified, coordinate means restriction or hospitalization, monitor the youth, and identify a culturally informed mental health professional for longer term care (Pilkington & D'Augelli, 1995).

EXAMPLES OF STUDIES USING WAIVED CONSENT PRACTICES

Over the years, researchers have documented instances in which the culturally informed practice of waived consent was used specifically for GSD youth. For instance, Remafedi (1994) waived parental/guardian consent in a study that taught cognitive and behavioral methods aimed to reduce HIV/AIDS among 139 sexual minority youth who were 13 to 21 years old. Participants were recruited from advertisements, flyers, and peer or professional referrals. They were compensated an unidentified amount for participating. Similarly, Heck (2015) attained a waiver of parental/guardian consent from their IRB for all minors when piloting an intervention with 10 GSD youth that sought to promote resilience in a mental health program based in a gay–straight alliance (GSA; most recently, this acronym refers to gender and sexuality alliance). At the beginning of each intervention session, an assent script was read, and participants provided verbal assent. Additional procedures on assent and consent were not provided.

In addition to waiving consent, some researchers have taken additional steps to help GSD youth participate in research. For example, Pilkington and D'Augelli (1995) contacted community-based organizations (CBOs) working with lesbian as well as gay youth (ages 15–21) and asked them to recruit participants ($N = 194$) who engaged in the CBOs' activities. Pilkington and D'Augelli (1995) acknowledged the constraints of requiring parental/guardian consent with lesbian as well as gay youth and enlisted an adult with professional counseling experience at each CBO to "assure that all replies were confidential and that youth were in no way coerced into participation" (Pilkington & D'Augelli, 1995, p. 36). Given the waiver of consent, a form was not signed by these adults nor was consent signed. The adult's purpose was to assist in the assent process for each youth (e.g., ensuring confidentiality, ensuring absence of coercion, answering questions) and to be available for questions throughout the study.

Similarly, Elze (2002) enlisted a youth advocate for the consent process to address in loco parentis requirements. Her study examined the risk factors of internalizing/externalizing problems with 184 lesbian, gay, and bisexual youth between 13 and 18 years old. The researcher met with each participant to determine whether consent should be waived to protect youth from having to come out to their parents/guardians. When consent was waived, the researcher worked with an advocate to "verify the youths' understanding of their rights, the assent procedures, and the voluntary nature of their participation" (Elze, 2002, p. 90). Waived consent indicated no forms were signed by an adult, only assent forms. Adults were available throughout the study to answer questions and to verify understanding.

Twenty high school students were enrolled in Lasser and Tharinger's 2003 study. Youth over 18 years of age provided informed consent, whereas youth under 18 signed assent when it was not considered harmful. If minors were not out to their parents/guardian, the researcher and director of a nonprofit agency had a discussion to determine if participating in the study interview would place the prospective participants at risk. Unlike other studies that included a third-party adult who monitored youth's assent, in this study, the minor and first author signed a consent form for the minor to participate. This demonstrates a potential conflict of interest because the first author enacted dual roles as a researcher and consent stand-in adult.

Kiperman (2018) conducted a dissertation that included an option for waived parental consent with the in loco parentis safeguard of an identified youth advocate. Kiperman sampled sexual and gender minority youth ($N = 135$) and explored how GSD youth experience support and nonsupport using mixed methods data. An eligibility screener was used to ensure participants met study inclusion criteria (between the ages of 14 and 17 years old, enrolled in school, did not identify as heterosexual and cisgender). In the eligibility screener, youth were asked if they were able to ask their parents for consent to participate. Those who said yes and were eligible were given a parental/guardian consent form to return, signed, before beginning their study involvement. Youth who indicated that they were unable to secure parental consent were provided access to the project's youth advocate who was a local CBO president for a group that served GSD youth. The youth advocate answered questions and was available to youth as neutral party who was not connected with the research study. The youth advocate was also available to determine if the GSD youth did not demonstrate the capacity to consent. In addition, a community therapist who had expertise working with this population served as a CMS for the project. The CMS was contacted if youth indicated any intent to harm themselves or others.

CONSENT/ASSENT PROCEDURES SPECIFIC TO GSD YOUTH

Thus far, we have defined consent and assent while addressing the barriers they present in promoting inclusion of vulnerable individuals, such as GSD youth, in research and practice. We also have reviewed alternative consent procedures that address these barriers and have provided examples of research that used various waived consent practices. In addition to identifying alternate consent procedures that promote GSD youth accessing services, a culturally informed framework calls for researchers to acknowledge additional ways we can foster relevant, meaningful practices when working with marginalized populations (Fisher-Borne et al., 2015; Sue, 2001). Therefore, this section addresses additional accommodations to informed consent/assent/waived consent practices when serving GSD youth to develop culturally informed and inclusive practice. We first review general recommendations followed by those specific to practice and research settings.

Confidentiality

When including GSD youth in research and practice, we must take every effort to protect their ethical right to confidentiality. Researchers and practitioners should be aware of the NASP (2010) ethics code I.2.6, which asks that

> school psychologists respect the right of privacy of students, parents, and colleagues with regard to sexual orientation, gender identity, or transgender status. They do not share information about the sexual orientation, gender identity, or transgender status of a student (including minors), parent, or school employee with anyone without that individual's permission. (p. 5)

This code indicates GSD youth have the right to manage their identity disclosure and to whom they are out. This code informs that it is not a practitioner or researcher's place to disclose their identity to others.

Nevertheless, when GSD youth are notified of the risks affiliated with participating in research or practice, they should be notified of times when confidentiality may be breached. Specifically, confidentiality is breached when youth endorse ideation or intent to harm themselves or others, require hospitalization, or when a parent/guardian contacts a researcher or practitioner to see if their child is participating in their study or services, respectively. While youth have an ethical right to confidentiality and privacy, parents and guardians may have rights to access their children's confidential information to which their consent was initially waived (APA, 2017; NASP, 2010). Although practitioners and researchers should remind parents of their child's right to confidentiality and privacy, they may be obligated to answer questions parents ask (e.g., Did my child participate in services or research?). Practitioners and researchers maintaining GSD youth's confidentiality should consult state guidelines to verify the expectation.

Gendered Language in the Consent/Assent/Waived Consent Process

Typically, the language of consent forms reflects binary gender norms whereby "he" and "she" are often used. Not all youth identify with these gender labels, and using "he" and "she" could ignite feelings of isolation or lack of acceptance for GSD individuals. Including "they" or avoiding labeling of "he" and "she" should be enacted to promote gender-inclusive practice when talking with youth and in written waived consent forms with which they are provided (Gustafsson Sendén et al., 2015).

Procedures in Practice

Informed consent is used in both research and practice. While the intent and application of informed consent involve similar processes in each, there are some differences to consider. The following is a discussion of considerations when enacting informed consent in practice.

Seeing School-Based Practitioners for Therapy

NASP (2010) ethics code I.1.2 states that if a student is not old enough to receive school psychological services independent of parental/guardian consent (based on findings presented in Table 5.1), the professional should obtain parental/guardian consent to provide continuing services to the student beyond preliminary meetings. Typically, students can be seen without parental/guardian consent in urgent situations and via self-referrals to establish the nature and degree of the presenting concern. NASP (2010) inferred that minors can be seen therapeutically without parent/guardian consent before forming a lasting clinical–client relationship in ongoing therapy, psychological diagnosis, and assessment for special education eligibility. Once these additional steps are taken, parental/guardian consent typically is required.

Conversely, Herlihy and Remley (2001) suggested that school counseling or therapy is a standard educational service to which students have the right to access. This means school-based therapy can be provided without parental consent despite youths' inability to legally consent for themselves. Herlihy and Remley discussed how youth have the right to confidentiality and privacy, but Family Educational Rights and Privacy Act (1974) policies identify a child's privacy and confidentiality as belonging to their parents. This confirms that parents can request information from practitioners and they can withdraw their child from services at any time. Therefore, children and youth should be made aware of these limitations in their service provisions.

Seeing School-Based Practitioners for Assessment

The NASP (2010) ethics code indicates that parental consent is required and cannot be waived before psychological diagnosis or assessment for special education eligibility. Additional challenges for practitioners in assessment include how to address an individual's sexual orientation or gender identity in a psychological report. Typically, there is no need to share this information, and best practice indicates that practitioners should not disclose this information on a GSD youth's behalf because disclosure should be managed by the youth themselves.

Accessing Provider Experience With GSD Youth

GSD youth should have access to practitioners' experience in working with GSD individuals (Allen et al., 1998). Useful information practitioners should make available to their clients includes the practitioner's framework (e.g., affirming cognitive behavior therapy), expected outcomes (e.g., whether the practitioner aims to affirm one's identity or "turn someone straight" with conversion therapy), how many years they have worked with GSD individuals, and the specific practices they enact to exhibit competence with GSD individuals (e.g., using safe space kits; adapting interventions to meet GSD youth needs; using gendered or nongendered pronouns; having experience in navigating GSD youth-specific topics, such as disclosure and transitioning).

Identifying the Costs

GSD youth should be notified of costs upfront. Costs may include parking, travel fees, and time (Fisher & Mustanski, 2014). There should be no difference in costs for GSD youth compared with those not identifying with their community. Nevertheless, a culturally informed framework involves acknowledging that GSD youth may not have similar resources as youth with access to parental/guardian consent (e.g., car rides, money). Given these may present as potential barriers, providers may seek funding options and resources (e.g., providing information on public transportation or travel funds), or troubleshoot around limitations. Promoting access to services could increase use and bolster culturally informed, sensitive, and fair practice with GSD youth.

Understanding the Benefits

When reviewing the consent/assent procedures, youth should be explicitly told about the benefits they may experience from therapy. Benefits can include a gained sense of hope around disclosure; sense of community membership with GSD peers, GSD adults, or allies; and an improved sense of identity development (Fisher & Mustanski, 2014).

Procedures in Research

While practice tends to be informed by empiricism and evidence, research tends to explore new phenomenon in which the results of studies are unknown and are, at times, exploratory. Given the nature of research, a separate discussion is warranted to inform how to navigate informed consent with youth.

Stigma Around "Minimal Risk" and GSD Youth

Minimal risk, according to the Protection of Human Subjects (2009), means "the probability and magnitude of harm or discomfort . . . are not greater . . .

than those ordinarily encountered in daily life or during the performance of routine or psychological examinations or tests" (p. 4). Research with GSD youth is often considered as more than minimal risk based on specific findings that indicate GSD youth are at greater risk of mental health, substance use, and victimization problems compared with their heterosexual, cisgender peers (Almeida et al., 2009; Hughes et al., 2010). Although many GSD individuals face hardships related to their marginalization, many GSD youth demonstrate resilience and lead well-adjusted lives (Fisher & Mustanski, 2014). Including GSD youth in research by demonstrating a range of their risk and resilience can help researchers deliver comprehensive, culturally informed service provision and advocacy on their behalf. Having opportunities for GSD youth to participate in research makes youth aware of advocates and support systems in their community that they may otherwise have not known (Wagaman, 2016).

Institutional Review Board

IRBs provide ethical and regulatory oversight of research involving human participants. An IRB aims to protect participant rights, welfare, and well-being; ensures compliance with local, state, and federal laws and regulations as well as agency regulations; and applies the highest ethical standards (National Institute of Environmental Health Sciences, 2019). Researchers have a responsibility to both enact consent procedures that meet the safety standards of the IRB as well as promote the IRB's culturally informed practice by sharing new approaches that aim to protect and to ensure the well-being of marginalized populations, such as GSD youth (Amdur, 2006). Researchers should also partner with IRBs to offer clear and concise information about in loco parentis procedures. They should be available to answer the IRB's questions and have an open dialogue to advocate for populations that historically have been underrepresented. It is important for researchers to provide psychoeducation to IRB members about the ethical and possible therapeutic benefits of this procedure (e.g., promoting self-determination, autonomy, beneficence, nonmaleficence) and the need to include missing voices in research (Amdur, 2006).

Reasons for Inclusion of GSD Youth

In explaining the purpose of the research during the consent process, discussion should address how the study specifically pertains to GSD youth and why they are included. An example would be identifying that a study seeks to explore GSD youth experiences of disclosure and coming out to oneself and others. Participants should be notified of the procedures involved (e.g., a qualitative interview or a survey with the specific question types and scales included) and how their GSD identity will be a part of the study (e.g., qualitative questions and follow-up prompts for specific details related to one's GSD identity).

Compensation

Research has rules and regulations that inform how one may be compensated for their participation. The expectation is that GSD youth should be compensated at equal rates as their heterosexual, cisgender peers. The American Academy of Pediatrics (Weise et al., 2002) recommended giving gifts rather than money to compensate for research participation; however, there are endless strategies and perspectives about how to compensate research participants. For instance, Bagley et al. (2007) discussed a wage model based on time and effort as appropriate with older adolescents. Wages should be commensurate with the effort exerted and should not present as coercive.

Risks and Costs in Research

Discussions of costs (e.g., travel, parking, time) and risks (e.g., instances when confidentiality may be breached similar to those discussed in the practice section) should be disclosed and carefully discussed. External resources also should be provided (e.g., local CBOs, GSD youth–friendly therapists, GSA programs, GSD youth summits or conferences in the region) to promote resilience among GSD youth. GSD youth–friendly crisis hotlines like The Trevor Project (a 24/7 service for GSD youth who have thoughts of suicide or who need a safe space to talk; 1-866-488-7386; https://www.thetrevorproject.org/) could be provided should peers or their friends be looking for resources.

RECOMMENDATIONS AND FUTURE DIRECTIONS

Few studies (e.g., Lasser & Tharinger, 2003; Pilkington & D'Augelli, 1995, Remafedi, 1994) have incorporated waived consent practice in social and behavioral sciences and in practice with GSD youth. Promoting culturally informed practice calls for researchers to advocate for waived parental/guardian consent to be standard practice with GSD youth to foster inclusive, ethical practice (e.g., Varjas et al., 2008, 2016). Furthermore, in research that has used waived consent procedures, the methods sections often present limited detail on the specific procedures used to execute this practice. Future research should present explicit consent/assent procedures to normalize and share possible culturally inclusive methods. Researchers can present explicit examples to their IRBs of approved consent practices with vulnerable communities so they may become more inclined to accept less familiar methods of waiving parental/guardian informed consent in the future.

While it is evident that youth without access to parental/guardian consent are limited in their ability to participate in research and practice compared with those with access to parental/guardian consent, whether or not there are differences in the lived experiences of these youth is unknown. Future research should seek to include youth (with and without access to parental/ guardian consent) to determine whether group differences exist. Researchers can also target samples of GSD youth without access to parental/guardian consent to inform our limited knowledge about their experiences.

In addition, future research should evaluate and advance the standards presented in this chapter to inform research and practice with GSD youth without access to parental/guardian consent. Preliminary standards for research were created based on methods presented in previous studies (Lasser & Tharinger, 2003; Pilkington & D'Augelli, 1995, Remafedi, 1994). Qualitative studies could evaluate how GSD youth, researchers/practitioners, parents/ guardians, and IRBs perceive the quality of the recommendations made, the integrity and acceptability of the recommended procedures, and additional recommendations for advancing the current standards. To inform practice with GSD youth, practitioners should consult state and local laws and regulations, and write explicit guidelines in a national document for practitioners to reference.

This chapter serves to promote the inclusion of GSD youth who have had limited ability to participate in practice and research. Nevertheless, limited research has explored how these practices may impact youth with intersecting marginalized statuses, such as youth who identify with a diverse gender identity, sexual orientation, or both; youth of color; youth from low socio-economic backgrounds; and so forth. There is also limited research on the variation of waived consent implantation for youth in middle school or high school. Future studies should explore how intersecting identities and GSD youth across age groups can be better included in research and practice. Further investigation of intersectionality related to waived consent procedures could expand the range of students' access to services.

Although consent procedures are mandatory in research (e.g., APA, 2017; NASP, 2010), mental health professionals in schools often do not require parental/guardian consent for students to participate unless risk or an ongoing therapeutic relationship has become present (Evans, 1999). However, GSD youth's ability to access services in schools (e.g., stigma around going to the counselor's office or seeking help, stigma about GSD identification, challenges of the coming out process) may be limited and should be explored in future research.

IRBs serve the purpose of ensuring ethical treatment of participants in research (Amdur, 2006). Given that parental/guardian consent acts as a safeguard for minor participants, waiving parental/guardian consent may not be permitted by some IRBs at this time. IRBs may view waiving parental/ guardian consent as harmful, or members of an IRB may be unaware of alternative consent procedures for parental/guardian consent when working with marginalized, vulnerable populations. Researchers should continue advocating for the GSD youth communities by educating their IRB, engaging in conversations with them about consent procedures, and sharing studies that have ethically waived consent for GSD youth.

CONCLUSION

As practice currently stands, consent/assent documents and processes are typically presented with gendered language, limited insight into how practitioners and researchers foster a safe and affirming space, and without the researcher/practitioners' personal pronoun preferences. Using waived consent and in loco parentis methods for research and clinical practice allows for historically silenced, excluded voices to be heard. By presenting examples in this chapter of research that used waived consent practice and also presenting ideas for clinicians to make their consent practices more inclusive of GSD youth, we hope to inform the progress that has been made thus far.

While studies have enacted waived consent procedures with GSD youth, IRBs, researchers, and practitioners should be encouraged to incorporate these procedures as standard practice. By doing so, professionals are taking steps toward removing barriers. In turn, GSD youth can have more access to services, be represented in research, and take steps toward addressing mental health and health disparities prevalent in their community. When professionals make these small changes, significant benefits for GSD youth can result—from improving their individual self-concept to fostering a national shift toward inclusion and acceptance.

TAKEAWAYS AND OPPORTUNITIES

Typical consent and assent procedures inherently exclude vulnerable populations, such as GSD youth. The good news is that there are culturally informed consent methods that promote inclusivity. We developed a flowchart (see Exhibit 5.1) as a step-by-step approach to ethical implementation of inclusive waived consent procedures as discussed in this chapter. Given how previous authors who used waived consent procedures provided insight around their recruitment procedures as well, we also developed a flowchart (see Exhibit 5.2) to inform how researchers and practitioners can practice inclusive recruitment procedures. Exhibits 5.3 and 5.4 depict examples of a recruitment flyer and screening script to use in recruitment, respectively. Additional questions beyond those posed in Exhibits 5.1 and 5.2 to guide your understanding of waived consent are the following:

- What are the differences between consent, assent, and waived consent?

- Why is it encouraged to use waived consent with GSD youth? When is waived consent not appropriate with GSD youth?

- What is a youth advocate? What purpose does this role serve in enacting waived consent procedures? Can a youth advocate be a research team member? Why or why not?

- In what instances may confidentiality be breached when working with GSD youth? What ethics codes protect and encourage confidentiality with GSD youth?

EXHIBIT 5.1

Flowchart to Guide Implementation of Waived Consent Procedures

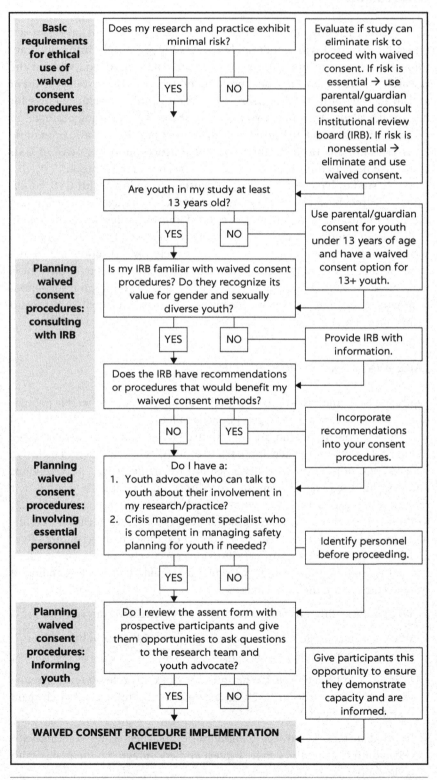

EXHIBIT 5.2

Inclusive Recruitment Procedure Recommendations

Materials

Recruitment Permission Scripts
Serves to ask permission to disseminate study flyers and recruitment efforts. Script content should include
- [ ] introduction:
  - o who presents the script
  - o their credentials
- [ ] summary of study purpose and tasks
- [ ] summary of perceived benefits and risks of participating
- [ ] eligibility criteria (who could participate)
- [ ] request to share recruitment flyer

Recruitment Flyers
Serves as visual aid to inform prospective participants of study. Flyer content should include
- [ ] summary of study purpose and tasks
- [ ] summary of perceived benefits
- [ ] eligibility criteria to participate
- [ ] contact information

Disseminate materials

Permission to Share
Get permission to share flyers from venues or websites.

Venues for Inclusive Dissemination
With goals of accessible and inclusive recruitment, we recommend recruiting/sharing flyers with the following wide range of venues:

GSD youth–specific venues
- [ ] community-based organizations
- [ ] fellow researchers/practitioners
- [ ] gender and sexuality alliances in schools
- [ ] social media groups for gender and sexually diverse (GSD) youth
- [ ] homeless shelters for GSD youth
- [ ] parent support groups for GSD youth

GSD youth–nonspecific venues
*Do not seek out of places have a history of not supporting the GSD youth community.
- [ ] schools, malls, parks, religious venues, information bulletins

Snowball sampling
- [ ] encourage participants to share flyer with friends (e.g., word of mouth)

Screening

Screening
Youth should contact researchers to be screened for eligibility to participate. In screening, youth should be asked if a parent/guardian can consent to their participation, or if they prefer using waived consent procedures.

EXHIBIT 5.3

Example Flyer for Recruitment

PROJECT SUPPORT

Are you 14–17 years old?

Are you a part of the LGBTQ+ community?

Are you in high school and live in the United States?

Make a difference by taking a survey and sharing your experience of feeling supported and not supported by others.

Participation involves a 25-minute survey.

To show our thanks, you get a $5.00 Starbucks gift card once you finish your survey!

Contact us to get started at:
teampswsu@gmail.com

Learn more about us at:
www.projectsupport.org

PROJECT
SUPPORT

WAYNE STATE
UNIVERSITY

Note. LGBTQ = lesbian, gay, bisexual, transgender, and queer or questioning.

EXHIBIT 5.4

Example Recruitment Script

Recruitment Screening Script

Present to people who can approve sharing your recruitment flyers and information.

"Hi. I'm [*insert first name*], an [*insert job title or academic position (e.g., assistant professor)*] at [*insert university name here*]. I am a researcher, and I focus on identifying ways we can promote gender and sexually diverse youth's physical, behavioral, and mental health. I am conducting a study in which GSD youth complete a survey that takes approximately 20 minutes to complete. The study shows how supportive relationships and other ideas, such as outness and identity development, inform positive outcomes for their community. Do you have any questions about the general purpose of the study?

"If youth who [*attend your community organization*] would be interested in participating, we are recruiting youth who identify as GSD or as not straight and cisgender. Participants must be between ages 14 and 17 years old and be in high school. Interested youth can contact us via my e-mail or phone number to see if they are eligible to participate. I will ask them a few questions to determine if they are eligible, and then they will complete the online survey. The survey asks them some demographic questions and includes measures, such as [*insert measures here*]. Do you have any questions about how youth can participate or about the study itself? [*Answer questions*]. Once they finish the survey, they are compensated $5 as a thank you for their time. Please to not hesitate to ask me questions. Thank you."

REFERENCES

Allen, L. B., Glicken, A. D., Beach, R. K., & Naylor, K. E. (1998). Adolescent health care experience of gay, lesbian, and bisexual young adults. *Journal of Adolescent Health, 23*(4), 212–220. https://doi.org/10.1016/S1054-139X(98)00022-6

Almeida, J., Johnson, R. M., Corliss, H. L., Molnar, B. E., & Azrael, D. (2009). Emotional distress among LGBT youth: The influence of perceived discrimination based on sexual orientation. *Journal of Youth and Adolescence, 38*(7), 1001–1014. https://doi.org/10.1007/s10964-009-9397-9

Amdur, R. J. (2006). *Institutional review board: Management and function.* Jones & Bartlett Learning.

American Psychological Association. (2017). *Ethical principles of psychologists and code of conduct.* http://www.apa.org/ethics/code/index.aspx

American Psychological Association. (2018). *APA resolution on support for the expansion of mature minors' ability to participate in research.* https://www.apa.org/about/policy/resolution-minors-research.pdf

American Psychological Association & National Association of School Psychologists. (2015). *Resolution on gender and sexual orientation diversity in children and adolescents in schools.* http://www.apa.org/about/policy/orientation-diversity.aspx

Bagley, S. J., Reynolds, W. W., & Nelson, R. M. (2007). Is a "wage-payment" model for research participation appropriate for children? *Pediatrics, 119*(1), 46–51. https://doi.org/10.1542/peds.2006-1813

Beahrs, J. O., & Gutheil, T. G. (2001). Informed consent in psychotherapy. *American Journal of Psychiatry, 158*(1), 4–10. https://doi.org/10.1176/appi.ajp.158.1.4

Bernhardt, B. A., Tambor, E. S., Fraser, G., Wissow, L. S., & Geller, G. (2003). Parents' and children's attitudes toward the enrollment of minors in genetic susceptibility research: Implications for informed consent. *American Journal of Medical Genetics, 116A*(4), 315–323. https://doi.org/10.1002/ajmg.a.10040

Bester, J., Cole, C. M., & Kodish, E. (2016). The limits of informed consent for an overwhelmed patient: Clinicians' role in protecting patients and preventing overwhelm. *American Medical Association Journal of Ethics, 18*(9), 869–886. https://doi.org/10.1001/journalofethics.2016.18.9.peer2-1609

Cohen, L. T., Millock, P. J., Asheld, B. A., & Lane, B. (2015). Minor patients: Consent to treatment and access to medical records. *Journal of the American College of Radiology, 12*(8), 788–790. https://doi.org/10.1016/j.jacr.2015.05.006

Coleman, D. L., & Rosoff, P. M. (2013). The legal authority of mature minors to consent to general medical treatment. *Pediatrics, 131*(4), 786–793. https://doi.org/10.1542/peds.2012-2470

DeKraai, M. B., & Sales, B. D. (1991). Liability in child therapy and research. *Journal of Consulting and Clinical Psychology, 59*(6), 853–860. https://doi.org/10.1037/0022-006X.59.6.853

Diamond, G. M., Diamond, G. S., Levy, S., Closs, C., Ladipo, T., & Siqueland, L. (2012). Attachment-based family therapy for suicidal lesbian, gay, and bisexual adolescents: A treatment development study and open trial with preliminary findings. *Psychotherapy, 49*(1), 62–71. https://doi.org/10.1037/a0026247

Dorn, L. D., Susman, E. J., & Fletcher, J. C. (1995). Informed consent in children and adolescents: Age, maturation and psychological state. *Journal of Adolescent Health, 16*(3), 185–190. https://doi.org/10.1016/1054-139X(94)00063-K

Elze, D. E. (2002). Risk factors for internalizing and externalizing problems among gay, lesbian, and bisexual adolescents. *Social Work Research, 26*(2), 89–100. https://doi.org/10.1093/swr/26.2.89

English, A., Bass, L., Boyle, A. D., & Eshragh, F. (2010). *State minor consent laws: A summary* (3rd ed.). Center for Adolescent Health & the Law.

Evans, S. W. (1999). Mental health services in schools: Utilization, effectiveness, and consent. *Clinical Psychology Review, 19*(2), 165–178. https://doi.org/10.1016/S0272-7358(98)00069-5

Family Educational Rights and Privacy Act, 20 U.S.C. § 1232g (1974).

Fisher, C. B., & Mustanski, B. (2014). Reducing health disparities and enhancing the responsible conduct of research involving LGBT youth. *Hastings Center Report, 44*(4, Suppl. 4), S28–S31. https://doi.org/10.1002/hast.367

Fisher-Borne, M., Cain, J. M., & Martin, S. L. (2015). From mastery to accountability: Cultural humility as an alternative to cultural competence. *Social Work Education, 34*(2), 165–181. https://doi.org/10.1080/02615479.2014.977244

Freedman, B., Fuks, A., & Weijer, C. (1993). In loco parentis. Minimal risk as an ethical threshold for research upon children. *Hastings Center Report, 23*(2), 13–19. https://doi.org/10.2307/3562813

Gustafsson Sendén, M., Bäck, E. A., & Lindqvist, A. (2015). Introducing a gender-neutral pronoun in a natural gender language: The influence of time on attitudes and behavior. *Frontiers in Psychology, 6*, 893–905. https://doi.org/10.3389/fpsyg.2015.00893

Heck, N. C. (2015). The potential to promote resilience: Piloting a minority stress-informed, GSA-based, mental health promotion program for LGBTQ youth. *Psychology of Sexual Orientation and Gender Diversity, 2*(3), 225–231. https://doi.org/10.1037/sgd0000110

Herlihy, B., & Remley, T. P. (2001). Legal and ethical challenges in counseling. In D. C. Locke, J. E. Myers, & E. L. Herr (Eds.), *The handbook of counseling* (pp. 69–90). Sage Publications. https://doi.org/10.4135/9781452229218.n5

Horng, S., & Grady, C. (2003). Misunderstanding in clinical research: Distinguishing therapeutic misconception, therapeutic misestimation, and therapeutic optimism. *IRB: Ethics & Human Research, 25*(1), 11–16. https://doi.org/10.2307/3564408

Hughes, T., McCabe, S. E., Wilsnack, S. C., West, B. T., & Boyd, C. J. (2010). Victimization and substance use disorders in a national sample of heterosexual and sexual minority women and men. *Addiction, 105*(12), 2130–2140. https://doi.org/10.1111/j.1360-0443.2010.03088.x

Kerwin, M. E., Kirby, K. C., Speziali, D., Duggan, M., Mellitz, C., Versek, B., & McNamara, A. (2015). What can parents do? A review of state laws regarding decision making for adolescent drug abuse and mental health treatment. *Journal of Child & Adolescent Substance Abuse, 24*(3), 166–176. https://doi.org/10.1080/1067828X.2013.777380

Kiperman, S. (2018). *Exploring a model of social support and nonsupport among LGBTQ youth with and without parent consent* [Doctoral dissertation, Georgia State University]. Counseling and Psychological Services Dissertations. https://scholarworks.gsu.edu/cps_diss/128

Lasser, J., & Tharinger, D. (2003). Visibility management in school and beyond: A qualitative study of gay, lesbian, bisexual youth. *Journal of Adolescence, 26*(2), 233–244. https://doi.org/10.1016/S0140-1971(02)00132-X

Mayberry, M. (2013). Gay–straight alliances: Youth empowerment and working toward reducing stigma of LGBT youth. *Humanity & Society, 37*(1), 35–54. https://doi.org/10.1177/0160597612454358

McConnell, E. A., Birkett, M., & Mustanski, B. (2016). Families matter: Social support and mental health trajectories among lesbian, gay, bisexual, and transgender youth. *Journal of Adolescent Health, 59*(6), 674–680. https://doi.org/10.1016/j.jadohealth.2016.07.026

Miller, V. A., & Nelson, R. M. (2006). A developmental approach to child assent for nontherapeutic research. *Journal of Pediatrics, 149*(1, Suppl.), S25–S30. https://doi.org/10.1016/j.jpeds.2006.04.047

Mustanski, B. (2011). Ethical and regulatory issues with conducting sexuality research with LGBT adolescents: A call to action for a scientifically informed approach. *Archives of Sexual Behavior, 40*(4), 673–686. https://doi.org/10.1007/s10508-011-9745-1

Mustanski, B., & Fisher, C. B. (2016). HIV rates are increasing in gay/bisexual teens: IRB barriers to research must be resolved to bend the curve. *American Journal of Preventive Medicine, 51*(2), 249–252. https://doi.org/10.1016/j.amepre.2016.02.026

National Association of School Psychologists. (2010). *Principles for professional ethics.* https://www.nasponline.org/assets/Documents/Standards%20and%20Certification/Standards/1_%20Ethical%20Principles.pdf

National Commission for the Protection of Human Subjects of Biomedical and Behavioral Research. (1979, April 18). *The Belmont report: Ethical principles and guidelines for the protection of human subjects of research.* https://www.hhs.gov/ohrp/regulations-and-policy/belmont-report/read-the-belmont-report/index.html

National Institute of Environmental Health Sciences. (2019). *NIEHS Institutional Review Board.* https://www.niehs.nih.gov/about/boards/irb/index.cfm

Pilkington, N. W., & D'Augelli, A. R. (1995). Victimization of lesbian, gay, and bisexual youth in community settings. *Journal of Community Psychology, 23*(1), 34–56. https://doi.org/10.1002/1520-6629(199501)23:1<34::AID-JCOP2290230105>3.0.CO;2-N

Ponterotto, J. G. (2010). Multicultural personality: An evolving theory of optimal functioning in culturally heterogeneous societies. *Counseling Psychologist, 38*(5), 714–758. https://doi.org/10.1177/0011000009359203

Protection of Human Subjects, 45 CFR § 46 (2009). https://www.hhs.gov/ohrp/sites/default/files/ohrp/policy/ohrpregulations.pdf

Redding, R. E. (1993). Children's competence to provide informed consent for mental health treatment. *Washington and Lee Law Review, 50*(2), 695–753. https://ssrn.com/abstract=2387941

Remafedi, G. (1994). Cognitive and behavioral adaptations to HIV/AIDS among gay and bisexual adolescents. *Journal of Adolescent Health, 15*(2), 142–148. https://doi.org/10.1016/1054-139X(94)90541-X

Richardson, L. A. (2001). Seeking and obtaining mental health services: What do parents expect? *Archives of Psychiatric Nursing, 15*(5), 223–231. https://doi.org/10.1053/apnu.2001.27019

Rossi, W. C., Reynolds, W., & Nelson, R. M. (2003). Child assent and parental permission in pediatric research. *Theoretical Medicine and Bioethics, 24*(2), 131–148. https://doi.org/10.1023/A:1024690712019

Roth-Cline, M., & Nelson, R. M. (2013). Parental permission and child assent in research on children. *Yale Journal of Biology and Medicine, 86*(3), 291–301. https://www.ncbi.nlm.nih.gov/pmc/articles/PMC3767214/

Ryan, C., Russell, S. T., Huebner, D., Diaz, R., & Sanchez, J. (2010). Family acceptance in adolescence and the health of LGBT young adults. *Journal of Child and Adolescent Psychiatric Nursing, 23*(4), 205–213. https://doi.org/10.1111/j.1744-6171.2010.00246.x

Sue, D. W. (2001). Multidimensional facets of cultural competence. *Counseling Psychologist, 29*(6), 790–821. https://doi.org/10.1177/0011000001296002

Tait, A. R., Voepel-Lewis, T., & Malviya, S. (2003). Do they understand? (Part I): Parental consent for children participating in clinical anesthesia and surgery research. *Anesthesiology, 98*(3), 603–608. https://anesthesiology.pubs.asahq.org/article.aspx?articleid=1943286

U.S. Department of Health & Human Services. (2001, August). *Mental health: Culture, race, and ethnicity—A supplement to mental health: A report of the surgeon general.* Rockville, MD: Substance Abuse and Mental Health Services Administration. https://www.ncbi.nlm.nih.gov/books/NBK44243/

Varjas, K., Dew, B., Marshall, M., Graybill, E., Singh, A., Meyers, J., & Birckbichler, L. (2008). Bullying in schools towards sexual minority youth. *Journal of School Violence, 7*(2), 59–86. https://doi.org/10.1300/J202v07n02_05

Varjas, K., Kiperman, S., & Meyers, J. (2016). Disclosure experiences of urban, ethnically diverse LGBT high school students: Implications for school personnel. *School Psychology Forum, 10*(1), 72–92. https://www.nasponline.org/publications/periodicals/spf/volume-10/volume-10-issue-1-(spring-2016)/disclosure-experiences-of-urban-ethnically-diverse-lgbt-high-school-students-implications-for-school-personnel

Wagaman, M. A. (2016). Promoting empowerment among LGBTQ youth: A social justice youth development approach. *Child & Adolescent Social Work Journal, 33*(5), 395–405. https://doi.org/10.1007/s10560-016-0435-7

Weise, K. L., Smith, M. L., Maschke, K. J., & Copeland, H. L. (2002). National practices regarding payment to research subjects for participating in pediatric research. *Pediatrics, 110*(3), 577–582. https://doi.org/10.1542/peds.110.3.577

Weithorn, L. A. (1983). Children's capacities to decide about participation in research. *IRB, 5*(2), 1–5. https://doi.org/10.2307/3563792

World Population Review. (n.d.). *Age of majority by state 2020.* Retrieved June 5, 2020, from https://worldpopulationreview.com/states/age-of-majority-by-state/

6

Using a Systems Approach to Creating Equitable Educational Environments for Gender and Sexually Diverse Families

Julie C. Herbstrith

Approximately one-half million households in the United States are headed by same-gender couples (United States Census Bureau, 2011). In a sample of people who identify as lesbian, gay, bisexual, transgender, and queer or questioning (LGBTQ), nearly half of the women and one fifth of the men reported that they had children (Gates, 2013). These numbers translate to as many as 7 million children who are being raised by gender and sexually diverse (GSD) parents. A preponderance of evidence documents the lack of preparedness by a number of systems (e.g., medicine, mental health, social services, schools) to support GSD families (Bishop & Atlas, 2015; Gibson, 2016; Moe & Sparkman, 2015; Romanelli & Hudson, 2017). The purpose of this chapter is to describe current issues that GSD families experience as they navigate school systems and to propose empirically supported interventions that can be implemented to create equitable school environments and positive home–school partnerships for these families.

TRANSLATIONAL SCIENCE FRAMEWORK

This chapter uses a translational science framework to examine problems and to posit solutions for creating equitable educational environments for GSD families. This approach is one that translates the findings from basic research

https://doi.org/10.1037/0000211-007
Supporting Gender Identity and Sexual Orientation Diversity in K–12 Schools, M. C. Lytle and R. A. Sprott (Editors)

into efficient, effective practice in field settings (Edwards & Shaw, 2018). A primary goal of translational science is to use what is learned from basic science to drive new approaches for prevention and intervention (Edwards, 2017; Guastaferro & Collins, 2019). In this chapter, readers are introduced to ways a translational science framework can draw connections across disciplines (e.g., social psychology, school psychology) to facilitate the development of an equitable school environment for GSD families.

ECOLOGICAL SYSTEMS APPROACH

In line with prior research (Jeltova & Fish, 2005), this chapter contextualizes problems and solutions using an ecological systems lens. This approach fits well within the translational science framework just described because it allows change to be conceptualized as occurring within the existing environment. From this perspective, interventions are deployed at natural entry points within extant ecological systems, and effectiveness is measured in the field.

Bronfenbrenner's (1979) model of ecological systems posits that human beings exist within the following set of nested systems: microsystem, mesosystem, macrosystem, exosystem, and chronosystem. Although a full review of ecological systems theory is beyond the scope of this chapter (see Bronfenbrenner, 1979, 2005), I provide brief definitions of these systems here. The *microsystem* is the smallest of systems and consists of the individual as well as their interactions and relations with people in their immediate environment. The microsystem includes the characteristics of the individual and the effects of their interactions with other systems. For GSD parents, this includes the (recurring) coming out process, experiences of prejudice, and other factors that create minority stress and may lead to mental health issues (Brooks, 1981; Meyer, 2003). The *mesosystem* consists of the interactions between microsystems and with people within the proximal environment, such as school and community. The *macrosystem* is the system that holds social and cultural norms, values, and expectations. Importantly, the macrosystem informs and influences other systems. The *exosystem* consists of policies, institutions, and laws. It is informed by the values and norms of the macrosystem, and it influences the microsystem. For example, GSD people who wish to adopt children in areas where adoption by GSD people is illegal can be affected negatively because of marginalization and exclusionary legislation. The *chronosystem* consists of time itself and an individual's life course, such as the effects of experiencing and being influenced by historical events that occur during one's life, by events that happened in the past that shape current attitudes and behaviors, and that influence the exosystem.

According to ecological systems theory, systems exert bidirectional influence on each other. Applying an ecological systems framework to the issues that GSD families face in the schools means that both the targets for change and the solutions may be found within these systems. Moreover, it means that ecological systems may be leveraged to create and maintain positive systems change. Berk (2000) described the broad ecological system as one that engages in a regulation process that maintains balance via rules, boundaries, and roles that are consistently reinforced via feedback loops. In line with ecological theory, interventions can be applied to systems to disrupt this balance and achieve a new homeostasis based on new roles and new norms so that the new system can then be maintained by new routines (e.g., feedback loops that maintain the new order).

SYSTEMS-LEVEL LANDSCAPE FOR GSD FAMILIES

At the school systems level, many issues are often detrimental to GSD families. A review of the extant literature reveals that these issues can be conceptualized as falling into three broad areas: (a) educators' lack of knowledge about GSD communities and related issues, (b) a climate of heteronormativity and cisnormativity, and (c) anti-GSD prejudice. Before providing a review of each area, it is important to provide some broad context in which to examine why school-based issues facing GSD families are critical to understand.

First, many school systems are generally unprepared to work with GSD families (Adams & Persinger, 2013; Cooley, 2015). This lack of preparation is observed in many ways: low levels of comfort with GSD parents reported by teachers and staff (Averett & Hegde, 2012), bullying of students who are or who are perceived to be GSD (Hillard et al., 2014; Kosciw et al., 2016; Prati et al., 2011), lack of awareness of bullying targeted at or associated with GSD students and families (Kosciw et al., 2016; Prati et al., 2011), and explicit anti-GSD prejudice among educators (Herbstrith et al., 2013; Mudrey & Medina-Adams, 2006).

The relationship between home and school is a central theme that underlies a number of problems. Home–school relationships are a documented predictor of a number of outcomes, including mental health and social–emotional well-being. (Pianta & Walsh, 1996; Swearer et al., 2004). Because schools play a central role in the lives of families, it is important that trust be established. Given the long history of prejudice and discrimination faced by the GSD communities (Herek, 2007), some GSD parents may be leery of trusting schools to provide a safe, supportive environment for their children. Furthermore, although attitudes toward people who are GSD have improved in the United States (Cooley, 2015; Kreitzer et al., 2015), in some areas within the country, acceptance may be the exception rather than the rule (D'Augelli, 2006; Hall & Rodgers, 2019; Marsack & Stephenson, 2017; S. J. McCann, 2011). It is also important to recognize that the experiences of families with transgender or non-binary parents may be particularly challenging because their identities may be pathologized; they may experience increased levels of isolation within their communities and their families of origin; and they may have less access to resources, such as health care (Downing, 2013). Therefore, the decision to come out to schools may be a difficult one because it may be met with negative reactions (Bishop & Atlas, 2015). There are potential ramifications for not coming out, which include increased levels of anxiety (Goldberg & Kuvalanka, 2012) and vigilant behavior designed to protect the family by keeping their GSD identity a secret (Gianino et al., 2009).

TARGETS FOR CHANGE

Taken together, the aforementioned issues provide some important context that is useful for understanding the difficulties that many GSD families face as they navigate school systems. The following section delineates three broad areas that, based on the literature, are presented as targets for change.

Educators' GSD Multicultural Competency

Preservice teacher training programs have mandated requirements about including courses that focus on diversity issues. The Council for the Accreditation of Educator Preparation (CAEP) is the accrediting body for teacher preparation programs and, as such, helps shape education programs. Notably, however, CAEP standards for diversity are limited, stating only that teachers should mirror the diversity of their students in terms of race, ethnicity, sexual orientation, and other characteristics (CAEP, n.d.). This lack of explication is troubling because it does not align with well-established models of diversity training (e.g., Banks, 2006; Sue, 1991), which call for learning the history and experiences of an array of cultural groups. It also ignores groups, including people who are transgender or gender diverse, to name a few.

Moreover, there is some evidence that multicultural courses in teacher training programs do not include education about the GSD communities, a problem noted by Herek (n.d., 1989) that still exists to some extent today. As an example, Gorski et al. (2013) found that syllabi of multicultural education courses in teacher training programs tended to omit GSD issues. Turning to the preservice teachers who take diversity courses, some reported having insufficient multicultural awareness, knowledge, and skills (Lehman, 2017). Specific to GSD issues, many studies (e.g., GLSEN [Gay, Lesbian and Straight Education Network] & Harris Interactive, 2012; Mudrey & Medina-Adams, 2006; Savage et al., 2004; Whitman et al., 2007) have found that educators do not think they have a sufficient depth or breadth of knowledge to work effectively with GSD people.

One finding that could drive the exclusion of GSD-focused training is that some people in education may hold the attitude that GSD topics are inappropriate in K–12 schools (DePalma & Atkinson, 2006). Kintner-Duffy et al. (2012) found that GSD families were "secret" in early childhood classrooms and that representation and acknowledgement of the existence of GSD families were perceived as irrelevant if there were no children of GSD parents in the class. Even when there is educator support for training on GSD topics, it may not be included for lack of institutional support or fear of community backlash (Amodeo et al., 2015). In addition, evidence suggests that some teachers are misinformed about GSD issues (Macgillivray & Jennings, 2008; Szalacha, 2004). Clark (2010) contended that, compared with those in other well-developed countries, schools in the United States lag behind in their inclusion of GSD issues in diversity courses and in school systems, generally. Altogether, the literature suggests that educators may still be underprepared to work with GSD parents and their children.

Heteronormative and Cisnormative School Climate

Heteronormativity is the cultural bias that heterosexuality is the only "normal" sexual orientation and that other-gender (e.g., male–female) pairings are assumed to be heterosexual. By extension, then, same-gender (e.g., male–male, female–female) couples are deemed "abnormal." *Cisnormativity* is the cultural bias that is based on the assumption that all people are born cisgender (e.g., with gender identity that matches the biological sex they were assigned at birth). In a cisnormative environment, people who are cisgender are considered normal, whereas people who are transgender are considered abnormal. Furthermore, all people are assumed to be cisgender and heterosexual.

Heteronormative and cisnormative environments place higher value and legitimacy onto people who fit its assumptions about sexual orientation and gender identity. There is little to no room for people who violate the norm, and people who do not fit may be ignored or denigrated. Heteronormativity and cisnormativity may contribute significantly to the creation and maintenance of environments that are highly amenable to *microaggressions*, defined as brief, commonplace behaviors that communicate hostile, derogatory insults to a person on the basis of their belonging to a particular outgroup (Sue, 2005; Sue et al., 2007).

Microaggressions can be unintentional and even invisible to perpetrator and target. They can be harmful because they send messages of lack of belongingness and delegitimization (Sue, 2010). Importantly, it is not just GSD parents who experience microaggressions. Farr et al. (2016) documented that children of GSD parents also experience microaggressions and that they may occur even more frequently for children who are adopted. For GSD families, microaggressions may be conceptualized as falling into three categories: (a) family legitimacy, (b) family values, and (c) gender role violations (Haines et al., 2017). Family legitimacy microaggressions target the "realness" of relationships between same-gender couples and portrays nonbiological parents as "less than" biological parents. For example, Haines et al. (2017) reported the experience of parents who had phone calls from the school asking to speak to a student's "real" mother. Microaggressions that invoke family values include statements intended to denigrate affectionate behavior (e.g., hand-holding in public) between same-gender parents as inappropriate or even to portray same-gender couples as immoral. Gender role violations, according to Haines et al. (2017), garner microaggressions that insult people who do not fit into traditional, binary male and female gender roles. For example, asking a same-gender female couple which one does the "man's" chores at home is a microaggression that targets people based on their lack of fit within traditional boundaries of what it means to be male or female.

Schools are organized to reflect macrosystem-level values and norms; thus, they reflect the broad societal norms of heteronormativity and cisnormativity. School systems often reinforce traditional family structures and gender roles, leaving little to no flexibility for families that fall outside of this norm (Haines et al., 2017; Kosciw & Diaz, 2008). Often, there is no institutional awareness that school systems are operating from a base of heteronormativity. This is problematic because of the negative effects that heteronormative and cisgender assumptions can have on those who are marginalized.

School policy, mission statements, and curricula often reflect microaggressions via the exclusion of GSD parents. Many schools do not have forms that reflect same-gender parents (Fox, 2007; S. Hicks, 2011), making it difficult to complete them accurately. This can lead to a feeling of delegitimization for families (Gibson, 2016). Furthermore, school policies and forms that exclude GSD parents inhibit informed educators from affirming GSD parents. School mission statements sometimes lack language about respect for diversity or exclude sexual orientation and gender diversity from their definition of diversity (Gorski et al., 2013; Herek, n.d.). Another example of the influence of macrosystem values on other ecological systems can be found in antidiscrimination policies that do not include language specific to bullying and harassment based on actual or perceived sexual orientation, gender identity, or gender expression (Jeltova & Fish, 2005; Lopez & Bursztyn, 2013).

Other omissions of GSD issues can be found in K–12 curricula and library holdings in which there is often a significant lack of representation of GSD issues (Bishop & Atlas, 2015; DePalma & Atkinson, 2006; Martino & Cumming-Potvin, 2011). As an example, despite the increasingly expanded inclusion of books about different family configurations (e.g., adoptive, blended, extended), Bishop and Atlas (2015) reported that GSD families are still consistently omitted. Furthermore, school libraries often do not have books that portray GSD youth. There is also an absence of books and curricular materials that feature or describe people who have intersectional identities (e.g., race, ability, religion; Blackburn & Smith, 2010). This is indicative of the tendency to conceptualize GSD families as one monolithic group rather than as an array of families with a spectrum of diverse identities (Few-Demo et al., 2016). This lack of representation can send a message to GSD parents and children that they are not recognized, are not valued, or both (Martino & Cumming-Potvin, 2011). Furthermore, it makes the GSD communities invisible to others, which can perpetuate prejudice and microaggressions.

When GSD issues are included in the school curriculum, they are often taught within the realm of sex education (Bishop & Atlas, 2015). This lack of infusion into the regular curriculum may perpetuate the overemphasis on sexual behavior that is often linked to the GSD communities and discount other aspects of sexual identity (Kite & Bryant-Lees, 2016). Moreover, the topics typically included in textbooks are often framed around problems rather than in a positive light. This only serves to perpetuate stereotypes about the GSD communities (Macgillivray & Jennings, 2008; Rasmussen, 2005).

Anti-GSD Prejudice and Behavior

School climate plays an important role in the academic and social well-being of students (Sugai et al., 2012). As heteronormative and cisnormative environments, school systems may reinforce negative societal attitudes toward GSD families. In the social–psychological literature, negative attitudes toward people that are based solely on membership in a marginalized group is referred to as *prejudice* (Devine, 1989). Compared to other types of prejudice, anti-GSD prejudice has been relatively understudied. In the school systems, research on anti-GSD prejudice has largely documented prejudiced attitudes via self-report measures of attitudes and experiences (e.g., Averett & Hegde, 2012; G. R. Hicks & Lee, 2006; Middleton, 2002; Sears, 1992; H. E. Taylor, 2000; Vogt & McKenna, 1998). My colleagues and I (Herbstrith et al., 2013) used a more rigorous research paradigm with both a well-established implicit measure of prejudice (e.g., Payne et al., 2005) and self-report measures, and found similar patterns. Although anti-GSD attitudes have improved over time (Hall & Rodgers, 2019; G. R. Hicks & Lee, 2006), there is substantial evidence that anti-GSD bullying and harassment continue to occur frequently in schools (Espelage et al., 2008; GLSEN & Harris Interactive, 2012; Hillard et al., 2014; Poteat et al., 2013). Justifiably, many students who are GSD, who are from GSD families, or both, do not feel safe at school (GLSEN & Harris Interactive, 2012; Peter et al., 2016). Kosciw et al. (2016) reported that about one-fourth of students with GSD parents felt unsafe at school, whereas one-half reported harassment because of the sexual orientation of their parent(s).

In line with ecological systems theory, which suggests that systems maintain a state of homeostasis, it is not surprising that one reason for the persistence of prejudice and its behavioral correlates of bullying, harassment, and violence is that incidents go unreported or are met with little to no response by teachers and administrators (GLSEN & Harris Interactive, 2012; Kosciw et al., 2016). Dragowski et al. (2016) reported that fewer than one-third of teachers intervened in such incidents. The lack of intervention is what serves to maintain the environment, in part, by sending a message to people within the system that anti-GSD prejudice is acceptable. It is also an example of the influence of the mesosystem, the system that contains the interactions between microsystems. Evidence suggests that educators may not respond to anti-GSD behaviors out of concern for negative responses from administrators (DePalma & Atkinson, 2010; Dragowski et al., 2016) and the community (Dessel, 2010).

GSD TALKING THE TALK: PRACTICE GUIDELINES

Professional organizations in the mental health arena have developed guidelines for working with GSD families and children. As an example, the American Psychological Association (APA, 2012) published the "Guidelines for Psychological Practice With Lesbian, Gay, and Bisexual Clients" (APA is currently updating these guidelines). Even though all 21 guidelines are potentially applicable to supporting families led by lesbian, gay, and bisexual (LGB) parents in school systems, a focus on Guidelines 8 ("Psychologists strive to understand the experiences and challenges faced by LGB parents"; p. 18); 9 ("Psychologists recognize that the families of LGB people may include people who are not legally or biologically related"; p. 18); and 19 ("Psychologists strive to include LGB issues in profession education and training"; p. 25) are especially warranted.

Guideline 8 specifically addresses unique concerns for LGB families in terms of (a) dispelling the myth that LGB people are unfit parents; and (b) a lack of support from their communities, extended families, and friends. Guideline 9 stipulates the recognition of family structures that, for many reasons, may be unique relative to traditional ones. This guideline has particular implications for the way schools often do business on a daily basis. As an example, families must complete a considerable amount of paperwork for their children, from registration and emergency contact information to individualized education programs for special education (APA, 2012). The forms used to collect this information are largely heterosexist in that they typically ask for identification of "mother" and "father" rather than "parent" or a different identifier. This method may exclude and ignore family members who play a significant role in a student's life, perhaps even a non-binary parent or guardian. The lack of representation of GSD families in paperwork or related policies has been cited as problematic in many studies (Bishop & Atlas, 2015; Byard et al., 2013; Fox, 2007; Gibson, 2016). Guideline 19 is a directive to include LGB issues in both graduate training of psychologists and subsequent professional development training. This guideline highlights the importance of instilling in psychologists the awareness of heterosexist environments as well as heterosexual privilege and further suggests that diversity be affirmed as a priority at the institutional level (APA, 2012). Unfortunately, the APA guidelines are not widely disseminated in school systems (Borden, 2014), which implies they are not used. As such, GSD families may feel unwelcome, excluded, and even mistreated (Bishop & Atlas, 2015).

In 2015, APA published its "Guidelines for Psychological Practice With Transgender and Gender Nonconforming People," which comprises a set of standards for practitioners who work with people who are transgender and gender diverse. Although each guideline should be applied when working with transgender and gender diverse parents and their families in the schools, of particular relevance are Guidelines 4, 5, 10, 11, and 13. Guideline 4 states that practitioners must be aware of how their own attitudes and knowledge about gender identity and gender expression affect their practice with people who are transgender and gender diverse.

Guideline 5 describes the importance of practitioner awareness of the extent to which stigma, prejudice, discrimination, and violence permeate the lives of transgender and gender diverse people. It is especially important to recognize that minority stress and oppression do not affect parents in isolation. Rather, they are experienced by children as well, both directly and indirectly (APA, 2015).

Guideline 10 states that practitioners should be aware that presenting concerns may or may not be related to a transgender or gender diverse person's gender identity. It is a common assumption that a GSD person who seeks the help of a mental health practitioner needs help because of their sexual orientation or gender identity. Practitioners must recognize any assumptions they may have about why a transgender or gender diverse parent or their child seeks their assistance (APA, 2015).

Guideline 11 recommends that practitioners understand the important connection between affirmative care and positive life outcomes for transgender and gender diverse people. In the context of schools, this guideline translates to the need for practitioners to be supportive and affirming in their direct work with, and in their advocacy efforts for, students whose parents are transgender or gender diverse (APA, 2015).

Guideline 13 states that practitioners must recognize that family formations among people who are transgender and gender diverse can take on many forms. This has many implications in the schools, where culture and climate tend to be highly heteronormative and cisnormative, and therefore non-affirming of these families. Practitioners should be cognizant of the different forms this lack of affirmation can take, from the language embedded in policies and forms to events and functions that are built on heterosexual and cisgender models of parenting (e.g., "Muffins With Mom Day," "Daddy–Daughter Dance"; APA, 2015).

The National Association of School Psychologists (NASP) also sets practice guidelines for school psychologists, who provide a wide range of mental health services to students and families in school settings. Similar to other school-based professionals, school psychologists are charged with practicing within the realm of multicultural competence (NASP, 2010; Thomas, 2010). To that end, NASP sets out clear expectations that schools be safe, inclusive places where every student is treated with dignity and respect (NASP, 2011). NASP calls on school psychologists specifically to take responsibility as allies to the GSD communities (McCabe, 2014; NASP, 2011).

Taken together, the aforementioned guidelines make it clear that mental health professionals are charged with providing service and support for GSD parents and their children. The following section details a systems approach to creating a safe and equitable learning environment for GSD families.

GSD WALKING THE WALK: DEVELOPING A POLICY INITIATIVE

This section describes a translational science approach to making schools an equitable, safe environment for GSD parents and families. Thus far, much of the literature on GSD parents and their children's schooling is descriptive in nature. That is, it describes GSD families' experiences as they navigate the school system and advocate for themselves. Using an ecological systems lens to examine the target areas for change that were outlined in the previous section, however, it is easy to envision a shift in thinking. That is, rather than trying to fit GSD families into a system that is not designed with them in mind, the focus should shift to fixing the system so that it includes GSD families. Rather than placing the onus on families to insert themselves into a heteronormative and cisnormative system, the focus should be on systems change. In line with ecological systems theory, there are multiple points of entry by which to effect this kind of change. This section describes interventions that focus primarily on the macrosystem and mesosystem with the understanding that the work will be done within the context of the exosystem and chronosystem.

Translational research posits that basic research should inform the development of treatment approaches and that researchers should facilitate the implementation of these approaches in the field (Guastaferro & Collins, 2019). The purpose of using a translational research perspective in writing this chapter is to envision a way to connect "what is known" about a problem from basic social sciences research to "what can be done" about the problem in the environment in which it exists. A review of the literature on prevention and intervention efforts to ameliorate problems for GSD families in the schools shows that, outside of research on the effects of gay–straight alliances (more recently referred to as "gender and sexuality alliances" or "genders and sexualities alliances") in schools (e.g., Fetner & Kush, 2008; Goodenow et al., 2006; Heck et al., 2013; Szalacha, 2003), which are directed primarily at helping GSD students, little else has been done on a systems level. With that in mind, the remainder of this chapter is a policy initiative that can be used to guide psychological systems consultants as they work to create equitable educational environments for GSD parents and their students.

The focus of this section is on linking the target areas for change that were identified earlier (educators' GSD multicultural competency, heteronormative and cisnormative school climate, anti-GSD prejudice and behavior) with interventions that have empirical support in the social sciences literature. The criteria for choosing interventions were that they are theory based, specific to GSD issues, and able to be transported into the school system and scaled up to intervention at the systems level. Each intervention is described within the context of ecological systems theory.

Receiving Multicultural Education and Training

Diversity training is a standard part of degree programs, and preservice teacher training is no exception (Gay, 2010; Tinkler & Tinkler, 2013). Many graduate programs also require coursework in multiculturalism as part of their degree plans. Diversity courses are typically part of accreditation standards (APA, CAEP, NASP) across higher education. Indeed, it has been long understood that to be a successful educator, one must have an understanding of the worldview of one's students (Banks, 2006; Gay, 2010).

In a meta-analysis of anti-GSD prejudice-reduction interventions, Bartoş et al. (2014) found that education was the most frequently used intervention for prejudice reduction. They reported that effect sizes for increasing knowledge reached highly effective ($d = 1.01$) and small to medium ($d = 0.36$) for reducing negative emotions. There are many examples of multicultural competency training efforts in various fields, including mental health, medicine, and social work. Moreover, efforts have been aimed at expanding knowledge and skills for a range of cultures. Health professionals have reported feelings of increased comfort in working with clients of different races (Jernigan et al., 2016), religions (Pedersen et al., 2011), and sexual orientation (Carabez et al., 2015; Hope & Chappell, 2015; Spanierman et al., 2011). This increased comfort is likely because of better developed knowledge base, more positive attitudes about different cultural groups, and a broader skill set in working with them (Sue et al., 1992).

Of particular relevance to this chapter, Choi et al. (2006) measured change in school psychologists' attitudes and feelings about gay and lesbian parents after diversity training. The results demonstrated that participants' beliefs were more positive but that their feelings about gay and lesbian parents did not change significantly. They found that diversity training led to more positive beliefs and cognitions but had no significant effect on feelings. This finding is consistent with Bezrukova et al.'s (2016) finding that training and education led to higher levels of cognitive learning than more positive attitudes. Although the relations between attitudes and behaviors toward GSD people are complex (Goodman & Moradi, 2008), these results suggest that behavior change is possible even when attitudes do not correspond. Said differently, people may be able to change their professional behavior even if their attitudes remain the same.

Turning to the three systems-level target areas for change identified earlier, multicultural education has the potential to influence each of them. There is evidence that many educators do not receive cultural competence training on GSD issues and therefore are likely to be uninformed or even misinformed. As Sue et al. (1992) stated, having an understanding and common language leads to increased comfort levels when working with people of different cultures. Multicultural training can build levels of comfort by imparting knowledge and skills, building empathy, and remediating misinformation. In addition, multicultural education is a tool that can disrupt heteronormative and cisnormative culture that permeates many school systems. It can impart perspective and empathy to educators, which may lead to more frequent recognition of heteronormative and cisnormative assumptions.

Multicultural competence in any area requires sustained attention and effort. Saunders et al. (2015) described the process as a journey with no end point. Successful training on GSD issues requires long-term follow-up with trainees so that new knowledge and skills can be integrated into practice (Whitman et al., 2007). Consultants and trainers in multicultural competence should be prepared to meet trainees "where they are" and then help them move from "knowing" to "doing" (Freeman et al., 2017).

Some GSD competency training programs already exist for pre-K–12 school staff. Some nonprofit organizations—including GLSEN (https://www.glsen.org/), the Human Rights Campaign (https://www.hrc.org/), and the Trevor Project (https://www.thetrevorproject.org/)—have training curricula on GSD issues in the school setting. In addition, national and state school psychology organizations provide excellent resources, support, and training on GSD issues. Universities that have faculty experts in this area are also an excellent resource for school systems seeking consultation and training related to creating equitable educational experiences for GSD families.

In ecological systems terms, having a meaningful understanding of culture aside from one's own is important because of the potential influence this knowledge has on one's worldview. Specifically, training educators on GSD issues by providing them with some cultural knowledge and shared language is likely to have effects at the micro- and mesosystem levels. It could effectively train educators to be GSD allies and, in turn, increase the frequency of positive interactions between GSD families and educators. This may then influence immediate relationships among others in the school system (e.g., other families, administrators, community members). According to Epstein and Van Voorhis (2010), it is the frequency of interactions across different stakeholders that creates positive systems change.

It is important to recognize the effect that multicultural education can have on the larger ecological systems. Children of GSD parents who have positive experiences in a school system that includes them are likely to feel more connected to it (Benner et al., 2008). This sense of belongingness has been shown to translate to higher levels of academic adjustment (Pittman & Richmond, 2007), lower levels of truancy (Demanet & Van Houtte, 2012), and better psychosocial adjustment (Jose et al., 2012). Moreover, children who attend a school that is equitable and accessible for every student have the potential to be able to positively influence the macrosystem and exosystem as they grow into adulthood because they value diversity.

Invoking Social Norms

Social norms are a set of collective behaviors that are established as acceptable within a particular culture. Social norms dictate the behavior of individuals; they serve as unwritten guidelines for what to do or how to behave in situations (Cialdini et al., 1991; Sherif, 1936). Crandall et al. (2002) used group norm theory (e.g., Sherif & Sherif, 1953) to posit that prejudice is a negative attitude that is formed and maintained at the group level by group norms. For individuals, then, prejudice is a negative attitude that is formed by adopting a valued group's attitude. For example, a person who identifies with a particular social group may adopt the attitudes and beliefs that are held by members of that group. This conceptualization of prejudice suggests that social norms can be leveraged and used to shape behavior within a system.

Indeed, the social–psychological literature is robust with findings related to group processes and the power of groups to reinforce behavior based on expectations (Festinger, 1950). Specifically, many studies suggest that manipulating social norms may be an effective way to reduce anti-GSD prejudice (Bartoş et al., 2014; Tankard & Paluck, 2017). In their meta-analysis, Bartoş et al. (2014) calculated a medium effect size ($d = 0.46$) for studies that used social norms to manipulate behavior directed at GSD people. Tankard and Paluck (2017) found that people's perceptions of the normative belief about marriage equality shifted after the U.S. Supreme Court ruled in its favor in *Obergefell v. Hodges* (2015). Specific to school settings, Goldberg et al. (2017) found that coaching school-based leaders to display inclusive, positive behavior about GSD issues applied normative pressure onto others within the system, thereby reducing anti-GSD behavior.

The empirical literature suggests that social norms are powerful in large part because group conformity (Festinger, 1950) is critical for group functioning (Cialdini et al., 1991; Sherif, 1936). In that light, it is simple to imagine how harnessing social norms can influence school systems. First, social norms already exist in schools. Students learn to line up at a very young age, for example. They stand and recite the Pledge of Allegiance. School systems also promote unwanted behavior, such as when bullying and name-calling go unpunished. Leveraging social norms to create positive behavior change within school systems would have the potential to influence the microsystem and mesosystem. At the microsystem level, changing social norms may reduce the minority stress for GSD families (Farr, 2017; Meyer, 2003), which is so often responsible for poor mental health outcomes (McConnell et al., 2015; Mustanski et al., 2010; Russell & Fish, 2016). Furthermore, it may improve the home–school relationships for GSD families by increasing the likelihood of GSD family engagement in schools. This, in turn, may create the opportunity for more frequent interactions among educators, administrators, and GSD families (e.g., intergroup contact), which would serve to create a more positive bidirectional influence at the mesosystem level. As L. Taylor and Adelman (2000) suggested, home–school partnerships can influence the worldview of all participants, which serves to send messages to GSD families that they are being included and valued. As social norms influence people's behavior, the ecosystem will be disrupted (Berk, 2000) and then will achieve balance again in accordance with the newly established boundaries and rules.

Invoking social norms maps onto two primary targets for intervention that were identified earlier. First, changing social norms could target the heteronormative and cisnormative climate that is typical in many school systems, which may reduce the amount of microaggressions perpetrated on GSD families. Similarly, changing social norms could reduce overt anti-GSD prejudice along the lines of Goldberg et al. (2017), who noted the effect of behavior change among the leadership on the behavior of other people within the system.

Promoting Intergroup Contact

Intergroup contact is a phenomenon that arose from the early years of prejudice research (Allport, 1954; Pettigrew, 1998). Essentially, intergroup contact is the social interaction of people who are from different social or cultural groups. Allport (1954) hypothesized that, under the proper conditions, increased levels of intergroup contact had the potential to reduce prejudice among members of different groups (e.g., heterosexual parents, GSD parents). Over the years, many researchers have examined group processes with regard to intergroup contact as a way to reduce anti-GSD prejudice, specifically. Pettigrew and Tropp (2006) conducted a meta-analysis and found that the intervention with the strongest influence on anti-GSD prejudice was inter-group contact. Similarly, Bartoş et al. (2014) examined eight studies and found that intergroup contact had an overall medium effect size ($d = 0.56$). While LaCosse and Plant (2019) found that imagined contact with famous gay men and lesbians reduced prejudice, Vezzali et al. (2015) conducted a study in which participants imagined contact with GSD people, which resulted in increased levels of willingness to have contact with members of the GSD communities in the future. Similarly, Burk et al. (2018) found that story-telling panels of GSD people reduced negative attitudes, and Burke et al. (2015) reported more positive attitudes in relation to more frequent and more positive contact with GSD people. Taken together, the social–psychological literature demonstrates that real or imagined intergroup contact may indeed reduce anti-GSD prejudice, which is one of the three targets for intervention identified earlier.

In the school system, this intervention is most clearly aimed at creating change at the microsystem and mesosystem levels. Epstein and Van Voorhis (2010) described the task of changing the worldview of stakeholders within a system as a way to effect change. This translates to the manipulation of interactions between people in microsystems with others within the proximal environment. Said differently, orchestrated social contact between different groups of people can help create positive changes. GSD families may feel more valued and better understood, and may have a heightened sense of belongingness in the system. Educators may experience a shift in their worldview based on interactions with GSD people, leading to less prejudiced attitudes and behaviors.

CONCLUSION

The purpose of this chapter was to describe a policy initiative that would use a translational science approach to transport empirically supported interventions that would promote an equitable, welcoming educational environment for GSD parents and their children. To that end, three broad targets for change were identified in the extant literature: educator knowledge about GSD issues, school climates that are heteronormative and cisnormative, and anti-GSD prejudice. Then, three interventions identified as effective at addressing those issues in other settings were described: providing GSD multicultural education, invoking social norms, and promoting intergroup contact. Each intervention has the potential to effect systems-level change in schools so that GSD parents and their children are afforded an equitable learning environment in which they feel included and affirmed.

TAKEAWAYS AND OPPORTUNITIES

- As many as 7 million children are being raised by GSD parents.

- Ecological systems theory is a valuable way to conceptualize how equitable educational environments can be created for GSD parents and their children.

- GSD professional organizations in psychology offer guidelines for working with people who are GSD; mental health professionals are responsible for following those guidelines in their practice settings.

- Three types of anti-GSD prejudice reduction interventions that have considerable empirical support in the social–psychological literature and are suitable for systemwide implementation in schools are providing educator multicultural education, invoking social norms, and promoting intergroup contact.

- How can you use your skills, role, or social capital in your professional environment to influence school social norms or intergroup contact, as described in this chapter?

REFERENCES

Adams, R., & Persinger, J. (2013). Research-based practice: School support and same-sex parents. *NASP Communique, 42*(2), 10–13.

Allport, G. W. (1954). *The nature of prejudice.* Doubleday.

American Psychological Association. (2012). Guidelines for psychological practice with lesbian, gay, and bisexual clients. *American Psychologist, 67*(1), 10–42. https://doi.org/10.1037/a0024659

American Psychological Association. (2015). Guidelines for psychological practice with transgender and gender nonconforming people. *American Psychologist, 70*(9), 832–864. https://doi.org/10.1037/a0039906

Amodeo, A. L., Vitelli, R., Scandurra, C., Picariello, S., & Valerio, P. (2015). Adult attachment and transgender identity in the Italian context: Clinical implications and suggestions for further research. *International Journal of Transgenderism, 16*(1), 49–61. https://doi.org/10.1080/15532739.2015.1022680

Averett, P. E., & Hegde, A. (2012). School social work and early childhood student's attitudes toward gay and lesbian families. *Teaching in Higher Education, 17*(5), 537–549. https://doi.org/10.1080/13562517.2012.658564

Banks, J. (2006). *Cultural diversity and education: Foundations, curriculum and teaching.* Allyn & Bacon.

Bartoş, S. E., Berger, I., & Hegarty, P. (2014). Interventions to reduce sexual prejudice: A study-space analysis and meta-analytic review. *Journal of Sex Research, 51*(4), 363–382. https://doi.org/10.1080/00224499.2013.871625

Benner, A. D., Graham, S., & Mistry, R. S. (2008). Discerning direct and mediated effects of ecological structures and processes on adolescents' educational outcomes. *Developmental Psychology, 44*(3), 840–854. https://doi.org/10.1037/0012-1649.44.3.840

Berk, L. E. (2000). *Child development* (5th ed.). Allyn & Bacon.

Bezrukova, K., Spell, C. S., Perry, J. L., & Jehn, K. A. (2016). A meta-analytical integration of over 40 years of research on diversity training evaluation. *Psychological Bulletin, 142*(11), 1227–1274. https://doi.org/10.1037/bul0000067

Bishop, C. M., & Atlas, J. G. (2015). School curriculum policies, and practices regarding lesbian, gay, bisexual, and transgender families. *Education and Urban Society, 47*(7), 766–784. https://doi.org/10.1177/0013124513508580

Blackburn, M. V., & Smith, J. M. (2010). Moving beyond the inclusion of LGBT themed literature in English language arts classrooms: Interrogating heteronormativity and exploring intersectionality. *Journal of Adolescent & Adult Literacy, 53*(8), 625–634. https://doi.org/10.1598/JAAL.53.8.1

Borden, K. (2014). When family members identify as lesbian, gay, or bisexual: Parent–child relationships. *Professional Psychology, Research and Practice, 45*(4), 219–220. https://doi.org/10.1037/a0037612

Bronfenbrenner, U. (1979). Contexts of child rearing: Problems and prospects. *American Psychologist, 34*(10), 844–850. https://doi.org/10.1037/0003-066X.34.10.844

Bronfenbrenner, U. (2005). *Making human beings human: Bioecological perspectives on human development.* Sage.

Brooks, V. R. (1981). *Minority stress and lesbian women.* Lexington Books.

Burk, J., Park, M., & Saewyc, E. M. (2018). A media-based school intervention to reduce sexual orientation prejudice and its relationship to discrimination, bullying, and the mental health of lesbian, gay, and bisexual adolescents in Western Canada: A population-based evaluation. *International Journal of Environmental and Public Health, 15*(11), Article 2447. https://doi.org/10.3390%2Fijerph15112447

Burke, S. E., Dovidio, J. F., Przedworski, J. M., Hardeman, R. R., Perry, S. P., Phelan, S. M., Nelson, D. B., Burgess, D. J., Yeazel, M. W., & van Ryn, M. (2015). Do contact and empathy mitigate bias against gay and lesbian people among heterosexual first-year medical students? A report from the medical student CHANGE study. *Academic Medicine, 90*(5), 645–651. https://doi.org/10.1097/ACM.0000000000000661

Byard, E., Kosciw, J., & Bartkiewicz, M. (2013). Schools and LGBT-parent families: Creating change through programming and advocacy. In A. E. Goldberg & K. R. Allen (Eds.), *LGBT-parent families: Innovations in research and implications for practice* (pp. 275–290). Springer. https://doi.org/10.1007/978-1-4614-4556-2_18

Carabez, R., Pellegrini, M., Mankovitz, A., Eliason, M. J., & Dariotis, W. M. (2015). Nursing students' perceptions of their knowledge of lesbian, gay, bisexual, and transgender issues: Effectiveness of a multi-purpose assignment in a public health nursing class. *The Journal of Nursing Education, 54*(1), 50–53. https://doi.org/10.3928/01484834-20141228-03

Choi, H., Thul, C. A., Berenhaut, K. S., Suerken, C. K., & Norris, J. L. (2006). Survey of school psychologists' attitudes, feelings, and exposure to gay and lesbian parents and their children. *Journal of Applied School Psychology, 22*(1), 87–107. https://doi.org/10.1300/J370v22n01_05

Cialdini, R. B., Kallgren, C. A., & Reno, R. R. (1991). A focus theory of normative conduct: A theoretical refinement and reevaluation of the role of norms in human behavior. In M. P. Zanna (Ed.), *Advances in experimental social psychology* (Vol. 24, pp. 201–234). Academic Press. https://doi.org/10.1016/S0065-2601(08)60330-5

Clark, C. T. (2010). Preparing LGBTQ-allies and combating homophobia in a U.S. teacher education program. *Teaching and Teacher Education, 26*(3), 704–713. https://doi.org/10.1016/j.tate.2009.10.006

Cooley, A. H. (2015). Constitutional representations of the family in public schools: Ensuring equal protection for all students regardless of parental sexual orientation or gender identity. *Ohio State Law Journal, 76*, 1006–1050.

Council for the Accreditation of Educator Preparation. (n.d.). *The CAEP standards.* http://caepnet.org/standards/introduction

Crandall, C. S., Eshleman, A., & O'Brien, L. (2002). Social norms and the expression and suppression of prejudice: The struggle for internalization. *Journal of Personality and Social Psychology, 82*(3), 359–378. https://doi.org/10.1037/0022-3514.82.3.359

D'Augelli, A. R. (2006). Coming out, visibility, and creating change: Empowering lesbian, gay, and bisexual people in a rural university community. *American Journal of Community Psychology, 37*(3–4), 365–376. https://doi.org/10.1007/s10464-006-9043-6

Demanet, J., & Van Houtte, M. (2012). School belonging and school misconduct: The differing role of teacher and peer attachment. *Journal of Youth and Adolescence, 41*(4), 499–514. https://doi.org/10.1007/s10964-011-9674-2

DePalma, R., & Atkinson, E. (2006). The sound of silence: Talking about sexual orientation and schooling. *Sex Education, 6*(4), 333–349. https://doi.org/10.1080/14681810600981848

DePalma, R., & Atkinson, E. (2010). The nature of institutional heteronormativity in primary schools and practice-based responses. *Teaching and Teacher Education, 26*(8), 1669–1676. https://doi.org/10.1016/j.tate.2010.06.018

Dessel, A. B. (2010). Effects of intergroup dialogue: Public school teachers and sexual orientation prejudice. *Small Group Research, 41*(5), 556–592. https://doi.org/10.1177/1046496410369560

Devine, P. G. (1989). Stereotypes and prejudice: Their automatic and controlled components. *Journal of Personality and Social Psychology, 56*(1), 5–18. https://doi.org/10.1037/0022-3514.56.1.5

Downing, J. B. (2013). Transgender-parent families. In A. Goldberg & K. Allen (Eds.), *LGBT-parent families* (pp. 105–115). Springer. https://doi.org/10.1007/978-1-4614-4556-2_7

Dragowski, E. A., McCabe, P. C., & Rubinson, F. (2016). Educators' reports on incidence of harassment and advocacy toward LGBTQ students. *Psychology in the Schools, 53*(2), 127–142. https://doi.org/10.1002/pits.21895

Edwards, O. W. (2017). Toward a framework for translational research in school psychology. *School Psychology Forum, 11*(1), 1–4.

Edwards, O. W., & Shaw, S. R. (2018). Publishing in *School Psychology Forum*: Research in practice. In R. G. Floyd (Ed.), *Publishing in school psychology and related fields: An insider's guide* (pp. 145–151). Routledge.

Epstein, J. L., & Van Voorhis, F. L. (2010). School counselors' roles in developing partnerships with families and communities for student success. *Professional School Counseling, 14*(1), https://doi.org/10.1177/2156759X1001400102

Espelage, D. L., Aragon, S. R., Birkett, M., & Koenig, B. W. (2008). Homophobic teasing, psychological outcomes, and sexual orientation among high school students: What influence do parents and schools have? *School Psychology Review, 37*(2), 202–216.

Farr, R. H. (2017). Does parental sexual orientation matter? A longitudinal follow-up of adoptive families with school-age children. *Developmental Psychology, 53*(2), 252–264. https://doi.org/10.1037/dev0000228

Farr, R. H., Crain, E. E., Oakley, M. K., Cashen, K. K., & Garber, K. J. (2016). Micro-aggressions, feelings of difference, and resilience among adopted children with sexual minority parents. *Journal of Youth and Adolescence, 45*(1), 85–104. https://doi.org/10.1007/s10964-015-0353-6

Festinger, L. (1950). Informal social communication. *Psychological Review, 57*(5), 271–282. https://doi.org/10.1037/h0056932

Fetner, T., & Kush, K. (2008). Gay–straight alliances in high schools. *Youth & Society, 40*(1), 114–130. https://doi.org/10.1177/0044118X07308073

Few-Demo, A. L., Humble, A. M., Curran, M. A., & Lloyd, S. A. (2016). Queer theory, intersectionality, and LGBT-parent families: Transformative critical pedagogy in family theory. *Journal of Family Theory & Review, 8*(1), 74–94. https://doi.org/10.1111/jftr.12127

Fox, R. K. (2007). One of the hidden diversities in schools: Families with parents who are lesbian or gay. *Childhood Education, 83*(5), 277–281. https://doi.org/10.1080/00094056.2007.10522932

Freeman, J., Sugai, G., Simonsen, B., & Everett, S. (2017). MTSS coaching: Bridging knowing to doing. *Theory into Practice, 56*(1), 29–37. https://doi.org/10.1080/00405841.2016.1241946

Gates, G. J. (2013). *LGBT parenting in the United States.* The Williams Institute. https://escholarship.org/uc/item/9xs6g8xx

Gay, G. (2010). Acting on beliefs in teacher education for cultural diversity. *Journal of Teacher Education, 61*(1–2), 143–152. https://doi.org/10.1177/0022487109347320

Gianino, M., Goldberg, A., & Lewis, T. (2009). Family outings: Disclosure practices among adopted youth with gay and lesbian parents. *Adoption Quarterly, 12*(3–4), 205–228. https://doi.org/10.1080/10926750903313344

Gibson, M. F. (2016). "This is real now because it's a piece of paper": Texts, disability, and LGBTQ parents. *Disability & Society, 31*(5), 641–658. https://doi.org/10.1080/09687599.2016.1197822

GLSEN & Harris Interactive. (2012). *Playgrounds and prejudice: Elementary school climate in the United States, a survey of students and teachers.* GLSEN.

Goldberg, A. E., Black, K., Sweeney, K., & Moyer, M. (2017). Lesbian, gay, and hetero-sexual adoptive parents' perceptions of inclusivity and receptiveness in early child-hood education settings. *Journal of Research in Childhood Education, 31*(1), 141–159. https://doi.org/10.1080/02568543.2016.1244136 (Corrigendum published 2017, *Journal of Research in Childhood Education, 31*(2), p. 312. https://doi.org/10.1080/02568543.2017.1305241)

Goldberg, A. E., & Kuvalanka, K. A. (2012). Marriage (in)equality: The perspectives of adolescents and emerging adults with lesbian, gay, and bisexual parents. *Journal of Marriage and Family, 74*(1), 34–52. https://doi.org/10.1111/j.1741-3737.2011.00876.x

Goodenow, C., Szalacha, L., & Westheimer, K. (2006). School support groups, other school factors, and the safety of sexual minority adolescents. *Psychology in the Schools, 43*(5), 573–589. https://doi.org/10.1002/pits.20173

Goodman, M. B., & Moradi, B. (2008). Attitudes and behaviors toward lesbian and gay persons: Critical correlates and mediated relations. *Journal of Counseling Psychology, 55*(3), 371–384. https://doi.org/10.1037/0022-0167.55.3.371

Gorski, P. C., Davis, S. N., & Reiter, A. (2013). An examination of the (in)visibility of sexual orientation, heterosexism, homophobia, and other LGBTQ concerns in U.S. multicultural teacher education coursework. *Journal of LGBT Youth, 10*(3), 224–248. https://doi.org/10.1080/19361653.2013.798986

Guastaferro, K., & Collins, L. M. (2019). Achieving the goals of translational science in public health intervention research: The multiphase optimization strategy (MOST). *American*

Journal of Public Health, 109, S128–S129. https://ajph.aphapublications.org/doi/abs/10.2105/AJPH.2018.304874

Haines, K. M., Reyn Boyer, C., Giovanazzi, C., & Paz Galupo, M. (2017). "Not a real family": Microaggressions directed toward LGBTQ families. *Journal of Homosexuality, 65*(9), 1138–1151. https://doi.org/10.1080/00918369.2017.1406217

Hall, W. J., & Rodgers, G. K. (2019). Teachers' attitudes toward homosexuality and the lesbian, gay, bisexual, and queer community in the United States. *Social Psychology of Education, 22*(1), 23–41. https://doi.org/10.1007/s11218-018-9463-9

Heck, N. C., Flentje, A., & Cochran, B. N. (2013). Offsetting risks: High school gay–straight alliances and lesbian, gay, bisexual, and transgender (LGBT) youth. *Psychology of Sexual Orientation and Gender Diversity, 1*(S), 81–90.

Herbstrith, J. C., Tobin, R. M., Hesson-McInnis, M. S., & Joel Schneider, W. (2013). Preservice teacher attitudes toward gay and lesbian parents. *School Psychology Quarterly, 28*(3), 183–194. https://doi.org/10.1037/spq0000022

Herek, G. M. (n.d.). *Definitions: Homophobia, heterosexism, and sexual prejudice.* https://psychology.ucdavis.edu/rainbow/html/prej_defn.html

Herek, G. M. (1989). Hate crimes against lesbians and gay men. Issues for research and policy. *American Psychologist, 44*(6), 948–955. https://doi.org/10.1037/0003-066X.44.6.948

Herek, G. M. (2007). Confronting sexual stigma and prejudice: Theory and practice. *Journal of Social Issues, 63*(4), 905–925. https://doi.org/10.1111/j.1540-4560.2007.00544.x

Hicks, G. R., & Lee, T. T. (2006). Public attitudes toward gays and lesbians: Trends and predictors. *Journal of Homosexuality, 51*(2), 57–77. https://doi.org/10.1300/J082v51n02_04

Hicks, S. (2011). *Lesbian, gay and queer parenting: Families, intimacies, genealogies.* Springer. https://doi.org/10.1057/9780230348592

Hillard, P., Love, L., Franks, H. M., Laris, B. A., & Coyle, K. K. (2014). "They were only joking": Efforts to decrease LGBTQ bullying and harassment in Seattle public schools. *Journal of School Health, 84*(1), 1–9. https://doi.org/10.1111/josh.12120

Hope, D. A., & Chappell, C. L. (2015). Extending training in multicultural competencies to include individuals identifying as lesbian, gay, and bisexual: Key choice points for clinical psychology training programs. *Clinical Psychology: Science and Practice, 22*(2), 105–118. https://doi.org/10.1111/cpsp.12099

Jeltova, I., & Fish, M. (2005). Creating school environments responsive to gay, lesbian, bisexual, and transgender families: Traditional and systemic approaches for consultation. *Journal of Educational & Psychological Consultation, 16*(1), 17–33. https://doi.org/10.1207/s1532768xjepc1601&2_2

Jernigan, V. B. B., Hearod, J. B., Tran, K., Norris, K. C., & Buchwald, D. (2016). An examination of cultural competence training in US medical education guided by the tool for assessing cultural competence training. *Journal of Health Disparities Research and Practice, 9*(3), 150–167.

Jose, P. E., Ryan, N., & Pryor, J. (2012). Does social connectedness promote a greater sense of well-being in adolescence over time? *Journal of Research on Adolescence, 22*(2), 235–251. https://doi.org/10.1111/j.1532-7795.2012.00783.x

Kintner-Duffy, V., Vardell, R., Lower, J., & Cassidy, D. (2012). "The changers and the changed": Preparing early childhood teachers to work with lesbian, gay, bisexual, and transgender families. *Journal of Early Childhood Teacher Education, 33*(3), 208–223. https://doi.org/10.1080/10901027.2012.705806

Kite, M., & Bryant-Lees, K. B. (2016). Historical and contemporary attitudes toward homosexuality. *Teaching of Psychology, 43*(2), 164–170. https://doi.org/10.1177/0098628316636297

Kosciw, J. G., & Diaz, E. M. (2008). *Involved, invisible, ignored: The experiences of lesbian, gay, bisexual and transgender parents and their children in our nation's K–12 schools.* GLSEN.

Kosciw, J. G., Greytak, E. A., Giga, N. M., Villenas, C., & Danischewski, D. J. (2016). *The 2015 National School Climate Survey: The experiences of lesbian, gay, bisexual, transgender, and queer youth in our nation's schools.* GLSEN.

Kreitzer, R., Doan, L., & Chatfield, S. (2015, June 26). Supreme Court rules in favor of same-sex marriage across the U.S.: USAPP experts react. *LSE US Centre.* http://blogs. lse.ac.uk/usappblog/2015/06/26/supreme-court-rules-in-favor-of-same-sex-marriage-across-the-u-s-usapp-experts-react/

LaCosse, J., & Plant, E. A. (2019). Imagined contact with famous gay men and lesbians reduces heterosexuals' misidentification concerns and sexual prejudice. *European Journal of Social Psychology, 49*(1), 141–156. https://doi.org/10.1002/ejsp.2391

Lehman, C. L. (2017). Multicultural competence: A literature review supporting focused training for preservice teachers teaching diverse students. *Journal of Education and Practice, 8*(10), 109–116.

Lopez, E. C., & Bursztyn, A. M. (2013). Future challenges and opportunities: Toward culturally responsive training in school psychology. *Psychology in the Schools, 50*(3), 212–228. https://doi.org/10.1002/pits.21674

Macgillivray, I. K., & Jennings, T. (2008). A content analysis exploring lesbian, gay, bisexual, and transgender topics in foundations of education textbooks. *Journal of Teacher Education, 59*(2), 170–188. https://doi.org/10.1177/0022487107313160

Marsack, J., & Stephenson, R. (2017). Sexuality-based stigma and depression among sexual minority individuals in rural United States. *Journal of Gay & Lesbian Mental Health, 21*(1), 51–63. https://doi.org/10.1080/19359705.2016.1233164

Martino, W., & Cumming-Potvin, W. (2011). "They didn't have *out there* gay parents—They just looked like normal regular parents": Investigating teachers' approaches to addressing same-sex parenting and non-normative sexuality in the elementary school classroom. *Curriculum Inquiry, 41*(4), 480–501. https://doi.org/10.1111/j.1467-873X.2011.00557.x

McCabe, P. C. (2014). The r(ally) cry: School psychologists as allies and advocates for the LGBTQ community. *School Psychology Forum, 8*(1), 1–9.

McCann, S. J. (2011). Do state laws concerning homosexuals reflect the preeminence of conservative-liberal individual differences? *Journal of Social Psychology, 151*(3), 227–239. https://doi.org/10.1080/00224540903366792

McConnell, E. A., Birkett, M. A., & Mustanski, B. (2015). Typologies of social support and associations with mental health outcomes among LGBT youth. *LGBT Health, 2*(1), 55–61. https://doi.org/10.1089/lgbt.2014.0051

Meyer, I. H. (2003). Minority stress and mental health in gay men. In L. D. Garnets & D. C. Kimmel (Eds.), *Psychological perspectives on lesbian, gay, and bisexual experiences* (2nd ed., pp. 699–731). Columbia University Press.

Middleton, V. A. (2002). Increasing preservice teachers' diversity beliefs and commitment. *Urban Review, 34*(4), 343–361. https://doi.org/10.1023/A:1021372801442

Moe, J. L., & Sparkman, N. M. (2015). Assessing service providers at LGBTQ-affirming community agencies on their perceptions of training needs and barriers to service. *Journal of Gay & Lesbian Social Services, 27*(3), 350–370. https://doi.org/10.1080/10538720.2015.1051687

Mudrey, R., & Medina-Adams, A. (2006). Attitudes, perceptions, and knowledge of pre-service teachers regarding the educational isolation of sexual minority youth. *Journal of Homosexuality, 51*(4), 63–90. https://doi.org/10.1300/J082v51n04_04

Mustanski, B. S., Garofalo, R., & Emerson, E. M. (2010). Mental health disorders, psychological distress, and suicidality in a diverse sample of lesbian, gay, bisexual, and transgender youths. *American Journal of Public Health, 100*(12), 2426–2432. https://doi.org/10.2105/AJPH.2009.178319

National Association of School Psychologists. (2010). *Model for comprehensive and integrated school psychological services.* https://www.nasponline.org/standards-and-certification/nasp-practice-model

National Association of School Psychologists. (2011). *Lesbian, gay, bisexual, transgender, and questioning youth* [Position statement]. Retrieved from https://www.nasponline.org/lgbtqi2-s

Obergefell v. Hodges, 135 S. Ct. 2584 (2015). https://www.supremecourt.gov/opinions/14pdf/14-556_3204.pdf

Payne, B. K., Cheng, C. M., Govorun, O., & Stewart, B. D. (2005). An inkblot for attitudes: Affect misattribution as implicit measurement. *Journal of Personality and Social Psychology, 89*(3), 277–293. https://doi.org/10.1037/0022-3514.89.3.277

Pedersen, A., Walker, I., Paradies, Y., & Guerin, B. (2011). How to cook rice: Ingredients for teaching anti-prejudice. *Australian Psychologist, 46*(1), 55–63. https://doi.org/10.1111/j.1742-9544.2010.00015.x

Peter, T., Taylor, C., & Edkins, T. (2016). Are the kids all right? The impact of school climate among students with LGBT parents. *Canadian Journal of Education, 39*(1), 1–25.

Pettigrew, T. F. (1998). Intergroup contact theory. *Annual Review of Psychology, 49*(1), 65–85. https://doi.org/10.1146/annurev.psych.49.1.65

Pettigrew, T. F., & Tropp, L. R. (2006). A meta-analytic test of intergroup contact theory. *Journal of Personality and Social Psychology, 90*(5), 751–783. https://doi.org/10.1037/0022-3514.90.5.751

Pianta, R. C., & Walsh, D. J. (1996). *High-risk children in schools: Constructing sustaining relationships.* Routledge & Kegan Paul.

Pittman, L. D., & Richmond, A. (2007). Academic and psychological functioning in late adolescence: The importance of school belonging. *Journal of Experimental Education, 75*(4), 270–290. https://doi.org/10.3200/JEXE.75.4.270-292

Poteat, V. P., DiGiovanni, C. D., & Scheer, J. R. (2013). Predicting homophobic behavior among heterosexual youth: Domain general and sexual orientation-specific factors at the individual and contextual level. *Journal of Youth and Adolescence, 42*(3), 351–362. https://doi.org/10.1007/s10964-012-9813-4

Prati, G., Pietrantoni, L., & D'Augelli, A. R. (2011). Aspects of homophobia in Italian high schools: Students' attitudes and perceptions of school climate. *Journal of Applied Social Psychology, 41*(11), 2600–2620. https://doi.org/10.1111/j.1559-1816.2011.00842.x

Rasmussen, M. L. (2005). *Becoming subjects: Sexualities and secondary schooling.* Routledge.

Romanelli, M., & Hudson, K. D. (2017). Individual and systemic barriers to health care: Perspectives of lesbian, gay, bisexual, and transgender adults. *American Journal of Orthopsychiatry, 87*(6), 714–728. https://doi.org/10.1037/ort0000306

Russell, S. T., & Fish, J. N. (2016). Mental health in lesbian, gay, bisexual, and transgender (LGBT) youth. *Annual Review of Clinical Psychology, 12*(1), 465–487. https://doi.org/10.1146/annurev-clinpsy-021815-093153

Saunders, J., Haskins, M., & Vasquez, M. (2015). Cultural competence: A journey to an elusive goal. *Journal of Social Work Education, 51*(1), 19–34. https://doi.org/10.1080/10437797.2015.977124

Savage, T. A., Prout, H. T., & Chard, K. M. (2004). School psychology and issues of sexual orientation: Attitudes, beliefs, and knowledge. *Psychology in the Schools, 41*(2), 201–210. https://doi.org/10.1002/pits.10122

Sears, J. T. (1992). Educators, homosexuality, and homosexual students: Are personal feelings related to professional beliefs? *Journal of Homosexuality, 22*(3–4), 29–80. https://doi.org/10.1300/J082v22n03_03

Sherif, M. (1936). *The psychology of social norms.* Harper & Brothers.

Sherif, M., & Sherif, C. W. (1953). *Groups in harmony and tension.* Harper.

Spanierman, L. B., Oh, E., Heppner, P. P., Neville, H. A., Mobley, M., Wright, C. V., & Navarro, R. (2011). The Multicultural Teaching Competency Scale: Development and initial validation. *Urban Education, 46*(3), 440–464. https://doi.org/10.1177/0042085910377442

Sue, D. W. (1991). A model for cultural diversity training. *Journal of Counseling and Development, 70*(1), 99–105. https://doi.org/10.1002/j.1556-6676.1991.tb01568.x

Sue, D. W. (2005). Racism and the conspiracy of silence. *Counseling Psychologist, 33*(1), 100–114. https://doi.org/10.1177/0011000004270686

Sue, D. W. (2010). *Microaggressions in everyday life: Race, gender, and sexual orientation.* John Wiley & Sons.

Sue, D. W., Arredondo, P., & McDavis, R. J. (1992). Multicultural counseling competencies and standards: A call to the profession. *Journal of Multicultural Counseling and Development, 20*(2), 64–88. https://doi.org/10.1002/j.2161-1912.1992.tb00563.x

Sue, D. W., Capodilupo, C. M., Torino, G. C., Bucceri, J. M., Holder, A. M. B., Nadal, K. L., & Esquilin, M. (2007). Racial microaggressions in everyday life: Implications for clinical practice. *American Psychologist, 62*(4), 271–286. https://doi.org/10.1037/0003-066X.62.4.271

Sugai, G., O'Keeffe, B. V., & Fallon, L. M. (2012). A contextual consideration of culture and school-wide positive behavior support. *Journal of Positive Behavior Interventions, 14*(4), 197–208. https://doi.org/10.1177/1098300711426334

Swearer, S. M., Cowan, R. J., & Sheridan, S. M. (2004). Home-school collaboration. In C. Spielberger (Ed.-in-Chief), *Encyclopedia of applied psychology* (Vol. 2, pp. 201–208). Elsevier.

Szalacha, L. A. (2003). Safer sexual diversity climates: Lessons learned from an evaluation of Massachusetts safe schools program for gay and lesbian students. *American Journal of Education, 110*(1), 58–88. https://doi.org/10.1086/377673

Szalacha, L. A. (2004). Educating teachers on LGBTQ issues: A review of research and program evaluations. *Journal of Gay & Lesbian Issues in Education, 1*(4), 67–79. https://doi.org/10.1300/J367v01n04_07

Tankard, M. E., & Paluck, E. L. (2017). The effect of a Supreme Court decision regarding gay marriage on social norms and personal attitudes. *Psychological Science, 28*(9), 1334–1344. https://doi.org/10.1177/0956797617709594

Taylor, H. E. (2000). Meeting the needs of lesbian and gay young adolescents. *The Clearing House: A Journal of Educational Strategies, Issues and Ideas, 73*(4), 221–224. https://doi.org/10.1080/00098650009600956

Taylor, L., & Adelman, H. S. (2000). Connecting schools, families, and communities. *Professional School Counseling, 3*(5), 298–307.

Thomas, J. T. (2010). *The ethics of supervision and consultation: Practical guidance for mental health professionals.* American Psychological Association. https://doi.org/10.1037/12078-000

Tinkler, B., & Tinkler, A. (2013). Experiencing the other: The impact of service-learning on preservice teachers' perceptions of diversity. *Teacher Education Quarterly, 40*(4), 41–62.

United States Census Bureau. (2011, September 27). *Census bureau releases estimates of same-sex married couples.* http://www.census.gov/newsroom/releases/archives/2010_census/cb11-cn181.html

Vezzali, L., Stathi, S., Crisp, R. J., Giovannini, D., Capozza, D., & Gaertner, S. L. (2015). Imagined intergroup contact and common ingroup identity: An integrative approach. *Social Psychology, 46*(5), 265–276. https://doi.org/10.1027/1864-9335/a000242

Vogt, W. P., & McKenna, B. J. (1998, April 13–17). *Teachers' tolerance: Their attitudes toward political, social, and moral diversity* [Paper presentation]. Annual Meeting of the American Educational Research Association, San Diego, CA, United States.

Whitman, J. S., Horn, S. S., & Boyd, C. J. (2007). Activism in the schools: Providing LGBTQ affirmative training to school counselors. *Journal of Gay & Lesbian Psychotherapy, 11*(3–4), 143–154. https://doi.org/10.1300/J236v11n03_08

7

Meeting a Need

The Respect Workshop—*Competency Training for School Health and Mental Health Professionals Serving Gender and Sexually Diverse Students*

Sam E. Greenberg, Jana E. Sharp, and Clinton W. Anderson

School-based mental health professionals consistently rank among the most trusted school professionals by gender and sexually diverse (GSD) students[1] (Kosciw et al., 2012, 2014, 2016). In *The 2015 National School Climate Survey* (Kosciw et al., 2016), 51.7% of GSD youth said they would be somewhat or very comfortable talking about lesbian, gay, bisexual, and transgender (LGBT) issues with a school-based mental health professional, 10.6% said they had talked to a school-based mental health professional many times about LGBT issues in the past year, 13.2% said they had talked to a school-based mental health professional a few times, and 12.3% had talked to a school-based

---

[1]A note on terminology: Over the 20-year history of the APA *Respect Workshop*, from its conception in 1999 to the most recent curriculum revision in 2018 (Rosenbaum et al., 2018), terminology used to describe "sexual orientation diversity" and "gender identity diversity" shifted several times. The variations in terminology used were a result of the availability of data, an emphasis on data-informed decision making, and APA's capacity to address the needs of specific populations. The terms "lesbian, gay, and bisexual (LGB)," "lesbian, gay, bisexual, and questioning (LGBQ)," "lesbian, gay, bisexual, and transgender (LGBT)," and "lesbian, gay, transgender, and questioning (LGBTQ)" were all used in the *Respect Workshop* materials and related literature at various times. Scientific research likewise has used various terminology over time based on which communities were included in studies. Throughout this chapter, we use terms such as "LGB," "LGBQ," "LGBT," and "LGBTQ" to describe study populations in accordance with the terms used by the original authors of studies. Similarly, we use these terms in descriptions of the historical development of the *Respect Workshop* at various stages consistent with usage at the stage being described.

https://doi.org/10.1037/0000211-008
Supporting Gender Identity and Sexual Orientation Diversity in K–12 Schools, M. C. Lytle and R. A. Sprott (Editors)

mental health professional one time. Similarly, in a 2015 survey of young men who have sex with men, school nurses were reported as the school staff member with whom respondents felt most comfortable talking about HIV and sexually transmitted infection (STI) testing as well as condoms (Rasberry et al., 2015).

The unique skills of school psychologists, school counselors, school social workers, and school nurses—if they have the requisite training—can be applied in the context of GSD students' distinct challenges. GSD students have specific health risks (Coker et al., 2010; Rafferty et al., 2018) that school nurses are uniquely positioned to address through strategies, such as HIV and STI prevention (National Association of School Nurses, 2016). School counselors and school psychologists are trained to address the effects of adverse experiences on academic performance and mental health (American School Counselor Association, 2017; National Association of School Psychologists [NASP], 2017), including those for which GSD students are at a higher risk (Coker et al., 2010; Rafferty et al., 2018), such as bullying. School social workers can intervene to address interactions of environmental factors that impact students' well-being, including those at home, such as parental rejection, and at school, such as harassment (Martin et al., 2014). All school-based mental health professionals can help schools to enforce antibullying policies specific to sexual orientation and gender identity, use their training to support GSD students who are bullied, and intervene with students who violate such policies. Moreover, these professionals can use their knowledge and experience to support competency among staff working with GSD students.

Formal training on issues faced by GSD students is recommended as a best practice for school health and mental health professionals (American Psychological Association [APA] & NASP, 2015; DeCrescenzo & Mallon, 2000; Goodrich et al., 2013). However, training specific to supporting GSD students is rarely a required part of the curricula for these professionals. According to a 2019 report that surveyed 1,741 school counselors, psychologists, and social workers, across 50 states and the District of Columbia, nearly 70% had received little to no competency training in school related to working with sexually diverse populations, and more than 80% received little to no training on working with gender diverse populations (Kull et al., 2019). In a stratified random sample of 500 members of NASP, fewer than one third had received any formal training in supporting sexually diverse students and their parents (Choi et al., 2006). Similarly, issues specific to GSD students are largely absent from the training curricula for school counselors (Goodrich & Luke, 2010; Jennings, 2014) and school nurses (Carabez et al., 2015). In a 2009 survey, 68% of social work program directors reported courses on diversity, including GSD content, but only 47% believed their programs trained students very or fairly well "to provide competent services to LGBT youth" (Martin et al., 2014, p. 14). When members of five professional associations were surveyed, school health and mental health professionals reported lack of training in issues specific to lesbian, gay, and bisexual (LGB) populations as a key barrier to providing services to these students (Sawyer et al., 2006). Furthermore, Case and Meier (2014) noted that even when professional training programs do incorporate GSD specific curricula, resources for transgender and gender diverse students are often excluded.

THE NEED FOR A RESOURCE

The need for training to increase the capacity of school health and mental health professionals to address the needs of LGB students (Sawyer et al., 2006) motivated APA to develop the *Respect Workshop: Preventing Health Risks and Promoting Healthy Outcomes Among Lesbian, Gay, Bisexual, Transgender and Questioning (LGBTQ) Students* (Anderson & Porter, 2004). The *Respect Workshop* is a professional development curriculum specifically designed to support middle and high school counselors, nurses, psychologists, and social workers in meeting the unique needs of GSD students. The workshop content addresses both direct services to students and system interventions within school environments, such as professional development opportunities and policy support.

APA developed and field tested the *Respect Workshop* between 1999 and 2004 during the first of five cooperative agreements between APA and the Centers for Disease Control and Prevention (CDC), Division of Adolescent and School Health. In subsequent cooperative agreements with CDC, the workshop was revised and updated twice, and was implemented as an online course. In the current cooperative agreement, which began in 2018 and runs until 2023, the *Respect Workshop* is one of the resources APA is using to assist schools in establishing safe and supportive environments (SSEs) for middle and high school students as an approach to preventing HIV and other STIs among adolescents (CDC, 2019b, p. 67). Grounded in the theory of planned behavior (Ajzen, 1991), the workshop aims to bolster professionals' ability to (a) assist GSD students in coping with their distinctive challenges; (b) promote safe school environments that nurture healthy and successful students; and (c) motivate all students to prevent HIV, STIs, and pregnancy.

RESPECT WORKSHOP DEVELOPMENT AND REFINEMENT

From 1999 to 2018, APA's *Respect Workshop* was developed (see Table 7.1) through a research and development process conducted in collaboration with six professional associations: (a) American Counseling Association, (b) American School Counselor Association, (c) National Association of School Nurses, (d) NASP, (e) National Association of Social Workers, and (f) School Social Work Association of America. The goal throughout the development of the *Respect Workshop* curriculum was to increase the capacity of school professionals (i.e., counselors, psychologists, social workers, and nurses) to promote the health and well-being of lesbian, gay, bisexual, and questioning (LGBQ)

TABLE 7.1. Development and Updating of the *Respect Workshop*, 1999–2018

Year(s)	Focus/developmental phase
1999–2002	Formative evaluation; *Respect Workshop* developed with a focus on LGBQ students
2002–2003	*Respect Workshop* field testing
2004	CDC clearance process and approval of the *Respect Workshop*, first edition
2005–2011	Implementation of first edition, including first edition of evaluation tools
2006	*Respect Workshop* featured in a publication of *Journal of HIV/AIDS Prevention in Children & Youth* (Sawyer et al., 2006)
2009–2011	Revision and update process, resulting in inclusion of gender diverse students
2013	CDC clearance process and approval of the *Respect Workshop*, second edition
2013–2017	Implementation of *Respect Workshop*, second edition
2015	Refined evaluation tools, including pretest, posttest, and follow-up
2015	Online modules and blended learning format developed for *Respect Workshop*
2016–2017	Added to online course: updated scientific information, learning assessments, and registration system for providing certification for use in seeking continuing education
2015–2018	Revision and update process, resulting in third edition of *Respect Workshop*
2018	CDC approval of the *Respect Workshop*, third edition, including online modules

Note. LGBQ = lesbian, gay, bisexual, and questioning; CDC = Centers for Disease Control and Prevention.

students. The curriculum development process began with an extensive education and training needs assessment conducted with members of each professional association. A mixed-method needs assessment was conducted, beginning with key informant interviews, focus groups with members of each professional group, and literature reviews of relevant scientific as well as professional literature. Qualitative data analyses were used to inform the development of a survey instrument that was then completed by 941 members of the four target professional groups (Sawyer et al., 2006). The survey instrument asked professionals from the four target groups about their perceptions of LGBQ students in their schools, including the health and mental health risk factors faced by these students in comparison with their peers. The survey also inquired about the professionals' attitudes toward LGBQ students and toward providing a set of support services relevant to LGBQ students. In addition, professionals were queried about their experience with and potential barriers to providing those relevant services.

Members of the professional associations who completed the survey largely indicated positive attitudes and beliefs toward LGBQ students; they indicated feeling that LGBQ students were an important population in their schools that faced higher risks than their non-LGBQ counterparts. Many respondents reported having provided support services to LGBQ students, and an even higher percentage said their professional roles should involve providing support to LGBQ students. Respondents also reported a number of barriers to supporting LGBQ students, including

- these students fearing disclosing their sexual orientation to school professionals,
- school climate among students tolerates harassment of LGBQ students,
- lack of support from school administrators on LGBQ issues,
- some school staff have negative attitudes toward LGBQ people,
- lack of adequate training of school staff regarding needs of LGBQ students,
- lack of knowledge and skills among school staff about working with LGBQ students,
- lack of adequate educational materials to use with LGBQ students,
- other work duties take precedence,
- staff believe or fear that they will be labeled as LGBQ if they address LGBQ issues or advocate for LGBQ students,
- school policies do not specifically address needs of LGBQ students,
- fear of parent or guardian objections, and
- fear of community opposition. (Sawyer et al., 2006, p. 45)

APA used the quantitative data collected from the survey and the qualitative data collected from focus groups and key informants, in conjunction with the research available on LGBQ populations at the time, to develop the *Respect Workshop* curriculum. In addition, APA commissioned representatives from each targeted profession to develop papers specifying their profession's role and scope of work in supporting students. These papers further informed curriculum development, which was grounded in the scope of work of each targeted professional group. Each professional representative assisted in drafting curriculum content and reviewed subsequent drafts of the curriculum to ensure it was professionally relevant to the audience. The new curriculum was field-tested 21 times in 2003 and 2004 with more than 600 attendees who completed formative evaluations used to hone the workshop curriculum and design. After revisions were made in response to the evaluation data, the workshop was submitted to the CDC for approval in 2004. Between 2005 and 2011, the workshop was a central resource for APA's work with the state education agencies (SEAs) and local education agencies (LEAs) that were also funded by CDC to increase their support for the health of LGBQ students.

Beginning in approximately 2009, APA began a workshop revision and update process, which most notably resulted in a second edition that was more inclusive of gender identity issues and transgender students. In the development of the second edition of the workshop, the decision to include transgender students and their needs was a response to feedback received in the evaluation of the *Respect Workshop* that indicated that the inclusion of transgender students was an important need for school personnel. While scientific research connecting positive outcomes among transgender students to safe and supportive school environments and specific interventions was limited at the time, APA decided that this need justified the assumption that interventions shown to be helpful to LGBQ students would also be help-ful to gender diverse students. Transgender issues were added to the *Respect Workshop* curriculum in an expanded terminology section, which included relevant high-quality scientific knowledge on transgender youth and specific school-based examples of curriculum concepts involving transgender students. The second edition (Bogden & Anderson, 2011) was approved by the CDC in 2013.

Until 2015, the *Respect Workshop* was exclusively offered as an in-person training, most often implemented as a 1-day, 7.5-hour workshop facilitated by two trainers from APA's training cadre. The training was offered to school health and mental health professionals in partnership with professional asso-ciations or with SEAs and LEAs funded by the CDC. The in-person training focused on four key modules: (a) understanding foundational knowledge on health risks and protective factors for lesbian, gay, bisexual, transgender, and questioning (LGBTQ) youth; (b) helping individual LGBTQ students; (c) helping schools adopt protective practices; and (d) planning follow-up action by partic-ipants after the workshop when they returned to their schools.

By 2015, APA had developed and piloted a 6.5-hour online course that consisted of three self-paced modules. Like the in-person training, the online course focused on foundational knowledge, direct services, and schoolwide protective practices. The online version of the *Respect Workshop* was designed to expand the reach of the curriculum by offering the online modules on demand, at no charge to participants, and with access to online resources. In addition, associations and agencies could request a blended learning format by incorporating a live action–planning webinar led an APA trainer in conjunc-tion with the online course modules.

Beginning in 2016, APA initiated a second comprehensive curriculum review process to ensure data and resources were current and that there was continued alignment with, and relevance to, the professional fields of school counseling, school psychology, school nursing, and school social work. From 2017 to 2018, APA partnered with ETR, a behavioral health organization specializing in the design of evidence-based programs and services, to update the *Respect Workshop* curriculum. In conducting the update, APA and CDC agreed to maintain the four core elements of the training: (a) presenting current scientific knowledge on the health and well-being of GSD students; (b) grounding the workshop in the duties and responsibilities of the targeted professions; (c) designing the workshop in line with the theory of planned behavior, which aims to influence participants' professional attitudes, norms, and perceived behavioral control; and (d) using evidence-based professional development practices, including active learning techniques, peer-to-peer edu-cation, and the presentation of information in a variety of formats.

The revision process was based on data obtained in surveys of two groups of relevant informants: (a) a survey of scientific experts on GSD youth seeking input on the knowledge needed to support school professionals working with GSD students and (b) a survey of representatives of each of the four target professional groups to collect their feedback on the curriculum's relevance to the professions' scopes of work. Nine content experts reviewed the current empirical data and research findings derived from scientifically credible sources on the health and well-being of GSD students, and proposed updated scientific information for the curriculum. Twenty expert school professionals shared feedback on the curriculum's relevancy to professionals in their field, specifically with respect to direct services and protective schoolwide factors; they provided recommendations for changes. In addition, ETR staff engaged *Respect Workshop* trainers in a focus group to gather their input on the workshop design and observed the workshop to gather real-time feedback from participants. APA staff and ETR analyzed the results from the surveys, the on-site training with participant feedback, and discussions with trainers to develop recommendations for what to keep, update, or revise in the workshop curriculum. The third edition of the *Respect Workshop* (Rosenbaum et al., 2018) was approved by CDC for continued use with its funded partners in 2018. The overall history of the development and revisions of the *Respect Workshop* are summarized in Table 7.1.

RESPECT WORKSHOP OUTCOME DATA: 2014–2017

From the initial development of the *Respect Workshop*, the evaluation design consisted of presurveys; postsurveys; and three, 6-month follow-up surveys. Over the years, *Respect Workshop* outcome evaluations have demonstrated that participants' intentions to engage in relevant professional behaviors increased from pre- to postworkshop, and self-reported performance of those behaviors increased from preworkshop to follow-up, but *Respect Workshop* evaluation tools have been modified over time and, therefore, are unable to be included in one comprehensive evaluation.

The most recent refinement in evaluation tools was made in 2014 and used consistently from 2014 to 2017. As presented in the annual reports, this evaluation included an analysis of data from presurveys and postsurveys for all workshops conducted by APA and its partners (2014–2015, 2015–2016, 2016–2017). These analyses demonstrated that professionals participating in the *Respect Workshop* increased their self-reported knowledge, skills, and self-efficacy in working with GSD youth at a statistically significant level ($p < .05$) across three core competencies: promoting SSEs; assisting GSD students in coping with their distinct challenges; and motivating students to prevent HIV, STIs, and pregnancy (Sharp Insight, 2017).[2]

---

[2]Findings from the 2014–2017 *Respect Workshop* analyses were limited by a small sample of matched pre–post surveys ($n = 66$). Of the 250 presurveys administered during this 3-year period, just over one quarter (26%) were matched because of implementation challenges, including the use of older survey versions and participants not consistently completing a unique identifier on handwritten surveys.

RESPECT WORKSHOP SATISFACTION DATA: 2014–2017

In addition to participant outcome evaluation data, the evaluation process also captured satisfaction data from workshop sponsors, SEA personnel in states funded by CDC for which APA provided capacity-building assistance. Organizers of the *Respect Workshop* from participating SEAs reported a positive overall experience with the *Respect Workshop* with 100% agreeing or strongly agreeing that they would "recommend the *Respect Workshop* to another SEA interested in increasing their capacity to improve SSEs for all students and staff." In the words of a *Respect Workshop* organizer,

> The *Respect Workgroup* provided professional development to a core group of priority district staff. It was beneficial to connect with people across the priority districts interested in taking leadership roles to create safe and supportive environments for youth. This workshop was a great way to kick off our work on the development of policy to support transgender youth.

In addition, 100% of *Respect Workshop* organizers agreed or strongly agreed that partnering with APA to offer the *Respect Workshop* increased their agency's capacity to meet the following goals:

- build the capacity of priority districts to lead district-level initiatives to increase the implementation of SSEs;

- provide leadership, guidance, and technical assistance to priority districts to improve the working relationships with strategic partners to achieve program impact and sustainability; and

- improve SSE for all students and staff.

Another organizer shared,

> We are currently offering a *Respect Workshop* training for the Department of Education staff. We will be offering *Respect* training every 3 months in different districts in the state. The locations will host the training, but the invite will be to all schools in the area.

Their feedback also indicated the workshop was perceived as useful for providing professional development to other school staff around issues specific to GSD students. For example, one organizer reported that "I . . . used resources from the *Respect Workshop* to put together a whole school presentation regarding the positive impact of having a GSA [this acronym has referred to 'gay–straight alliance' but more recently refers to 'gender and sexuality alliance' or 'genders and sexuality alliances'] in our school."

RESPECT WORKSHOP REACH

From the initial field testing in 2002 through 2017, APA has maintained internal records of the implementation of the *Respect Workshop* as a preventive intervention. In that time, more than 2,000 school professionals have

FIGURE 7.1. Locations of *Respect Workshop* Cohorts: 2002–2017

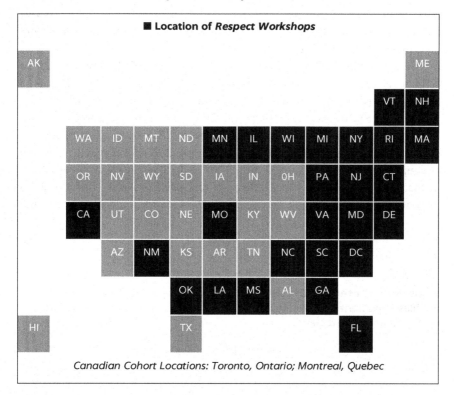

■ Location of *Respect Workshops*

Canadian Cohort Locations: Toronto, Ontario; Montreal, Quebec

participated in the in-person workshop in 82 cohorts across 26 U.S. states, the District of Columbia, and Canada (see Figure 7.1). The number of *Respect Workshops* implemented in each state or territory ranged from one to 12 and averaged 3.1 workshops per locale. In-person workshops were most often conducted in partnership with SEAs and LEAs or as part of national or state professional association conferences.

RESPECT WORKSHOP PARTICIPATION AND *SCHOOL HEALTH PROFILES* TRENDS

The available evaluation data for the *Respect Workshop* indicate that both participants and sponsors benefit from the workshop. Furthermore, the dissemination of the workshop has been geographically extensive. Given the positive evaluation results and extensive dissemination of the *Respect Workshop*, an effort was made to evaluate whether the workshop has had any impact on the adoption of supportive practices related to GSD students by school systems in the jurisdictions where the workshop has been conducted. The CDC conducts a biennial survey of school health policies and practices and publishes the results in a report called *School Health Profiles* (CDC, 2017). In 2010, seven items specifically focused on positive practices related to LGBTQ youth (see Exhibit 7.1) were added to the *School Health Profiles* questionnaire. These items from the 2010 profiles were repeated in 2012, 2014, and 2016 (CDC, n.d.-a). As such, trends in positive practices related to GSD youth in school environments can be observed over time.

The percentage of schools that engage in each GSD competency in Exhibit 7.1 varies widely across states and territories. For example, in 2016, the percentage of schools that provided curricula or supplementary materials that include HIV, STI, or pregnancy prevention information relevant to GSD youth ranged from 20.0% to 67.5% across states, whereas the percentage that provided curricula or supplementary materials and engaged in all five practices related to supporting GSD youth ranged from 2.6% to 40.5% (Brener et al., 2017).

States that participated in the *Respect Workshop* from 2002 through 2016 experienced greater overall increases in *School Health Profiles* scores for the

---

EXHIBIT 7.1

Items From Centers for Disease Control and Prevention *School Health Profiles* Questionnaires Relevant to Lesbian, Gay, Bisexual, Transgender, and Questioning Students

Teacher Questionnaire

- Does your school provide curricula or supplementary materials that include HIV, sexually transmitted infection, or pregnancy prevention information that is relevant to lesbian, gay, bisexual, transgender, and questioning youth (e.g., curricula or materials that use inclusive language or terminology)?

Principal Questionnaire

- Does your school have a student-led club that aims to create a safe, welcoming, and accepting school environment for all youth, regardless of sexual orientation or gender identity? These clubs are sometimes called "gay–straight alliances."

- Does your school engage in each of the following practices related to lesbian, gay, bisexual, transgender, and questioning (LGBTQ) youth?

  - Identify safe spaces for LGBTQ youth, such as a counselor's office, designated classroom, or student organization where LGBTQ youth can receive support from administration, teachers, or other school staff.

  - Prohibit harassment based on student's perceived or actual sexual orientation or gender identity.

  - Encourage staff to attend professional development on safe and supportive school environments for all students.

  - Facilitate access to providers not on school property who have experience in providing health services to LGBTQ youth, including HIV/sexually transmitted infection testing and counseling.

  - Facilitate access to providers not on school property who have experience in providing social and psychological services to LGBTQ youth.

Note. Questionnaire items adapted from *Profile Questionnaires*, by Centers for Disease Control and Prevention, 2019b, July 9. U.S. Department of Health & Human Services (https://www.cdc.gov/healthyyouth/data/profiles/questionnaires.htm). In the public domain.

FIGURE 7.2. Comparison of Percentages of Schools Reporting Curricula and Practices Supportive of LGBTQ Youth (2010–2016) in Jurisdictions Where the *Respect Workshop* Had Occurred With Those in Jurisdictions Where No *Respect Workshop* Had Occurred

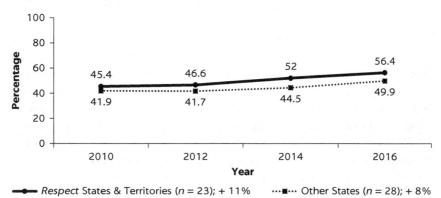

●— *Respect* States & Territories (*n* = 23); + 11%   ···■··· Other States (*n* = 28); + 8%

Note. LGBTQ = lesbian, gay, bisexual, transgender, and questioning.

GSD-supportive practices than states that did not participate in the *Respect Workshop* (CDC, n.d.-a; see Figure 7.2).[3] Across the GSD competencies measured, states that implemented the *Respect Workshop* (2002–2016) saw a larger overall 6-year growth in *School Health Profiles* scores. It is encouraging that the *Respect Workshop* is associated with improved school practices, but this association is correlational. The majority of the jurisdictions in which the *Respect Workshop* was conducted were funded—as APA was—by the CDC to address health disparities among groups of youth at disproportionate risk of HIV and STIs. Thus, they were likely to have engaged in supportive activities to promote healthy outcomes for GSD students in addition to the *Respect Workshop*. Furthermore, these jurisdictions may have already had better uptake of the GSD-supportive practices before the workshop took place. It may have been the greater supportiveness to GSD students in these jurisdictions that led to the *Respect Workshop* being conducted there.

RESPECT WORKSHOP IN PRACTICE: TWO STATE EDUCATION AGENCIES' EXPERIENCES

The research and development efforts invested in the *Respect Workshop* curriculum resulted in a robust resource for SEAs and LEAs to use in training school health and mental health professionals. Addressing sexual orientation and

---

[3]Although the *Respect Workshop* implementation began in 2002, *School Health Profiles* began to include items related to GSD-supportive practices in 2010; as such, the data presented in Figure 7.2 range from 2010 to 2016.

gender diversity in schools is complex even with access to the best of resources. Facilitating training on these issues involves consideration of the unique needs of students and families within a school's local context; attention to the level of sociopolitical support for GSD issues at the local and state levels; and incorporating culturally relevant concepts appropriate to the training's audience, among other factors.

All the participating SEAs that collaborated with APA from 2014 to 2018 adapted the *Respect Workshop* to some extent. Many SEAs used local data from the Youth Risk Behavior Survey (CDC, n.d.-b) to give workshop attendees a better understanding of risk factors faced by GSD youth in their state. Some SEAs incorporated testimonies from GSD youth to bring abstract concepts into focus as the everyday reality of students. For example, one state in the Northeast with high political acceptance of sexual and gender diversity included the presence of a local transgender youth and her family at the *Respect Workshop* to ground the conceptual material in tangible experiences. This allowed attendees to engage with a young person personally affected by issues that were of central focus in the curriculum. Another SEA in a Midwestern state with a large Native American population added culturally relevant content to the *Respect Workshop* that emphasized the Two-Spirit identity. In collaboration with an organization in the state that specialized in GSD Native issues, the SEA selected definitions and resources that were created by the Two-Spirit community.

The remainder of this section explores the unique experiences of two SEAs implementing the *Respect Workshop* in different parts of the country. Each SEA's experience adapting the content, format, and delivery of the *Respect Workshop* to suit the needs of their particular audience is discussed. Challenges that arose during implementation of the *Respect Workshop* and how each SEA addressed them are included.[4]

Case Study 1: Providing Respect in a Culture of Uncertainty

Our educators want to know how to handle these issues that are coming up with students, but we just don't have the resources. Some of our districts are very poor. They can't even afford to travel to another part of the state for training. The school professionals want to help, but they're scared, they're scared of handling the situation wrong and getting sued. If they had a textbook or reference guide, they can take themselves out of it and defer to that resource.

—SEA REPRESENTATIVE

The level of political support for GSD students in this rural state could be described as variable according to geography: Some parts of the state are

---

[4]Case studies were developed from in-depth interviews conducted with SEA personnel in each state that was funded to implement the *Respect Workshop*. Interviews were conducted confidentially to encourage interviewees to be forthcoming, and the data are reported here anonymously. Where quotations appear in the case studies, the text is directly from the interviews.

largely supportive of such diversity and other parts are largely opposed. The SEA representative shared that

> it's an oil and water mix so to speak. . . . It's about half and half. You've got some folks that are recognizing that there is change, recognizing that there is a new day, new age, so to speak, and then some are very traditional where it's like, hey, this is the way I've been taught. This is the way that my parents taught or my grandparents, and this is the way it's got to be.

It was in this mixed political environment that the *Respect Workshop* took place. The SEA became interested in facilitating the *Respect Workshop* based on requests from local districts. The districts noticed a pattern of issues arising in their schools related to GSD students and were often unsure of the best way to handle them. Individuals within the districts sought guidance and a template from the SEA.

The SEA worked with LEAs to ensure professionals who were interested could access the *Respect Workshop*. The state faces high rates of poverty; lack of access to professional development opportunities; and even lack of resources, such as broadband internet in many areas. As such, educators often do not have access to the information they need for supporting GSD populations. "They were very eager to come and learn," said the SEA representative.

Given attendees' eagerness to learn and that professionals' context for understanding GSD issues was limited to their everyday experiences in schools, the SEA believed the best course of action would be to start from the lived experiences of those in the room. To set the stage for the *Respect Workshop,* the SEA representative and expert training facilitators asked the attending educators and school health and mental health professionals in the room about their everyday experiences with GSD students. Real-life experiences of the group were then used as examples of how to apply the concepts from the *Respect Workshop* curricula. The SEA representative elaborated:

> The primary goal was to present a topic, talk about the topic, and then part of the trainers' goals was to teach the staff and the faculty how to implement . . . what they learned in these trainings. We encouraged them to speak out or speak up because we don't know how to help what they don't know. If you have a child in your district who identifies as being trans and they wanted to use [a certain] bathroom, what did you do? If it has come up in your district, then let's make it an open discussion with the experts there.

Bringing these real-world experiences to the training space first began an open dialogue in which the content of the *Respect Workshop* curricula was more likely to have an impact.

The SEA viewed the primary barrier to providing support to GSD students in this state as lack of access to information about how best to do this. In addition, school personnel felt fearful that they might mishandle a situation related to students' distinct challenges and that this mishandling could result in consequences that would negatively impact their job, school, or district. As a result, personnel often felt ill equipped. The SEA noted a need for resources to reference that could be deferred to as the experts on GSD students' issues.

That way, regardless of the political climate or even a staff member's personal feelings about sexual and gender diversity, they could defer to expert resources and remove themselves from liability by referring to "what the textbook says."

The state also offered continuing education credits as an incentive for educators to attend trainings they might not otherwise have attended. In reflecting on the high level of attendance and participant engagement in the *Respect Workshop*, the SEA emphasized that the professionals in this state desired knowledge but often did not have access to it. The SEA also stated the need to continue to provide access to information to everyday professionals because the upper levels of school administrations might not be in support of GSD student issues for political reasons.

To cater to each LEA following the *Respect Workshop*, the SEA held a series of follow-up trainings that drew from various aspects of the *Respect Workshop* curriculum to reach the districts that didn't have the means to travel. SEA representatives geographically traveled to poorer districts to offer them the training without requiring the expenses of travel. As the SEA representative put it,

> We made the access more central to them. . . . We were watchful and mindful: "We know you don't have all the resources to come here. We're going to come to you. We're going to make it easy," and I think once we did that, that's why it grew so fast.

Case Study 2: Accommodating and Supporting Professionals Through Respect

[The Respect Workshop*] is a way to bring people together in school districts that are interested and may already be the go-to adults in the school for creating safe and supportive environments for kids to talk to and be that kind of safe place. This kind of training is providing them with additional knowledge and expertise to be able to share that message with other staff within the school.*

—SEA REPRESENTATIVE

In a state with high competency in supporting GSD students, the *Respect Workshop* served a support role. The political environment in the state is favorable to sexual and gender diversity both in terms of popular opinion and with respect to statutes and policies at the board of education level. State laws include protections against harassment and discrimination based on sexual orientation, gender identity, and gender expression.

The SEA in this state valued the format of the *Respect Workshop*, which allowed participants to investigate their own perceptions and come to their own conclusions. "When people come to their own conclusions and begin to ask themselves questions based on new information, that's . . . the most powerful," said an SEA lead.

One way the state bolstered the material of the *Respect Workshop* was to offer follow-up support and technical assistance. For example, after personnel from one LEA attended the training, the agency asked for guidance in how to reflect GSD students in their curriculum and what books to make available to students such that students would see themselves reflected in class materials. To personalize the *Respect Workshop* training, the state included a panel of youth speakers who attended the school that hosted the training,

To accommodate the needs of school health and mental health professionals, the SEA offered the *Respect Workshop* in two places, one in the southern part of the state and one in the northern part of the state, so that attendees would not have to travel prohibitively far. The SEA worked closely with expert trainers and facilitators who were not from the state to make sure they understood the state and local political and legal climate surrounding GSD issues. Higher level administrators, including assistant school superintendents, attended the training, which permitted trainers to incorporate a broader policy lens.

CHALLENGES OF IMPLEMENTATION

The *Respect Workshop* has faced challenges related to in-person implementation; the evaluation implementation; and implementation of the self-paced, online modules. Over time, APA has developed the following approaches to addressing these challenges.

Implementing the in-person *Respect Workshop* sometimes meant competing with myriad other professional development requirements and interests at the state and local levels. In some cases, workshop organizers struggled to secure a 7.5-hour window for the training within the school calendar. In other jurisdictions, the greatest challenge was receiving authorization to host professional development focused specifically in support of GSD students. Across all locales, there was the challenge of ensuring consistent funding to implement a national training model. APA worked to address these challenges by partnering closely with SEAs and LEAs, managing controversy around SSEs, and securing federal funding for the *Respect Workshop* and trainer cadre from CDC.

The *Respect Workshop* also faced implementation challenges related to the evaluation. From 2002 to 2017, the *Respect Workshop* evaluation approach was relatively burdensome for a 7.5-hour training event, including three participant instruments: a presurvey, a postsurvey, and a follow-up survey. Furthermore, the evaluation tools were revised at least three times, limiting the ability to compare survey findings over many years. Evaluation participation was variable with difficulties in gathering follow-up survey data and matching surveys through confidential unique identifiers. These difficulties limited analyses and introduced potential bias to the evaluation sample. APA worked to address these challenges by encouraging presurvey completion before the event and tightening online procedures for the development of unique identifiers. In 2019, APA began to explore other survey methods, such as a postsurvey with retrospective presurvey items to further reduce evaluation implementation challenges.

Although the online *Respect Workshop* was primarily developed in response to existing implementation challenges, its development and initial rollout faced unique challenges. More specifically, the online modules were developed as standard modules and are unable to be customized to meet the specific needs of jurisdictions. In addition, the modules are hosted on a platform that requires individuals to register and establish an account to participate. Still, APA has accepted these barriers to provide a scientifically accurate course for school health and mental health professionals that is both free of charge and accessible on demand. In addition, learning assessments for the modules were added in 2018 to provide valid certificates of learning to participants for them to use in seeking continuing education credits. For schools or districts specifically interested in a customized, online experience, APA has begun to provide an optional, personalized, action-planning module led in real time by a *Respect Workshop* trainer.

FUTURE DIRECTIONS: WHAT'S NEXT FOR *RESPECT*?

Going forward, APA will continue to offer the *Respect Workshop* to LEAs and to other institutions and individuals. In 2018, APA was funded by the CDC through a 5-year cooperative agreement on promoting adolescent health through school-based HIV prevention (CDC, 2019b). The work of APA is focused on strengthening the capacity of LEAs funded by the CDC to create SSEs for all students. Under the cooperative agreement, funded education agencies promote annual professional development for all school staff on supporting GSD students. The revised and updated *Respect Workshop* curriculum serves as a resource in APA's support of LEAs to meet this professional development requirement. A new direction being considered is adapting the curriculum for other groups of school personnel, for example, teachers. In addition, the *Respect Workshop* could be further adapted in the future to specifically address the needs of GSD students across cultures.

RECOMMENDATIONS

The *Respect Workshop* is grounded in the understanding that school health and mental health professionals are in a unique position to support GSD students and all other students in the school environment. The following recommendations outline four professional groups poised to specifically support the needs of GSD students and five protective, schoolwide practices that promote a systemwide approach to SSEs:

- The *Respect Workshop* encourages professional education programs, school districts, and schools to provide initial training and continuous learning opportunities to specialized instructional support professionals—including members of the following four professions—who directly address the needs of GSD students:
  - school counselors
  - school nurses

    – school psychologists

    – school social workers

- The *Respect Workshop* encourages the promotion of the following five research-based, protective, schoolwide practices that provide SSEs for GSD and all other students:

    – Maintain a GSD-inclusive school climate because as students do better when they feel welcome and safe at school.

    – Facilitate access to supportive GSD peers because students benefit when they interact with accepting peers.

    – Assist families to be supportive because family acceptance has a protective effective for GSD children and youth.

    – Provide GSD-sensitive health education because health and sexuality education are more effective when relevant to students' concerns.

    – Facilitate access to STI, HIV, and reproductive health services because students with opportunities to access health services learn responsibility.

CONCLUSION

Overall, the *Respect Workshop* fills a unique need by focusing competency training for GSD youth on four core groups of professionals: (a) school nurses, (b) school counselors, (c) school psychologists, and (d) school social workers. These professionals are among the most trusted professionals by GSD students and are uniquely trained to provide supports relevant to these students' specific needs. Although these professional groups are essential supports for GSD students in school, they have little access to consistent competency training for this population.

    Preliminary data on the *Respect Workshop* reveal increases in knowledge, skills, and self-efficacy among professionals working with GSD youth. In addition, organizers of the *Respect Workshop* from SEAs report that the *Respect Workshop* increased their capacity to provide leadership, guidance, and capacity building to districts and to support SSEs for students and staff.

    In the 20 years it has been working with the CDC to improve schools' capacity to promote health and well-being of GSD students, APA has found in that there is a desire among school health and mental health and other support professionals to address the disproportionate risks faced by GSD students across widely varied political contexts. Access to reliable resources that could be turned to as a scientific standard is highly desired, not only for use in directly supporting students but to rely on as a safety net if controversies arise. The *Respect Workshop* and similar resources thus play multiple roles in the changing landscape of addressing sexual and gender diversity in schools. In states and districts with more access to knowledge about issues relevant to GSD students, the *Respect Workshop* is an APA-endorsed standard curriculum that SEAs and LEAs can build on when training school health and mental health professionals. In areas of the country with less access to resources about issues relevant to GSD students, the *Respect Workshop* serves as a conversation starter for complex discussions at the intersection of professionals' political, social, and spiritual beliefs and environments. Although there has been great change during these past 20 years, APA sees a continued need for high-quality training to help schools to provide safety and support to GSD students, and will be using the *Respect Workshop* to meet that need.

TAKEAWAYS AND OPPORTUNITIES

- School psychologists, school social workers, school counselors, and school nurses play an especially important role in creating a supportive school environment for GSD students because they consistently rank among the most trusted school professionals by GSD students.

- Formal training on issues faced by GSD students is recommended as a best practice for school health and mental health professionals; however, training specific to supporting GSD students is rarely a required component of their professional training.

- APA's *Respect Workshop* fills a unique need for increasing capacity of school health and mental health professionals to promote SSEs for GSD students in schools.

- School health and mental health professionals may engage with the following questions as opportunities for exploration and discussion: If you serve as a school psychologist, school social worker, school counselor, or school nurse, what are the types of concerns around gender identity and sexual orientation that students bring to you most often? What opportunities does your professional role make available to you in supporting families of GSD youth? How might training, such as the *Respect Workshop*, equip you to support teachers, administrators, coaches, or other school personnel with understanding GSD students' needs? As you read through this chapter, how can you adapt this or similar trainings for the unique and intersecting identities among GSD students within your school district (e.g., racial and ethnic diversity, religious affiliations)?

REFERENCES

Ajzen, I. (1991). The theory of planned behavior. *Organizational Behavior and Human Decision Processes, 50*(2), 179–211. https://doi.org/10.1016/0749-5978(91)90020-T

American Psychological Association & National Association of School Psychologists. (2015). *Resolution on gender and sexual orientation diversity in children and adolescents in schools*. https://www.apa.org/about/policy/orientation-diversity

American School Counselor Association. (2017). School counselors transforming schools for lesbian, gay, bisexual, transgender, and queer (LGBTQ) students [Special Issue]. *Professional School Counseling, 20*(1a). https://journals.sagepub.com/toc/pcxa/20/1a

Anderson, C. W., & Porter, J. D. (2004). *Preventing health risks and promoting healthy outcomes among LGBQ youth: A training workshop for school counselors, nurses, psychologists, and social workers.* American Psychological Association.

Bogden, J. F., & Anderson, C. W. (2011). *RESPECT: Preventing health risks and promoting healthy outcomes among lesbian, gay, bisexual, transgender, and questioning students: A training workshop for specialized instructional support services professionals in middle and high schools* (2nd ed.). American Psychological Association.

Brener, N. D., Demissie, Z., McManus, T., Shanklin, S. L., Queen, B., & Kann, L. (2017). *School Health Profiles 2016: Characteristics of health programs among secondary schools.* Centers for Disease Control and Prevention. https://www.cdc.gov/healthyyouth/data/profiles/pdf/2016/2016_Profiles_Report.pdf

Carabez, R., Pellegrini, M., Mankovitz, A., Eliason, M., Ciano, M., & Scott, M. (2015). "Never in all my years . . .": *Nurses' education about LGBT health. Journal of Professional Nursing, 31*(4), 323–329. https://doi.org/10.1016/j.profnurs.2015.01.003

Case, K. A., & Meier, S. C. (2014). Developing allies to transgender and gender-nonconforming youth: Training for counselors and educators. *Journal of LGBT Youth, 11*(1), 62–82. https://doi.org/10.1080/19361653.2014.840764

Centers for Disease Control and Prevention. (n.d.-a). *Profiles results.* https://www.cdc.gov/healthyyouth/data/profiles/results.htm

Centers for Disease Control and Prevention. (n.d.-b). *Youth Risk Behavior Surveillance System (YRBSS) overview.* https://www.cdc.gov/healthyyouth/data/yrbs/overview.htm

Centers for Disease Control and Prevention. (2017, November 2). *School Health Profiles.* https://www.cdc.gov/healthyyouth/data/profiles/index.htm

Centers for Disease Control and Prevention. (2019b). *PS18-1807 program guidance: Guidance for school-based HIV/STD prevention (component 2) recipients of PS18-1807SSE Rationale.* U.S. Department of Health and Human Services. https://www.cdc.gov/healthyyouth/fundedprograms/1807/resources/PS18-1807-GUIDANCE508.pdf

Choi, H.-S., Thul, C. A., Berenhaut, K. S., Suerken, C. K., & Norris, J. L. (2006). Survey of school psychologists' attitudes, feelings, and exposure to gay and lesbian parents and their children. *Journal of Applied School Psychology, 22*(1), 87–107. https://doi.org/10.1300/J370v22n01_05

Coker, T. R., Austin, S. B., & Schuster, M. A. (2010). The health and health care of lesbian, gay, and bisexual adolescents. *Annual Review of Public Health, 31*(1), 457–477. https://doi.org/10.1146/annurev.publhealth.012809.103636

DeCrescenzo, T., & Mallon, G. P. (2000). *Serving transgender youth: The role of child welfare systems—Proceedings of a colloquium.* Child Welfare League of America.

Goodrich, K. M., Harper, A. J., Luke, M., & Singh, A. A. (2013). Best practices for professional school counselors working with LGBTQ youth. *Journal of LGBT Issues in Counseling, 7*(4), 307–322. https://doi.org/10.1080/15538605.2013.839331

Goodrich, K. M., & Luke, M. (2010). The experiences of school counselors-in-training in group work with LGBTQ adolescents. *Journal for Specialists in Group Work, 35*(2), 143–159. https://doi.org/10.1080/01933921003705966

Jennings, T. (2014). Sexual orientation curriculum in U.S. school counselor education programs. *Journal of LGBT Issues in Counseling, 8*(1), 43–73. https://doi.org/10.1080/15538605.2014.853639

Kosciw, J. G., Greytak, E. A., Bartkiewicz, M. J., Boesen, M. J., & Palmer, N. A. (2012). *The 2011 National School Climate Survey: Key findings on the experiences of lesbian, gay, bisexual, and transgender youth in our nation's schools.* GLSEN. https://www.glsen.org/sites/default/files/2020-04/2011%20GLSEN%20National%20School%20Climate%20Survey.pdf

Kosciw, J. G., Greytak, E. A., Giga, N. M., Villenas, C., & Danischewski, D. J. (2016). *The 2015 National School Climate Survey: The experiences of lesbian, gay, bisexual, transgender and queer youth in our nation's schools.* GLSEN. https://www.glsen.org/article/2015-national-school-climate-survey

Kosciw, J. G., Greytak, E. A., Palmer, N. A., & Boesen, M. J. (2014). *The 2013 National School Climate Survey: The experiences of lesbian, gay, bisexual and transgender youth in our nation's schools.* GLSEN. https://www.glsen.org/sites/default/files/2020-03/GLSEN-2013-National-School-Climate-Survey-Full-Report.pdf

Kull, R. M., Greytak, E. A., & Kosciw, J. G. (2019). *Supporting safe and healthy schools for lesbian, gay, bisexual, transgender, and queer students: A national survey of school counselors, social workers, and psychologists.* GLSEN. https://www.glsen.org/article/supporting-safe-and-healthy-schools-lgbtq-students

Martin, J. I., Messinger, L., Kull, R., Holmes, J., & Bermudez, F. (2014). *Sexual orientation and gender expression in social work education: Results from a national survey.* Council on Social Work Education. https://www.cswe.org/CSWE/media/APM-2012/SexualOrientationAndGenderExpression.pdf

National Association of School Nurses. (2016). *LGBTQ students: The role of the school nurse.* https://www.nasn.org/nasn/advocacy/professional-practice-documents/position-statements/ps-lgbtq

National Association of School Psychologists. (2017). *Safe schools for transgender and gender diverse students* [Position statement]. https://www.nasponline.org/lgbtqi2-s

Rafferty, J., Committee on Psychosocial Aspects of Child and Family Health, Committee on Adolescence, & Section on Lesbian, Gay, Bisexual, and Transgender Health and Wellness. (2018). Ensuring comprehensive care and support for transgender and gender-diverse children and adolescents. *Pediatrics, 142*(4), Article e20182162. https://doi.org/10.1542/peds.2018-2162

Rasberry, C. N., Morris, E., Lesesne, C. A., Kroupa, E., Topete, P., Carver, L. H., & Robin, L. (2015). Communicating with school nurses about sexual orientation and sexual health: Perspectives of teen young men who have sex with men. *Journal of School Nursing, 31*(5), 334–344. https://doi.org/10.1177/1059840514557160

Rosenbaum, L., Anderson, C., Christopher, D. & Wright, T. (2018). *The Respect Workshop trainer manual* (3rd ed.). American Psychological Association.

Sawyer, R. J., Porter, J. D., Lehman, T. C., Anderson, C., & Anderson, K. M. (2006). Education and training needs of school staff relevant to preventing risk behaviors and promoting health behaviors among gay, lesbian, bisexual, and questioning youth. *Journal of HIV/AIDS Prevention in Children & Youth, 7*(1), 37–53. https://doi.org/10.1300/J499v07n01_03

Sharp Insight. (2017). Respect Workshop *pre–post findings (2015–2017)* [Unpublished evaluation report]. Available on request from the American Psychological Association or Sharp Insight, LLC.

8

Addressing Gender and Sexual Orientation Diversity Within Youth Populations

An Evaluation of Health Disparities and Recommendations on Affirmative School Policy

Amie R. McKibban and Austin R. Anderson

Across the literature and throughout this book (e.g., Gower et al., 2018; Poteat, 2008), it is clear that schools can offer a protective environment for gender and sexually diverse (GSD) youth. At this juncture, it has also likely become clear to you as the reader that structuring a protective school environment takes multiple, coordinated efforts, including training for teachers and teacher support; curricula that are GSD inclusive and sensitive; enumerated antibullying/harassment policies (i.e., policies that clearly specify sexual orientation and gender identity); policies that ensure equity in gender expression at school and school-related events (e.g., prom, sporting events); and access to gender-neutral or all-gender spaces, such as bathrooms (Kosciw et al., 2018; Russell et al., 2010). One strategy alone is insufficient for wide-scale change. There is a strong theoretical basis for why larger scale change, such as reducing health disparities in the GSD youth population, requires multiple and coordinated efforts. The basis for this lies within an understanding of minority stress and the levels at which that stress occurs.

In this chapter, we review the health disparities discussed in this book; discuss the mechanisms behind the health disparities; offer a theoretical framework for understanding these mechanisms; and explore how inclusive policy has been shown to impact health disparities in three main areas: (a) antiharassment policy, (b) curricular policy, and (c) policy that impacts gendered events and spaces. We end with a summary of our findings and

https://doi.org/10.1037/0000211-009
Supporting Gender Identity and Sexual Orientation Diversity in K–12 Schools, M. C. Lytle and R. A. Sprott (Editors)

recommendations moving forward as you consider the different ways in which to offer a supportive climate in your own school.

UNDERSTANDING HEALTH DISPARITIES IN SEXUAL ORIENTATION AND GENDER DIVERSE YOUTH POPULATIONS

Stigma and social disparities related to health have been well documented in the literature. Here, we explore the connections between minority stress and health disparities.

Understand Minority Stress Theory

It is helpful to frame discussions of health disparities in light of social stigma, minority stress, and their relationship to health disparities. As Hatzenbuehler and Pachankis (2016) discussed in their extensive review of the literature, the minority stress theory was developed to conceptualize health disparities often experienced by minority populations. Hatzenbuehler and Pachankis described how this theory helps explain health disparities in the GSD population:

> Drawing on insights from the stigma literature, Meyer (2003) developed the minority stress theory, which refers to the "excess stress to which individuals from stigmatized social categories are exposed as a result of their social, often a minority, position." Meyer conceptualized these stressors as unique (in that they are additive to general stressors that are experienced by all people and therefore require adaptations above and beyond those required of the non-stigmatized), chronic (in that they are related to relatively stable social structures such as laws and social policies), and socially based (in that they stem from social/structural forces rather than individual events or conditions). Minority stress theory there-fore posits that health disparities observed in LGBT [lesbian, gay, bisexual, and transgender] populations do not reflect psychological issues inherent to LGBT individuals, but rather are the end result of persistent stigma directed toward them. Originally developed to explain sexual orientation disparities in mental health, the theory has recently been applied to physical health disparities and to understanding health disparities related to gender identity. (p. 986)

Adapting to the stressors experienced by GSD youth requires sustained effort and energy to a level at which many of our youth are not yet equipped to do. Likewise, these stressors are chronic (continue across the lifetime) and occur at the individual level (e.g., coming out), the interpersonal level (e.g., rejection from peers), and the structural level (e.g., unequitable policies). As such, intervention and prevention strategies must be developed in a way that addresses different stressors at different levels.

Explore the Impact of Minority Stress on Health

Disparities in health as well as higher rates of risk behaviors (Kann et al., 2018; Savage & Schanding, 2013) among GSD youth have been established in the literature using multiple and national samples across time (Kosciw et al., 2016,

2018). Identifying the mechanisms linking minority stress (stigma) and health is an important step in understanding what strategies will reduce these health disparities. Extensive work has been done by Hatzenbuehler and Pachankis (2016) with sexually diverse populations to document these mechanisms, which include vigilance, rumination, loneliness, and physiological stress response. Taking a closer look at these mechanisms is the first step in developing strategies at your school that are effective in promoting supportive and healthy environments.

Environments that feel unsafe produce higher levels of vigilance among sexually diverse youth—that is, such environments increase the need to be alert to potential threats, whether those threats are relational (e.g., name-calling) or physical (e.g., assault). A substantial body of research by Hatzenbuehler (2009) and colleagues (Hatzenbuehler et al., 2013, 2015) has supported this increase in perceptual vigilance as well as its effects on health in youth and adult populations, including a negative impact on cardiovascular functioning and adverse effects on mental health. This increase in perceptual vigilance is closely tied to rumination when environments are perceived as stressful and unsafe. Not only have Hatzenbuehler and colleagues demonstrated that sexually diverse youth ruminate to a greater extent (e.g., focusing on the causes of stress), rumination has been associated with psychological distress, particularly when the focus of the rumination (e.g., name-calling) is related to their sexual orientation.

Further compounding these mechanisms is loneliness. When environmental stressors are directly related to youth's sexual orientations and gender identities, they tend to conceal these aspects of themselves and subsequently avoid interpersonal relationships for fear of being discovered (Ryan et al., 2010). Youth who identify as GSD are already at higher risk of rejection from peers and family (Kosciw et al., 2018), and avoidance of interpersonal relationships to avoid further rejection and victimization only increases the physical and psychological distress thus far documented.

As we have known for a long time, stress has a direct and immediate impact on physical health via our body's stress response—predominantly in the release of the steroid hormone cortisol. For GSD youth (and adults), research is beginning to demonstrate how chronic environmental stress, such as feeling unsafe at school, leads to a dysregulation of the cortisol response. To investigate exposure to structural stress (e.g., unsupportive schools), Hatzenbuehler and McLaughlin (2014) looked at 74 youth located in 24 states and, subsequently, the schools the participants attended. These areas were divided into two categories: high structural stress and low structural stress based on the presence or absence of supportive mechanisms in the environment (e.g., inclusive policy). The authors found that those youth raised in environments with high structural stress had a blunted cortisol response by early adulthood, similar to the type of response we see in children who have experienced maltreatment and those with posttraumatic stress disorder. Those raised in environments with low structural stress did not exhibit this response.

The authors' work provides us with documented evidence that minority stress affects the body's overall health response to stress, which can impact both physical and mental health over time.

We are starting to understand the underlying mechanisms of health disparities among GSD youth and how these mechanisms are related to supportive and unsupportive environments, particularly over the past 2 decades. Likewise, this research further helps us understand why multiple, coordinated efforts within our schools are necessary to decrease negative health outcomes GSD youth. We now turn our attention to ways in which structural stressors can be decreased by focusing on policy.

CHANGING STRUCTURAL STRESSORS BY CHANGING POLICY

Research in health disparities of sexually diverse adult populations suggests that policy change can alter environments in a way that reduces minority stressors and, in turn, reduces health disparities, both physical and mental (Chaudoir et al., 2017). For example, following the legalization of same-sex marriage in Massachusetts, the number of visits to medical clinics for mental and physical health difficulties decreased substantially among gay men. More telling of the impact policy can have, the result held regardless of whether these men were partnered or single (Hatzenbuehler et al., 2012). Although studies that investigate the impact of policy change using large-scale data, such as the Hatzenbuehler and McLaughlin (2014) study described earlier, are difficult to come by, current research does suggest that enumerated policies are related to better health outcomes in smaller samples.

Unfortunately, youth are often invisible in enumerated policies at the state and federal levels (Wardenski, 2005). This is self-evident in federal rulings, such as marriage equality. It may be, at first glance, less evident in state anti-discrimination laws. However, at the time of this writing, only 15 states and the District of Columbia have nondiscrimination laws designed to protect students on the basis of sexual orientation and gender identity. Furthermore, very few states have recognized the impact of bullying by creating antibullying laws that protect students; only 17 states and the District of Columbia have enumerated such laws (GLSEN [originally known as the Gay, Lesbian, and Straight Education Network], 2019). As Russell et al. (2010) pointed out, "Enumeration that is inclusive of sexual orientation and gender identity/expression is often at the forefront of the challenges in these state laws being passed" (p. 8). This is unfortunate because longitudinal research (Kosciw et al., 2018) has found a decrease in victimization based on sexual orientation and gender expression in states that had enumerated safe school laws. More illuminating, the same study (Kosciw et al., 2018) found no such decrease in victimization for GSD students in states with either no laws, or nonenumerated laws, from year to year.

Despite a lack of state-level laws, district and school policies can be developed in a way that may decrease minority stressors for GSD youth within the school setting (Chaudoir et al., 2017). In the next section, we review the research on policy change within schools, districts, or both. We further discuss how these policy changes may have a positive effect on the physical and mental health of GSD students as well as non-GSD students—a necessity in creating equitable policy change.

PROTECTING STUDENTS VIA NONDISCRIMINATION AND ANTIHARASSMENT/ANTIBULLYING POLICY

School-based harassment and bullying—both physical and relational—has been linked to negative, long-term consequences, including suicidality (Kann et al., 2018; Nansel et al., 2001; Russell et al., 2012), delinquency (Kosciw et al., 2018), poor academic outcomes (Schwartz et al., 2005), and poor health outcomes (e.g., Hatzenbuehler & Pachankis, 2016). Furthermore, rates of negative health outcomes as a result of bullying are higher for GSD students than their non-GSD peers who also face bullying (Goodenow et al., 2016), which is in line with research on minority stress and health. As many have expressed throughout this book, it is clear that schools and districts have a responsibility to address school-based harassment/bullying.

The state of antibullying policies across the nation is complex and incomplete; the most recent data on demographics were obtained in 2011 (Kull et al., 2015). However, the available data can provide us with useful information. Specifically, 70.5% of districts in the United States at that time had antibullying policies; only 42.6% included sexual orientation; and even fewer (14.1%) enumerated gender identity, gender expression, or both. This snapshot becomes even more complex when considering regional and state differences. We discuss the complexity and differences between states and regions in the next section of this chapter. But first, let us take a look at what the literature says about the relationship between enumerated antibullying policies and health outcomes for students.

As Russell and McGuire (2008) discussed, enumerated nondiscrimination and antibullying/harassment laws at the district and school levels may provide more immediate protections for students and also pave the way for other programs and initiatives, such as teacher training and gender and sexuality alliances (or GSAs, an acronym that has referred to "gay–straight alliances" but more recently refers to "gender and sexuality alliances" or "genders and sexualities alliances"). The impact of such policies is a bit more difficult to discern because there tends to be an interplay between state- and district-level policies. However, some conclusions suggest that in districts with enumerated antibullying/harassment policies, students report a more positive school climate (Szalacha, 2003) and feel safer (O'Shaughnessy et al., 2004), and schools within these districts have fewer reported suicide attempts (Goodenow et al., 2016). It appears that the most measurable impact policy has at the district level is that of students' perceptions of safety and well-being.

The impact of this difference in perception on health outcomes is, however, less clearly articulated in the literature. This should not suggest that enumerated antibullying/harassment policy at the district level does not matter; it does inasmuch as it can influence students' perceptions of school climate. Given the interplay between state- and district-level policies, however, measuring the impact of these policies on health outcomes is more difficult and nuanced. The key takeaway here is the positive shift in students' perceptions of school climate, and one of the key factors in shifting those perceptions are students' knowledge and understanding of the policies that do apply to them (Hansen, 2007).

Although enumerated antibullying/harassment policies may play a role in overall school climate for GSD and non-GSD students, other strategies appear to be more proximal in their association with students' experiences of bullying and victimization at school, and, hence, their mental and physical health. Next, we discuss two of these strategies: inclusive curricula and gendered events and spaces.

DEVELOPING POLICY RELATED TO INCLUSIVE CURRICULA

Policy that requires state-funded schools to incorporate GSD figures into the curricula (e.g., history curriculum), and GSD-sensitive curricula (e.g., sex education, social studies) are relatively new and, as Russell (2011) pointed out, probably one of the more contentious. Indeed, the landscape in the United States supports this notion: Only four states require such a curriculum—California, Colorado, Illinois, and New Jersey—whereas five states have passed laws prohibiting the teaching of a GSD curriculum. To further illustrate the contentiousness, it is noteworthy that these anti-GSD curricula laws have been challenged, and defeated, at the state and district levels in some places (e.g., North Carolina, Wisconsin).

Although these policy shifts are relatively new, examples of GSD issues being incorporated into multiple areas of school curricula have been available in the literature for the past 2 decades (see Russell, 2011). As such, studies are beginning to illuminate the potential benefits of GSD-inclusive curricula, particularly at the middle and high school levels. For example, Russell et al. (2006) found that California students who learned about sexual orientation and gender diversity reported less relational bullying and, subsequently, felt safer. These results appear to hold across time. Specifically, *The 2017 National School Climate Survey* (Kosciw et al., 2018) indicated that students who learned about GSD issues reported less relational bullying (e.g., name-calling, rumors), heard fewer GSD slurs, experienced increased feelings of safety, and had more productive conversations with teachers.

Curricular inclusion not only appears to improve school climate and subsequently student mental health, but it may also impact physical health. Although data on physical health outcomes are scant, Blake et al. (2001)

demonstrated that lesbian, gay, and bisexual (LGB) youth who received LGB-sensitive education on HIV and access to LGB-sensitive resources, and were taught by teachers who demonstrated more confidence in meeting their needs, were less likely to engage in risky sexual behaviors. Furthermore, the authors found that LGB students in schools that did not provide such education and materials were at greater risk when compared with all youth for HIV infection, pregnancy, suicide, and victimization.

In reviewing the available literature, and as articulated by Russell (2011), this strategy—that of inclusive and sensitive curricula—may have the strongest impact on GSD and non-GSD student outcomes. More specifically, inclusive curricula not only improve student well-being outcomes across the literature but also account for average differences in school climate between schools, as demonstrated in large-scale studies in California (Russell et al., 2006) and Massachusetts (Szalacha, 2003). As Russell clearly pointed out, it is unclear what mechanism is responsible for the effect of inclusive curricula. That is, inclusive curricula take many forms across studies, ranging from formal classroom content to informal aspects, such as posters and student–teacher interactions. As such, the implications of curricular inclusion may differ depending on implementation, and future research needs to flush out these differences to better understand what types of curricular changes have the most beneficial impact.

CREATING POLICY RELATED TO SCHOOL SPORTS AND GENDERED SPACES

As discussed so far, GSD students in K–12 educational settings often report higher levels of harassment and fear of violence than their non-GSD counterparts. When we look at *The 2017 National School Climate Survey* (Kosciw et al., 2018), GSD students are likely to experience negative aspects of climate as it relates to athletic and gender-related spaces, specifically. In these spaces, normative gender and sexuality roles are often strictly enforced, and the dominance of hegemonic masculinity threatens any deviation from these normative expectations. As indicators of such, *The 2017 National School Climate Survey* (Kosciw et al., 2018) reported the following statistics:

- More than 40% of GSD students avoided bathroom and locker-room spaces within schools because they felt unsafe or uncomfortable. (p. xviii)

- More than three quarters (75.4%) of GSD respondents avoided participation in school events (e.g., prom), and 70.5% avoided extracurricular activities because they felt unsafe. (p. xviii)

- Of GSD respondents, 11.3% reported being prevented or discouraged from participation in interscholastic athletics because they identified as GSD. (p. xx)

- Of transgender students, 43.6% reported being required to use the locker room or bathroom of their assigned gender at birth, as opposed to their current gender identity. (p. xx)

The pervasive nature of negative educational climates for GSD students has a variety of effects, seen and unseen, both inside and outside of the traditional classroom. Overall, there is a general lack of research regarding policy initiatives that directly impact the educational climate surrounding GSD individuals in sports and gendered spaces at the K–12 level. However, a number of sport-related GSD advocacy programs have shown promising inroads in creating open and accepting sporting cultures on implementation. These programs, such as Athlete Ally (https://www.athleteally.org/) and the You Can Play project (http://www.youcanplayproject.org/), share common objectives in promoting equal access, openness, and acceptance within sports settings. School systems would be well served by considering open participation within one of these GSD sports ally programs to outwardly project an environment of support within sporting spaces that are often unwelcoming to students of nonnormative sexualities and gender identities.

Aim for Inclusive Environments

The aim of any policies implemented around sporting and gendered spaces in school settings should be to create inclusive environments. For these environments to become inclusive, staff and student leaders must create norms around excellence in sports and gendered spaces that encourage inclusion. That is to say, the norms that are vital to success in sports (e.g., teamwork, dedication, goal setting) should be expanded to include and encourage inclusion. For example, *inclusive excellence* is an approach introduced by Kauer and Krane (2010) that places valuing diversity as a central athletic team goal that will help the team be more successful. If sports participants see inclusion of GSD athletes, coaches, and supporters as normative and vital to the success of their athletic pursuits, acceptance may follow naturally.

In addition, important language issues at play in sporting spaces can give them the appearance of being unwelcoming to participants with GSD identities. Often, the language used within sports mirrors the hegemonic masculinity that permeates through competitive athletic settings. Phrases like "You throw/run like a girl" or encouragement to "man up" emphasize the importance of cisnormative masculinity within sports while deemphasizing all aspects of femininity. Administrators and leaders within school athletic spaces should discourage this type of language while encouraging language that is more inclusive of all possible identities to create spaces that are, conceptually, more open to participants of varying identities.

Sports spaces, specifically, are implicitly vulnerable to direct reflections of the leadership that exists within them (i.e., coaches, team captains, and so on). Leadership within sports settings tends to have a direct and high-magnitude impact on the overall sporting environment. As such, leaders are vitally important in reinforcing and shaping inclusive cultures for GSD participants in sports (Cunningham, 2015a). Cunningham (2015b) noted,

> [Leaders can reinforce inclusive cultures] through their advocacy [of] the topic and by setting expectations for inclusion in the department. Strong leadership has a trickle-down effect (Ruiz et al., 2011), as people take note of leader expectations and modeling, and behave accordingly. This is particularly the case when it comes to the deinstitutionalization of organizational practices, systems, and values (Parish, 2005). (p. 51)

Allow Transgender Participation in Sports

Gender segregation is a particularly innate part of most sports settings: Boys play with and compete against boys, and girls play with and compete against girls. This makes sports an area that is firmly grounded in a binary definition of gender. To move from this grounding into a more inclusive setting for sports, regardless of gender identity, leaders and administrators must focus on the ideals of fair play and competition within sports; the role of *participation* in sports must be seen as the paramount goal of scholastic sports settings. In some settings, this has been occurring over the course of the past decade. For instance, in Washington State in 2009, the Washington Interscholastic Activities Association (WIAA, 2009) developed a groundbreaking policy that stated, "All students should have the opportunity to participate in WIAA activities in a manner that is consistent with their gender identity, irrespective of the gender listed on a student's records" (p. 47). This statement allows all athletes to compete as the gender with which they identify regardless of anatomy and without mandating legal or surgical status. This is perhaps the most inclusive policy for transgender competitors and serves as a model for secondary schools and colleges (Lucas-Carr & Krane, 2011).

When it comes to inclusion of transgender athletes in competitive sporting environments, scholastic sporting organizations often look to the National Collegiate Athletic Association (NCAA) for guidance concerning eligibility requirements at the "next level." NCAA policies regarding transgender athlete participation in intercollegiate athletics revolves around the use (or nonuse) of hormonal treatment related to gender transition. For transgender student athletes who are not undergoing any hormonal treatment related to gender transition, a transgender male athlete (female to male) can compete on any men's or women's team, whereas a transgender female athlete (male to female) may compete only on men's teams. For transgender student athletes who are undergoing hormonal treatment, the eligibility guidelines are slightly modified. A transgender male athlete (female to male) undergoing hormonal treatment for gender transition may compete on a men's team but may no longer compete on a female intercollegiate athletic team. A transgender female athlete (male to female) undergoing hormonal treatment for gender transition can participate immediately on any men's team but cannot participate on a female athletic team until completion of 1 calendar year of testosterone suppression treatment (NCAA, 2011).

This policy can be of assistance in interscholastic athletic models that closely mirror those of elite-level athletics, such as those based on the NCAA inter-collegiate athletics model or Olympics-level model. However, inclusive policy implementation should accompany a thorough examination of the inherent format of scholastic sports offerings. That is, in many cases, it may be possible to alter the format of sports offerings in other ways that may be more gender inclusive. Where possible, sports that can be modified for multigender partici-pation without sacrificing the integrity of the experience should be so modi-fied. Administrators within scholastic sporting environments should carefully examine their sports offerings and participatory needs to determine whether their programs can be modified for open participation regardless of gender identity.

EVALUATING THE IMPACT OF NEW POLICIES

As Marx and Kettrey (2016) and others have mentioned, the solutions discussed in this chapter have yielded mixed results in the literature. This may, in part, be due to the differences across districts and between schools. Indeed, regional differences result in variability with which efforts are adopted, implemented, and received (Graybill et al., 2015). Furthermore, local and state laws, district policies, and community characteristics impact such efforts in different ways—or in some cases, restrict such efforts, as we saw in the prohi-bition of GSD-inclusive curricula (GLSEN, 2019). Kull et al. (2015) helped to illuminate some of these differences in the success of implementing policy across districts depending on region and locale. For example, they found that district policies were more inclusive, particularly with student protections and professional development requirements related to sexual orientation and gender identity/expression in Northeast, nonrural areas. This, and other key findings, can be found in Table 8.1.

When we consider districts in states with existing antibullying state policies—which function to establish a statewide standard for how districts address bullying/harassment—disparity exists in how district policies are subsequently implemented. However, Kull et al. (2015) found that many of the districts in states with these mandates did not have antibullying policies in place, and for those that did, many of the policies did not include the enumerated standards set forth within state policy. These findings, noted in Table 8.2, help to elucidate why a decrease in negative health outcomes is not as evident when district-level policies are analyzed in the literature and also why changes to individual level factors, such as inclusive curricula, appear to have a more noticeable measured impact.

The success and ease of implementing any policy change within your school, your district, or both will depend on the region in which you are located as well as existing state policy, because state policy mandates how district policies are implemented. Furthermore, to assess the efficacy of inclusive school policy,

TABLE 8.1. Differences Between Districts, by Other Characteristics

Characteristics	Observational differences
Region	Districts in the Northeast were most likely to have antibullying policies, to have LGBT-inclusive policies, and to have policies that included professional development requirements.
	Districts in the South were least likely to enumerate protections for LGBT students in their policies.
	Districts in the West were least likely to have districts enumerating protections to any group of students in their antibullying policies.
Locale	Rural districts were least likely to have antibullying policies in general, to enumerate protections to any group of students, to have policies that were LGBT inclusive, and to include professional development requirements.
District	Districts that had an antibullying policy in general and had policies that were LGBT inclusive and required professional development were more likely to have a larger student population, higher student-to-teacher ratios, more spending per pupil, and higher socioeconomic status.
	Districts including accountability requirements were more likely to be in the South, in rural than suburban districts, and in districts with lower socioeconomic indicators.

Note. LGBT = lesbian, gay, bisexual, and transgender. Data from Kull, Kosciw, and Greytak (2015).

intentional efforts must be in place before implementation for the adequate measurement of health outcomes. Doing so will enable the district to gather data throughout the process and modify new policies according to their district and regional needs as well as across time. Most important, it will allow you to ensure that the changes being implemented protect students' well-being and educational growth and are not having an unforeseen negative impact on student well-being.

TABLE 8.2. Variation in District Policies Based on Presence of Antibullying State Law

Enumeration	District findings
Presence of district policy	Over a quarter (26.3%) of districts did not have an antibullying policy.
Sexual orientation	38.7% of districts were not providing protections to students based on actual or perceived sexual orientation in their antibullying policies.
Gender identity/expression	60.3% of districts were not providing protections to students based on gender identity/expression in their antibullying policies.
Professional development	For staff on bullying and harassment: 76.0% of districts were not requiring professional development in their antibullying policies.
Accountability	To the district and/or state for bullying incidents: 55.2% of districts were not requiring accountability in their antibullying policies.

Note. Data from Kull, Kosciw, and Greytak (2015).

CONCLUSION

Unsupportive and hostile school climates create minority stress for students in the GSD population. Moreover, minority stress has been linked to a variety of disparities, both immediate and long term, with poor physical and mental health outcomes (e.g., Hatzenbuehler & Pachankis, 2016). When we consider that the Equal Protection Clause of the 14th Amendment guarantees no child can be denied equal access to schooling, it becomes necessary for schools to consider whether a hostile environment prevents equal access for these students. This is especially important given the relationship between hostile environments and physical health outcomes that is due in large part to the need for increased vigilance on the student's part and results in an increase in rumination and higher rates of rejection and loneliness. Students should not have to decide between obtaining a public education and remaining healthy, particularly when creating an inclusive educational environment for GSD youth holds the potential to reduce mental and physical health difficulties within our schools.

As you consider restructuring your school environment, it is important to remember that creating an inclusive environment has the potential to not only reduce poor health outcomes for GSD youth but also to benefit non-GSD students. In an analysis of a large sample of ninth and 11th graders, for example, Gower et al. (2018) demonstrated that the schools using more supportive measures, specifically implementing multiple and coordinated efforts, experienced significantly less bullying—both relational and physical—compared with schools implementing fewer supportive measures. Furthermore, they demonstrated that these results held for non-GSD students. That is, purposefully creating a multifaceted, supportive environment that embraces sexual orientation and gender diversity benefits all students (Konishi et al., 2013). This, when carefully considered, makes sense given that all students have a sexual orientation and a gender identity regardless of how their identities may be categorized.

Unfortunately, creating an inclusive environment is not straightforward because many factors have to be considered with regard to what will work for your school, district, and state. It is a complex undertaking but not an impossible one. We conclude this chapter with a list of considerations and recommendations specific to the content of this chapter as you begin your journey toward full inclusion.

Understand Your School's Needs

If you have the resources to do so, establish a team to measure school climate, the health outcomes of students, or both. This can take significant resources, so we encourage working with your district in understanding what resources may be present. We also encourage you to reach out to your local or nearby university for assistance. Many universities have offices dedicated to community outreach and research. Doing so will assist you in establishing relevant policies based on the unique needs of your school.

Establish a Policy Committee

Develop a committee comprising students, faculty, support staff, and administrative staff who have an interest in rethinking your school policies. Having students on the committee is important and should not be dismissed, because the policy changes will ultimately affect them and they can offer insights that may be overlooked or not readily obvious. It is especially important to include students who represent the diversity within your school's GSD community, including but not limited to students of color, students of low socioeconomic status, non-binary students, and students who identify as bisexual. Make sure your committee is large enough to be representative of these categories but small enough to be effective and efficient in their decision making. We recommend no more than 12 to 15 members.

Know Your District and State Policies

Next, review the existing policies within your state and district. Does your state have an enumerated policy? If so, is the district policy in line with its recommendations? If district policy is misaligned with state policy, this will offer you a starting point for establishing policy change. If your state and district do not have enumerated policies, take the time to really tailor your efforts to your school's needs.

Determine the Content to Be Covered in Your Policies

Establish the content that your enumerated policies will include. This part can initially be overwhelming, but remember: You do not need to reinvent the wheel. Look at model policies at other schools in your region or refer to the model policies put forth by GLSEN (n.d.). Regardless of which model policy you use, we recommend including the following: (a) operational definitions of harassment, bullying, and cyberbullying; (b) definitions of sexual orientation and gender identity that are inclusive of all identities—including heterosexual and cisgender identities; (c) access to gender-segregated activities and spaces, including bathrooms, locker rooms, and gendered events, such as sports and prom; (d) dress code and dress code alternatives; (e) professional development and student training; (f) responsibilities, complaint procedures, and notifications; and (g) disciplinary procedures.

Compose Your Proposal

Compose your proposed policy, including a rationale and justification for why the policy is needed and important. This is where you want to ensure that your justification and rationale have established support from the scientific literature. Use what you have learned throughout this book and through reviewing model policies.

Propose Your New Policies

Your steps here will depend on your state and district boards. Most likely, you will need to present your proposal to your district's superintendent and board of education members for approval. This can be intimidating, but hold strong. Change is possible as long as you are willing to work with those in power who may not initially understand the necessity of policy change. This is when you may also receive some pushback from community members. You can consider asking students and parents, as well as experts in the field, to speak in favor of the proposal at the board meeting(s). Personal stories can make a big difference.

Measure and Modify

If you are successful in implementing enumerated and inclusive policies, keep in mind that it is best to measure the impact of these policies systematically and regularly, modifying as needed to ensure the efficacy of your policies. We again recommend contacting your local or nearby university for assistance with ensuring proper measurement and analysis. At the end of the day, policy change is a complex and ongoing process—and when done correctly will prove to be rewarding and, quite literally, life changing.

TAKEAWAYS AND OPPORTUNITIES

- The minority stress theory helps to explain and conceptualize GSD youth health disparities and can be linked to the presence of supportive environments, unsupportive environments, or both.

- Inclusive policy has the ability to create environments that are seen as supportive for GSD people, increase students' perceptions of safety and well-being, and potentially help address health disparities.

- GSD-inclusive curricula have strong impacts on student outcomes for both GSD and non-GSD students.

- Sporting and gendered spaces often present policy challenges for schools, particularly when it comes to transgender inclusion and participation.

- Regional and state differences will often impact the efficacy of policy and, thus, how it impacts health disparities. Effective policy requires intentional effort and adequate outcome measurement.

- What needs to be in place for you, in your context, to begin forming a policy committee? Whom will you ask to partner with you in creating it?

- Have you ever attended a meeting of your district school board? Consider attending a few meetings so you understand how they are structured. Then, sign up for the email list so you will see an agenda of topics to be discussed in upcoming meetings.

- Is there a member of the school board who is already interested in inclusive school environments? Identifying a potential "champion" for your cause can go a long way in your efforts for your students.

REFERENCES

Blake, S. M., Ledsky, R., Lehman, T., Goodenow, C., Sawyer, R., & Hack, T. (2001). Preventing sexual risk behaviors among gay, lesbian, and bisexual adolescents: The benefits of gay-sensitive HIV instruction in schools. *American Journal of Public Health, 91*(6), 940–946. https://doi.org/10.2105/AJPH.91.6.940

Chaudoir, S. R., Wang, K., & Pachankis, J. E. (2017). What reduces sexual minority stress? A review of the intervention "toolkit." *Journal of Social Issues, 73*(3), 586–617. https://doi.org/10.1111/josi.12233

Cunningham, G. B. (2015a). Creating and sustaining workplace cultures supportive of LGBT employees in college athletics. *Journal of Sport Management, 29*(4), 426–442. https://doi.org/10.1123/jsm.2014-0135

Cunningham, G. (2015b). LGBT inclusive athletic departments as agents of social change. *Journal of Intercollegiate Sport, 8*(1), 43–56. https://doi.org/10.1123/jis.2014-0131

GLSEN. (n.d.). *GLSEN Public Policy Office.* https://www.glsen.org/policy

GLSEN. (2019). *Policy maps: Enumerated anti-bullying laws by state.* Retrieved June 1, 2020, from https://www.glsen.org/article/state-maps

Goodenow, C., Watson, R. J., Adjei, J., Homma, Y., & Saewyc, E. (2016). Sexual orientation trends and disparities in school bullying and violence-related experiences, 1999–2013. *Psychology of Sexual Orientation and Gender Diversity, 3*(4), 386–396. https://doi.org/10.1037/sgd0000188

Gower, A. L., Forster, M., Gloppen, K., Johnson, A. Z., Eisenberg, M. E., Connett, J. E., & Borowsky, I. W. (2018). School practices to foster LGBT-supportive climate: Associations with adolescent bullying involvement. *Prevention Science, 19*(6), 813–821. https://doi.org/10.1007/s11121-017-0847-4

Graybill, E. C., Varjas, K., Meyers, J., Dever, B. V., Greenberg, D., Roach, A. T., & Morillas, C. (2015). Demographic trends and advocacy experiences of gay–straight alliance advisors. *Journal of LGBT Youth, 12*(4), 436–461. https://doi.org/10.1080/19361653.2015.1077770

Hansen, A. L. (2007). School-based support for GLBT students: A review of three levels of research. *Psychology in the Schools, 44*(8), 839–848. https://doi.org/10.1002/pits.20269

Hatzenbuehler, M. L. (2009). How does sexual minority stigma "get under the skin"? A psychological mediation framework. *Psychological Bulletin, 135*(5), 707–730. https://doi.org/10.1037/a0016441

Hatzenbuehler, M. L., Jun, H. J., Corliss, H. L., & Bryn Austin, S. (2015). Structural stigma and sexual orientation disparities in adolescent drug use. *Addictive Behaviors, 46*, 14–18. https://doi.org/10.1016/j.addbeh.2015.02.017

Hatzenbuehler, M. L., & McLaughlin, K. A. (2014). Structural stigma and hypothalamic–pituitary–adrenocortical axis reactivity in lesbian, gay, and bisexual young adults. *Annals of Behavioral Medicine, 47*(1), 39–47. https://doi.org/10.1007/s12160-013-9556-9

Hatzenbuehler, M. L., O'Cleirigh, C., Grasso, C., Mayer, K., Safren, S., & Bradford, J. (2012). Effect of same-sex marriage laws on health care use and expenditures in sexual minority men: A quasi-natural experiment. *American Journal of Public Health, 102*(2), 285–291. https://doi.org/10.2105/AJPH.2011.300382

Hatzenbuehler, M. L., & Pachankis, J. E. (2016). Stigma and minority stress as social determinants of health among lesbian, gay, bisexual, and transgender youth: Research evidence and clinical implications. *Pediatric Clinics of North America, 63*(6), 985–997. https://doi.org/10.1016/j.pcl.2016.07.003

Hatzenbuehler, M. L., Phelan, J. C., & Link, B. G. (2013). Stigma as a fundamental cause of population health inequalities. *American Journal of Public Health, 103*(5), 813–821. https://doi.org/10.2105/AJPH.2012.301069

Kann, L., McManus, T., Harris, W. A., Shanklin, S. L., Flint, K. H., Queen, B., Lowry, R., Chyen, D., Whittle, L., Thornton, J., Lim, C., Bradford, D., Yamakawa, Y., Leon, M., Brener, N., & Ethier, K. A. (2018). Youth risk behavior surveillance—United States, 2017. *Morbidity and Mortality Weekly Report Surveillance Summaries, 67*(8), 1–114. https://doi.org/10.15585/mmwr.ss6708a1

Kauer, K. J., & Krane, V. (2010). Inclusive excellence: Embracing diverse sexual and gender identities in sport. In S. J. Hanrahan & M. B. Andersen (Eds.), *Handbook of applied sport psychology* (pp. 764–779). Routledge.

Konishi, C., Saewyc, E., Homma, Y., & Poon, C. (2013). Population-level evaluation of school-based interventions to prevent problem substance use among gay, lesbian and bisexual adolescents in Canada. *Preventive Medicine, 57*(6), 929–933. https://doi.org/10.1016/j.ypmed.2013.06.031

Kosciw, J. G., Greytak, E. A., Giga, N. M., Villenas, C., & Danischewski, J. (2016). *The 2015 National School Climate Survey: The experiences of lesbian, gay, bisexual, transgender, and queer youth in our nation's schools.* GLSEN. https://www.glsen.org/article/2015-national-school-climate-survey

Kosciw, J. G., Greytak, E. A., Zongrone, A. D., Clark, C. M., & Truong, N. L. (2018). *The 2017 National School Climate Survey: The experiences of lesbian, gay, bisexual, transgender, and queer youth in our nation's schools.* GLSEN. https://www.glsen.org/research/2017-national-school-climate-survey-0

Kull, R. M., Kosciw, J. G., & Greytak, E. A. (2015). *From statehouse to schoolhouse: Anti-bullying policy efforts in U.S. states and school districts.* GLSEN.

Lucas-Carr, C. B., & Krane, V. (2011). What is the T in LGBT? Supporting transgender athletes through sport psychology. *Sport Psychologist, 25*(4), 532–548. https://doi.org/10.1123/tsp.25.4.532

Marx, R. A., & Kettrey, H. H. (2016). Gay–straight alliances are associated with lower levels of school-based victimization of LGBTQ+ youth: A systematic review and meta-analysis. *Journal of Youth and Adolescence, 45*(7), 1269–1282. https://doi.org/10.1007/s10964-016-0501-7

Meyer, I. H. (2003). Prejudice, social stress, and mental health in lesbian, gay, and bisexual populations: Conceptual issues and research evidence. *Psychological Bulletin, 129*(5), 674–697. https://doi.org/10.1037/0033-2909.129.5.674

Nansel, T. R., Overpeck, M., Ramani, S. P., Ruan, W. J., Simons-Morton, B., & Scheidt, P. (2001). Bullying behaviors among US youth: Prevalence and association with psychosocial adjustment. *JAMA, 285*(16), 2094–2100. https://doi.org/10.1001/jama.285.16.2094

National Collegiate Athletic Association. (2011). *NCAA inclusion of transgender athletes.*

O'Shaughnessy, M., Russell, S. T., Heck, K., Calhoun, C., & Laub, C. (2004). *Safe place to learn: Consequences of harassment based on actual or perceived sexual orientation and gender non-conformity and steps for making schools safer.* California Safe Schools Coalition and 4-H Center for Youth Development.

Parish, S. L. (2005). Deinstitutionalization in two states: The impact of advocacy, policy, and other social forces on services for people with developmental disabilities.

Research and Practice for Persons with Severe Disabilities, 30(4), 219–231. https://doi.org/10.2511/rpsd.30.4.219

Poteat, V. P. (2008). Contextual and moderating effects of the peer group climate on use of homophobic epithets. *School Psychology Review, 37*(2), 188–201.

Ruiz, P., Ruiz, C., & Martínez, R. (2011). Improving the "leader–follower" relationship: Top manager or supervisor? The ethical leadership trickle-down effect on follower job response. *Journal of Business Ethics, 99*(4), 587–608. https://doi.org/10.1007/s10551-010-0670-3

Russell, S. T. (2011). Challenging homophobia in schools: Policies and programs for safe school climates. *Educar em Revista, 39*(39), 123–138. https://doi.org/10.1590/S0104-40602011000100009

Russell, S. T., Kosciw, J., Horn, S., & Saewyc, E. (2010). Safe schools policy for LGBTQ students. *Social Policy Report, 24*(4), 1–25. https://doi.org/10.1002/j.2379-3988.2010.tb00065.x

Russell, S. T., Kostroski, O., McGuire, J. K., Laub, C., & Manke, E. (2006). LGBT issues in the curriculum promotes school safety. *California Safe Schools Coalition Research Brief, 4.* http://www.casafeschools.org/FactSheet-curriculum.pdf

Russell, S. T., & McGuire, J. K. (2008). The school climate for lesbian, gay, bisexual, and transgender (LGBT) students. In M. Shinn & H. Yoshikawa (Eds.), *Changing schools and community organizations to foster positive youth development* (pp. 133–149). Oxford University Press. https://doi.org/10.1093/acprof:oso/9780195327892.003.0008

Russell, S. T., Sinclair, K. O., Poteat, V. P., & Koenig, B. W. (2012). Adolescent health and harassment based on discriminatory bias. *American Journal of Public Health, 102*(3), 493–495. https://doi.org/10.2105/AJPH.2011.300430

Ryan, C., Russell, S. T., Huebner, D., Diaz, R., & Sanchez, J. (2010). Family acceptance in adolescence and the health of LGBT young adults. *Journal of Child and Adolescent Psychiatric Nursing, 23*(4), 205–213. https://doi.org/10.1111/j.1744-6171.2010.00246.x

Savage, T. A., & Schanding, T., Jr. (2013). Creating and maintaining safe and responsive schools for lesbian, gay, bisexual, transgender, and queer youths: Introduction to the special issue. *Journal of School Violence, 12*(1), 1–6. https://doi.org/10.1080/15388220.2012.724357

Schwartz, D., Gorman, A. H., Nakamoto, J., & Toblin, R. L. (2005). Victimization in the peer group and children's academic functioning. *Journal of Educational Psychology, 97*(3), 425–435. https://doi.org/10.1037/0022-0663.97.3.425

Szalacha, L. A. (2003). Safer sexual diversity climates: Lessons learned from an evaluation of Massachusetts safe schools program for gay and lesbian students. *American Journal of Education, 110*(1), 58–88. https://doi.org/10.1086/377673

Wardenski, J. (2005). A minor exception? The impact of *Lawrence v. Texas* on LGBT youth. *Journal of Criminal Law & Criminology, 95*(4), 1363–1410.

Washington Interscholastic Activities Association. (2009). *2009–2010 official handbook.*

Walking the Walk

Progress in Translation and Implementation, and an Agenda Going Forward

Richard A. Sprott and Megan C. Lytle

In this final chapter, we'd like to share our summary of findings and lessons about interventions and programs that directly address the needs of gender and sexually diverse (GSD) students. Taken together, these programs and interventions have been found to be effective in reducing risks to well-being and in promoting health (Gower et al., 2018; Hatzenbuehler et al., 2019; Heck et al., 2013; Ioverno et al., 2016; Russell et al., 2010; Ryan et al., 2009), which is important because GSD populations experience notable health disparities and problematic relations with school. In the recent past, several programs, interventions, and policies have been designed, implemented, and evaluated (e.g., Espelage, 2016; Gower et al., 2018; Hatzenbuehler et al., 2019; Ioverno et al., 2016; Russell et al., 2010). This is hopeful news and grounds for optimism in addressing the challenges. However, studies have also noted variability among GSD populations in terms of health outcomes, school experiences (Allen et al., 2020; McGuire et al., 2010), and the impact of intersecting identities for GSD youth (Poteat et al., 2011; Toomey et al., 2017). Gaps remain in how these differences among GSD students are translated to programs and interventions.

These programs and interventions target different levels of the socioecological systems that GSD students inhabit. We summarize these findings and lessons at different levels: interventions that are aimed at the individual level by targeting students or staff, programs at the system level that are geared toward the whole school or school district, and policies and programs at the state level.

https://doi.org/10.1037/0000211-010
Supporting Gender Identity and Sexual Orientation Diversity in K–12 Schools, M. C. Lytle and R. A. Sprott (Editors)

INTERVENTIONS AT THE LEVEL OF THE INDIVIDUAL STUDENT AND SCHOOL STAFF

Although a few individual (microlevel) interventions are designed specifically to address the needs of GSD students, a multitude of general programs that are aimed at changing all students' behaviors can be adapted to meet the specific needs of GSD youth. For instance, interventions that involve modeling or the practicing of antibullying behavior for students (Polanin et al., 2012), programs that provide knowledge and resources for school personnel to work with individual students, and campaigns to display GSD-affirming content may have broad effects (Gower et al., 2018).

A first step for many schools is to train educators, school-based mental health professionals, and staff to be allies. This approach may be especially useful in locations where gender and sexuality alliances (or "genders and sexualities alliances" [GSAs]; this acronym also has referred to "gay–straight alliances") or other school-level interventions are culturally or politically problematic, as previously discussed throughout this book (see Chapters 1–5 and 8). In Chapter 3, Meadows and Shain highlighted how even within conservative school systems, counselors, psychologists, teachers, and staff can take small but powerful steps (e.g., using inclusive language, identifying local affirming resources, displaying support) toward creating safer and more affirming schools. Similarly, McKibban and Anderson walked us through the process of how individual educators and school personnel can foster policy change (see Chapter 8).

No matter how big or small our actions are, creating a more inclusive environment is a protective factor for all students. Indeed, research has consistently demonstrated that small displays of affirming content, such as hanging rainbow, bisexual, or transgender flags, or all three, can help students identify trusted adults and improve the school climate (Gower et al., 2018; Griffin et al., 2004). Similarly, the artwork we hang in our offices, classrooms, and hallways speaks volumes. An image of Sylvia Rivera, Marsha P. Johnson, James Baldwin, or Wanda Sykes in our work environments may become a discussion point and an opportunity to celebrate historical GSD individuals of color. Working at this level may be the starting point for efforts aimed at other levels of the social environment, laying the foundation for cultural and political support for systemic interventions.

In addition, programs for school staff and mental health professionals that focus on promoting inclusive language can help provide support to GSD students (Kull et al., 2016). Often, inclusive language needs to be modeled, discussed, and practiced before it becomes a behavioral norm in a particular school. As Herbstrith suggested in Chapter 6, changing the language about marriage equality or having positive discussions about GSD issues may shift social norms and reduce anti-GSD behaviors (Bartoş et al., 2014; Goldberg et al., 2017). This language shift is especially important to do in elementary school classrooms, where GSD individuals and experiences are rarely discussed.

Trainings to promote the use of language and terminology that are respectful and accurate about GSD youth, such as using pronouns that honor a student's gender identity, can also help form a foundation for future actions, laying the groundwork for more comprehensive interventions and programs that might be implemented.

As Theodore and Chiasson described in Chapter 4, individual-level anti-bullying interventions have both advantages and disadvantages. Although scholars have noted the relational nature of in bullying in which youth may use pejorative language they have observed their peers or family members use (e.g., Espelage, 2016), individual change often occurs through strength-based campaigns or programs (Cahill et al., 2013). Interventions that understand the reciprocal dynamics between the roles of aggressor, target, and bystander—that individuals can shift between these roles and that each role impacts the enactment of other roles—mean that newer interventions are not focused just on the aggressor. These approaches do not fuse the behavioral role with the individual student as an unchanging identity (bully or victim) to the exclusion of the context or the changing dynamics of peer interactions. Being more sensitive to the dynamic system involved in bullying, interventions have become more effective. The Social Skills Training program is one such intervention designed to help youth, regardless of their role, to develop positive relationships with their peers by promoting prosocial behaviors, coping strategies, and social skills (Kõiv, 2012). Similarly, teachers are being trained to include social–emotional learning in their lessons, and they are receiving guidelines to address bullying in their classrooms (Espelage, 2016; van Verseveld et al., 2019). These strategies have been found to not only reduce bullying in general but also decrease the victimization of targeted groups (Espelage, 2016; Espelage et al., 2015).

Whether individual-level interventions are informal (e.g., being an ally, requesting that policies be enumerated and updated) or formal (e.g., professional development, antibullying programs), they tend to be effective in promoting change. There are numerous examples throughout this book about individuals, such as Virginia Uribe, who have played an instrumental role in making GSD students feel safer and affirmed. Specifically, in Chapter 2, Chiasson described how as an ally, Uribe helped champion numerous efforts (e.g., Project 10, gay prom, Models of Pride) within her school district that have inspired schools across the country to follow suit. Therefore, all it takes is one person to make a *big* difference.

INTERVENTIONS AT THE LEVEL OF THE SCHOOL OR DISTRICT

Interventions developed at the school or district level (mesolevel) may not only change individual behaviors but also potentially shift the overall climate of the educational environment. For instance, developing schoolwide programs, such as GSAs, gay proms, and enumerated policies that explicitly protect

GSD youth, have been found to protect against bullying and victimization (Hatzenbuehler et al., 2019; Russell et al., 2010). As previously discussed throughout this book, when we create safe and affirming environments for GSD youth, all students reap the benefits (Konishi et al., 2013).

GSAs are among the school-based programs that have been proven to increase school engagement, resiliency, and academic achievement as well as lower rates of absenteeism and bullying (Baams et al., 2018; Johns et al., 2019; Kosciw et al., 2018; Poteat et al., 2016; Toomey et al., 2011). While some schools have easily established GSAs to support their GSD students and allies, in other schools, this process may be more challenging. As Meadows and Shain discussed in Chapter 3, it is possible to establish GSAs in conservative districts! See the Appendix for additional resources; in addition, more detailed information on school-based GSA programs is outlined in Chapter 2 by Chiasson and Chapter 4 by Theodore and Chiasson.

Programs and interventions designed to help youth in general may be adapted for target populations, such as GSD youth. For instance, Sources of Strength (https://sourcesofstrength.org/) was developed to reduce adverse outcomes (e.g., suicide, bullying, violence) by connecting youth with peer leaders and caring adults, and although this program has not been adapted for GSD students, it is among the few evidence-based interventions for reducing suicide risk (Marshall, 2016). Hatchel et al. (2019) appear to be the first scholars to examine GSD youth using Sources of Strength data; however, the findings are based on baseline data rather than a pretest–posttest design. According to that study, both GSD youth and their non-GSD peers are more likely to endorse suicide ideation and attempts if they have experienced peer victimization or depressive symptoms (Hatchel et al., 2019). Additional research is needed to determine whether or not programs like Sources of Strength can reduce adverse risks among GSD youth and whether particular adaptations of this program to better meet the needs of GSD students are effective.

Aside from developing school-based resources specifically for students, training school and district staff about issues can also lay the groundwork for developing policies and resources to foster future actions to establish GSAs or create safe spaces at schools. If a school has little history of addressing the needs of GSD students, important and strategic first steps include staff trainings focused on legal mandates that schools are obligated to educate all students and cannot discriminate against some groups of students. Specifically, educating school staff about the federal Equal Access Act (1984) may be helpful if one expects resistance or backlash from the community about establishing a GSA. Similarly, it may be important to inform students, families, and staff about laws that directly pertain to them. As noted by Kiperman, DeLong, Varjas, and Meyers in Chapter 5, the Family Educational Rights and Privacy Act (1974) provides youth and families the right to confidentiality and privacy, but how this law is applied may vary based on district. Therefore, it may be helpful to provide teachers and staff with information from the American Civil Liberties Union's (2015) *Open Letter to Schools About LGBT [Lesbian, Gay, Bisexual, and Transgender] Student Privacy* to help them better understand their student's rights.

Training administrators, educators, and staff about health disparities can also emphasize the responsibility of schools and districts to address the unique needs of GSD students. However, it is critical that these trainings highlight how the disproportionate rates of adverse outcomes are the result of minority stress rather than the pathologizing of GSD youth and how staff can create affirming environments to ameliorate these issues. Because few articles and information address training elementary school staff, case studies may be a great way to help individuals and schools recognize specific strategies they can use. One such case study described how a mother proactively reached out to her local school district and collaborated with administrators, counselors, teachers, and staff about her child's strengths and unique needs and how the staff evolved from lacking self-efficacy to feeling prepared (Slesaransky-Poe et al., 2013). Moreover, as Greenberg, Sharp, and Anderson discussed in Chapter 7, professional training of school mental health providers and school nurses is particularly important because these are among the most trusted school professionals for GSD students. As a result of such trainings, some school districts have taken the initiative to form a core group of district staff who are champions and can lead the development of resources across schools to support GSD students. Moreover, professional training about policies that address issues, such as bathrooms, locker rooms, and sports as well as harassment and bullying, can also help clarify the actions that schools can take, especially when it comes to gender diversity.

As with individual-level interventions, school-based programs can be either formal or informal. Something as simple as broad training on inclusivity and diversity can help teachers, staff, and mental health professionals across the school system identify areas of growth, such as developing enumerated policies or learning how to use current laws to advocate for such student groups as GSAs. Similarly, more formal efforts, such as developing a GSA or bringing Sources of Strength to your school, can have a broad impact.

DEVELOPMENTS AT THE MACROLEVEL OF STATE EDUCATIONAL SYSTEMS

State-level professional organizations and educational agencies have resources available to school personnel, and these resources can be leveraged for interventions and programs in local educational agencies. In addition, some state governments have a vested interest in making professionals, including teachers, counselors, and psychologists, more prepared to work with diverse populations. For instance, New York State's Office of Children and Family Services (n.d.) as well as New Jersey's Department of Children and Families (State of New Jersey Department of Children and Families, n.d.) provide a list of resources specific to GSD youth and families.

Of particular usefulness are state education agencies or state professional organizations that often have resources and trainings about cultural humility readily available, especially as articles archived in their periodicals (e.g., *The California Psychologist, The New Jersey Psychologist*). Moreover, some licensing boards for health providers list available trainings and resources for increasing competencies in working with GSD students. For example, the Minnesota Professional Educator Licensing and Standards Board (n.d.) has free cultural competency trainings available, and Washington, DC, now requires professionals within health occupations to complete lesbian, gay, bisexual, transgender, and queer or questioning cultural competence training (Biologix Solutions, n.d.).

Cultural humility as a framework for training school professionals can often include GSD issues, and many resources have been developed for this purpose as discussed throughout this book (Chapters 2–8). Another recent example of developments in this area is the State of California, whose governor, Gavin Newsom, signed into law Assembly Bill Number 493, also known as the Safe and Supportive Schools Act of 2019, on October 12, 2019. This law directs the California Department of Education to develop resources or update current resources for in-service training about GSD concerns. In addition, the law encourages each school (including charter schools) in the state to provide training at least once every 2 years to teachers and other certified employees who work with students in Grades 7 through 12. Resources can include peer support or affinity clubs, such as a GSAs; safe spaces for GSD students; antibullying and harassment policies as well as complaint procedures; counseling services; the identification of school staff who have received antibias training or other training; health and other curriculum materials that are inclusive of, and relevant to, GSD youth; suicide prevention policies and related procedures; policies and procedures to protect the privacy of GSD students; information on local community-based organizations that support GSD youth; information on local physical and mental health providers with experience in treating and supporting GSD youth; and policies relating to the use of school facilities, including bathrooms and locker rooms.

Many recent state laws and policies directed toward the civil rights of GSD adults also have implications for schools at the local level. California, New Jersey, New York City, Oregon, and Washington recognize people as nonbinary as a gender identification (Fitzsimons, 2019); eventually, this recognition by the state will impact policies and practices in school districts. Other developments, however, such as the Religious Freedom Restoration Act of 1993 (1994) and subsequent state laws adopted to address religious freedom in the administration of state laws, can make programs and interventions focused on the educational needs of GSD students a contested area—or at least confusing for school personnel if schools are challenged. At the time this chapter was written, only 15 states (California, Colorado, Connecticut, Hawaii, Illinois, Iowa, Maine, Massachusetts, Minnesota, New Hampshire, New Jersey, New York, Oregon, Vermont, and Washington) and the District of Columbia have nondiscrimination laws designed to protect GSD students, and only 21 states (Arkansas, California, Colorado, Connecticut, Delaware, Illinois,

Iowa, Maine, Maryland, Massachusetts, Minnesota, Nevada, New Hampshire, New Jersey, New Mexico, New York, North Carolina, Oregon, Rhode Island, Vermont, and Washington) and the District of Columbia have antibullying laws that enumerate based on sexual orientation, gender identity, and gender expression (GLSEN, 2019; see Chapter 8).

Although numerous initiatives at the macrolevel create safer and more affirming schools, clearly, much work is needed to expand the reach of this promising beginning. All too often, advocates within the school system need to use state laws to garner support for GSD students; so, until every state has an enumerated law against bullying, there will be GSD youth at risk within their own schools. And while the rate of change is increasing (four more states added enumerated antibullying laws while this book was being written), for youth who do not feel safe, change cannot come soon enough.

CUTTING EDGES OF INTERVENTION

Several areas stand out as cutting edges in terms of implementation of programs and translation of research into practice. Using curricula that incorporate the discussion of GSD historical figures or topics sensitive to GSD concerns in social studies as well as sex education is not only an avenue to address health disparities, harassment, and bullying but also an opportunity to highlight strengths among GSD individuals. Similarly, whether GSD individuals are formally included within the curricula or informally discussed from a positive perspective, these forms of intergroup contact can reduce negative attitudes toward GSD people and families (see Chapter 6, this volume; LaCosse & Plant, 2019; Vezzali et al., 2015). However, this avenue remains highly controversial in many locales and is a current cutting edge with little research or evaluation data available at this time, as noted in earlier in this book (Chapters 2, 4, 6, and 8). Currently, only five states (California, Colorado, Illinois, New Jersey, and Oregon) require incorporation of GSD issues in curricula, whereas five states (Alabama, Louisiana, Mississippi, Oklahoma, and Texas) have passed laws prohibiting the teaching of this material (GLSEN, n.d.). These anti-GSD curricula laws have been challenged in some states, and, slowly, fewer states are prohibiting this valuable information.

It is also important for programs and interventions to be sensitive to the particular complex issues of consent in providing interventions or encouraging participation in research efforts. Trying to get informed consent from parents or legal guardians might "out" youth when they are not ready to disclose or expose them to rejecting behaviors from family that were not present before consent procedures were initiated. Alternative methods of informed consent were explored in Chapter 5. As previously discussed, part of the issue in terms of disclosing a students' sexual orientation, gender identity, or both, to their parents often relates to how schools and districts are interpreting Family Educational Rights and Privacy Act of 1974. While the American Civil Liberties Union, among other organizations, has offered guidance about this issue, some schools still have and continue to out youth without considering the harmful implications (Orman & Walsh, 2017).

Another cutting edge involves addressing school policies around the participation of students with gender and sexual diversities in sports, and addressing the needs of GSD students in gendered spaces, as discussed in Chapters 2 and 8. All too often, schools do not have policies about sports, bathrooms, and locker rooms until it becomes an issue, and as Chiasson noted (see Chapter 2), this issue is further complicated by building codes that require certain proportions of sex-segregated facilities to be available. While developing new inclusive policies and procedures may feel like a daunting task, a number of resources provide guidance, such as Athlete Ally (https://www.athleteally.org/) and a trans equality fact sheet (National Center for Transgender Equality, 2016).

Areas that still need innovations and development are programs and interventions focused on bisexual students, non-binary, gender-fluid youth, and questioning students. As discussed by Chiasson in Chapter 2, Meadows and Shain in Chapter 3, and Theodore and Chiasson in Chapter 4, these students are at higher risk compared with other GSD youth because of unique sources of minority stress. Because bisexual, non-binary, or questioning youth challenge some fundamental assumptions about gender and sexuality in ways that even gay and lesbian identities do not, programs and interventions often overlook their unique concerns or needs. For instance, many schools look to the National Collegiate Athletic Association and Athlete Ally for guidelines about transgender youth and sports, but even these affirming rules do not fully address the needs of non-binary youth. Although the National Collegiate Athletic Association focuses on binary forms of transition and whether or not a student has medically transitioned with hormones to determine which team someone can join, non-binary youth may also seek puberty-blocking hormones, hormone replacement therapy, or a nonmedical transition. Therefore, research by scholars, such as Jones et al. (2017), suggesting that there is insufficient evidence about whether medical interventions (i.e., hormone replacement therapy or surgical interventions) are an advantage and thus shouldn't be used to exclude athletes should be used to inform school policies on sports.

Another cutting edge in the work is addressing how multiple minority identities are associated with outcomes of programs and interventions for GSD students, especially intersecting racial or ethnic identities (Toomey et al., 2017). This cutting edge also includes the question of how awareness of intersecting identities is incorporated most effectively into the design and implementation of future interventions and programs. Work in this area done in the recent past has highlighted the effect of intersectionality on school outcomes—for example, that racial identity significantly predicted less positive attitudes toward school for heterosexual youth—but among youth with same-sex attractions, race did not predict school attitudes (Battle & Linville, 2006). However, this work is still being developed, and translating the basic research into programs and interventions remains a cutting edge.

WHAT'S MISSING? GAPS IN OUR UNDERSTANDING

The authors in this book have discussed both the historical roots and the latest developments in school programs and interventions to improve the health and well-being of GSD students. However, we can see gaps in our knowledge when designing programs and interventions. Two gaps include (a) our understanding of the mechanisms that explain the clear, positive outcomes of some programs and interventions; and (b) our understanding of the impact of the socioecological context on school-based interventions and programs. Both are crucial to address if we are to create stronger, more effective school-based programs and interventions, especially in light of the diversity of GSD students and the changes in social trends affecting acceptance or rejection of gender and sexual diversity.

Some of the latest efforts incorporate the socioecological theory in their philosophy and design, and this approach highlights the need for research about community connections and involvement as it relates to particular kinds of school programs relevant to GSD students. Specifically, to directly address the ecological context of programs and interventions, we need additional research and programs that examine how positive messages about gender and sexual diversity in school are enhanced or detracted by messages from family and community as well as how students navigate these sometimes conflicting messages. In addition, more work needs to be done to understand the fear and community backlash to implementing more affirming programs, especially because negative reactions from the community could impact or prevent the development or enactment of affirming interventions. Paying attention to these connections will improve the general models used for interventions and perhaps explain any differences in impact of school programs on youth well-being and health behaviors.

Research on family rejection or support as a context (or a moderator) for the effectiveness of school-based programs and interventions is another gap in our understanding of how these programs work. There are some possibilities to investigate. Incorporating information and strategies from the Family Acceptance Project (Ryan et al., 2009) as an aspect of school-based interventions might lead to more effective school-based interventions if families are included in some way in the design and implementation of programs. The inclusion of Family Acceptance Project strategies (Ryan et al., 2009) may be especially effective in conservative or religious areas, where intergroup contacts between schools and families may help educators as well as parents to focus on the well-being of youth. Another area to further explore is whether lessons from implementation of the American Psychological Association's *Respect Workshop* (Rosenbaum et al., 2018) could inform future program development. Although the research on transgender and gender diverse individuals is starting to increase, sometimes it may help to develop a more inclusive research design based on educated guesses, as the developers of the *Respect Workshop* did when they expanded their focus from lesbian, gay, and bisexual to GSD (see the description in Chapter 7).

Another challenge and opportunity for future work in this area is studying how changes in the macrosystem, including national social trends and policy developments, can impact the outcomes of school-based programs and interventions. More states are banning conversion therapies for GSD youth, for example. Do these bans have any effect on the levels of support from communities for school-based interventions? Do they affect the motivation and knowledge of school health professionals? We saw that the earlier passage of laws involving civil unions and the passage of marriage equality improved the health and well-being of GSD adults (Buffie, 2011). However, Hatzenbuehler et al. (2019) found that as a ban on marriage equality was proposed, homophobic bullying in schools increased significantly, whereas other forms of bullying decreased. The question, then, is this: Will local, state, and national policies related to GSD individuals, students, and families have the same impact or work the same way?

PROPOSED AGENDA FOR RESEARCH AND ADVOCACY TO IMPROVE INTERVENTIONS

The social trends that help shape the experience of GSD students have been rapidly changing, thus leading to challenges and opportunities for research on the role of schools in the health and well-being of these students. On the basis of the programs and interventions outlined in this book, we propose a possible agenda for research:

- Measure the impact of changes in attitudes and policies about gender identity and gender expression in schools—especially non-binary gender identities—on school adjustment and success. Include an examination of attitudes and policies related to school sports and gendered spaces.

- Assess the impact of various components of programs and interventions to create a model of the mechanisms by which these programs/interventions improve outcomes for GSD students. This assessment should include evaluating the impact of inclusive curricula, examining components of professional training for school personnel, and exploring components of GSAs.

- Conduct careful comparisons of diverse settings and with diverse samples to understand the ways in which the socioecological context impacts the implementation of programs and interventions, and affects the outcomes of these programs and interventions.

Advocacy efforts also need to adapt in the face of rapid changes in social trends. On the basis of the work reviewed in this book, we propose a possible agenda for advocacy:

- Work on policies around informed consent, privacy, and confidentiality as they relate to gender and sexual diversity.

- Support efforts to include sexual orientation and gender identity and expression information in the collection of school performance data at the level of state education agencies as well as in national efforts, such as through the Centers for Disease Control and Prevention's (n.d.) *Youth Risk Behavior Survey*, part of the Youth Risk Behavior Surveillance System, and the U.S. Department of Education, Office for Civil Rights's (n.d.) mandatory Civil Rights Data Collection.

- Help to create resources for addressing the needs of GSD students, including the establishment of GSAs—but going beyond, to focus this effort especially at organizational and institutional levels above individual schools.

- Advocate to have trainings specific to the needs of GSD students across age groups and cultures become a required component of professional training and continuing education for school health and mental health professionals.

- Work toward state-level nondiscrimination laws that protect students based on gender identity and sexual orientation.

STRATEGIES FOR SCHOOL PSYCHOLOGISTS AND SCHOOL COUNSELORS

How can school psychologists and counselors improve the lives of GSD students by putting what we know into practice? Lessons from the history of the Los Angeles Unified School District (see Chapter 2) indicate that efforts to make GSD students from ethnically and racially diverse backgrounds visible to the school can help. School psychologists and counselors can translate the latest research on the experience of GSD students in schools when issues of school climate and safety are discussed, and help inform staff about strategies to make their schools more affirming. While there are complications and ethical issues to consider in asking youth to identify as GSD or come out (see Chapter 5), school-level efforts to track bullying, assess school climate, and give the opportunity for students and families to self-identify as GSD can start the process. In school policy discussions and in staff training, it is important to accompany those school-level efforts with an emphasis on the rights of all students to have safe and supportive schools as well as to have equal access to education. In addition, it may be helpful to not only train school staff about how to speak up when they witness GSD bully but also to proactively role model inclusivity.

School psychologists and counselors in many schools might clearly signal that they are "safe" adults by using respectful and inclusive language around gender identity and sexual orientation diversity and by confronting stigmatizing language, even in socially conservative communities (see Chapter 3). School psychologists and counselors can offer staff training and support by pulling in the resources that this book has identified (see Chapters 1, 3, 4, 6, 7, and the Appendix). In some communities, school psychologists and counselors may find opportunities to advocate for inclusive curricula (e.g., recognizing GSD historical figures, authors, and artists in a variety of subjects), acknowledging that this is an area that is cutting edge for most states (see Chapter 8). Another cutting edge is around school sports and gendered spaces (see Chapters 2 and 8) and different strategies that schools can use to be more inclusive of non-binary, transgender, and gender diverse students. Aside from focusing on the locker room, coaches and teams can explore different strategies to be more inclusive. Rather than talking about the girl's team, athletes can be encouraged to talk about the soccer team. In these areas, though, advocacy rests on the same overarching arguments about the rights of all students to fully participate in school and about the benefit that school connectedness has on the development and well-being of all students, especially GSD students. Actions at the individual level and at several institutional levels are available to school psychologists and counselors, and many of these actions call for developing our advocacy and leadership skills in addition to knowing the latest research and latest resources for improving the lives of GSD students.

CONCLUSION

The chapters in this book have outlined the latest effective, successful approaches to improve the health and well-being of GSD students. The approaches are grounds for optimism that we can address the educational and health disparities of GSD students within the context of schools. Cutting edges of current work in research, practice, and policy are discussed, pointing the way to an agenda for the next steps in these efforts. Understanding the impact of the socioecological context on school programs and interventions as well as understanding the components of programs that make the most impact are two areas that need to be addressed if we are to increase the reach and the effectiveness of school programs and interventions for GSD students.

This book's main goals were to integrate what we know about the translation of basic research on GSD students into practical efforts to address the needs of GSD youth and also to integrate what we know about the implementation of programs and interventions in light of differing social contexts for schools and changing social trends affecting GSD students. These goals are about "walking the walk"—not just pronouncing what should be done but focusing on how to do it. We hope that key insights will emerge from this attempt to integrate across the current efforts in the field. And we hope that the models discussed in this book will nurture hope and enthusiasm for the work. Walking the walk means that our words match our actions—which will benefit the health and well-being of all of the students in our care.

TAKEAWAYS AND OPPORTUNITIES

- Interventions and programs are best approached using a socioecological framework that addresses micro-, meso-, and macrolevels.

- Cutting edges of interventions are inclusion of GSD information in school curricula; policies about privacy and consent that are sensitive to GSD concerns; inclusion in sports and gendered spaces; programs or interventions directed toward bisexual, queer, and questioning students; and how intersecting multiple minority identities are addressed in the design and implementation of programs and interventions.

- Two gaps include (a) our understanding of the mechanisms that explain the clear, positive outcomes among programs and interventions and (b) our understanding of the impact of the socioecological context on school-based interventions and programs.

- Now that you have read this chapter, please consider: Are some of these recommendations already implemented in your school? What additional steps can we take to better support GSD students at the individual, community, school, or state level? Do the laws in your state and the policies in your school protect GSD youth?

REFERENCES

Allen, B. J., Andert, B., Botsford, J., Budge, S. L., & Rehm, J. L. (2020). At the margins: Comparing school experiences of nonbinary and binary-identified transgender youth. *Journal of School Health, 90*(5), 358–367. https://doi.org/10.1111/josh.12882

American Civil Liberties Union. (2015, December 7). *Open letter to schools about LGBT student privacy.* https://www.aclu.org/letter/open-letter-schools-about-lgbt-student-privacy

Baams, L., Pollitt, A. M., Laub, C., & Russell, S. T. (2018). Characteristics of schools with and without gay–straight alliances. *Applied Developmental Science.* https://doi.org/10.1080/10888691.2018.1510778

Bartoş, S. E., Berger, I., & Hegarty, P. (2014). Interventions to reduce sexual prejudice: A study-space analysis and meta-analytic review. *Journal of Sex Research, 51*(4), 363–382. https://doi.org/10.1080/00224499.2013.871625

Battle, J., & Linville, D. (2006). Race, sexuality and schools: A quantitative assessment of intersectionality. *Race, Gender, & Class, 13*(3/4), 180–199.

Biologix Solutions. (n.d.). *LGBTQ cultural competency training for healthcare professionals.* Retrieved June 1, 2020, from https://blxtraining.com/lgbtq-cultural-competency/

Buffie, W. C. (2011). Public health implications of same-sex marriage. *American Journal of Public Health, 101*(6), 986–990. https://doi.org/10.2105/AJPH.2010.300112

Cahill, S., Valadéz, R., & Ibarrola, S. (2013). Community-based HIV prevention interventions that combat anti-gay stigma for men who have sex with men and for transgender women. *Journal of Public Health Policy, 34*(1), 69–81. https://doi.org/10.1057/jphp.2012.59

Centers for Disease Control and Prevention, Department of Adolescent and School Health. (n.d.). *Youth Risk Behavior Surveillance System (YRBSS).* https://www.cdc.gov/healthyyouth/data/yrbs/index.htm

Equal Access Act, 20 U.S.C. § 4071 (1984).

Espelage, D. L. (2016). Leveraging school-based research to inform bullying prevention and policy. *American Psychologist, 71*(8), 768–775. https://doi.org/10.1037/amp0000095

Espelage, D. L., Rose, C. A., & Polanin, J. R. (2015). Social–emotional learning program to reduce bullying, fighting, and victimization among middle school students with disabilities. *Remedial and Special Education, 36*(5), 299–311. https://doi.org/10.1177/0741932514564564

Family Educational Rights and Privacy Act, 20 U.S.C. § 1232g; 34 CFR Part 99 (1974).

Fitzsimons, T. (2019). *N.J. to become fourth state with gender-neutral birth certificate option.* https://www.nbcnews.com/feature/nbc-out/n-j-become-fourth-state-gender-neutral-birth-certificate-option-n964601

GLSEN. (n.d.). *Laws that prohibit the "promotion of homosexuality": Impacts and implications.* https://www.glsen.org/article/laws-prohibit-promotion-homosexuality-impacts-and-implications

GLSEN. (2019). *State policy maps.* Retrieved June 1, 2020, from https://www.glsen.org/article/state-maps

Goldberg, A. E., Black, K., Sweeney, K., & Moyer, M. (2017). Lesbian, gay, and heterosexual adoptive parents' perceptions of inclusivity and receptiveness in early childhood education settings. *Journal of Research in Childhood Education, 31*(1), 141–159. https://doi.org/10.1080/02568543.2016.1244136 (Corrigendum published 2017, *Journal of Research in Childhood Education, 31*(2), p. 312. https://doi.org/10.1080/02568543.2017.1305241)

Gower, A. L., Forster, M., Gloppen, K., Johnson, A. Z., Eisenberg, M. E., Connett, J. E., & Borowsky, I. W. (2018). School practices to foster LGBT-supportive climate: Associations with adolescent bullying involvement. *Prevention Science, 19*(6), 813–821. https://doi.org/10.1007/s11121-017-0847-4

Griffin, P., Lee, C., Waugh, J., & Beyer, C. (2004). Describing roles that gay–straight alliances play in schools: From individual support to school change. *Journal of Gay & Lesbian Issues in Education, 1*(3), 7–22. https://doi.org/10.1300/J367v01n03_03

Hatchel, T., Ingram, K. M., Mintz, S., Hartley, C., Valido, A., Espelage, D. L., & Wyman, P. (2019). Predictors of suicidal ideation and attempts among LGBTQ adolescents: The roles of help-seeking beliefs, peer victimization, depressive symptoms, and drug use. *Journal of Child and Family Studies, 28*(9), 2443–2445. https://doi.org/10.1007/s10826-019-01339-2

Hatzenbuehler, M. L., Shen, Y., Vandewater, E. A., & Russell, S. T. (2019). Proposition 8 and homophobic bullying in California. *Pediatrics, 143*(6), Article e20182116. https://doi.org/10.1542/peds.2018-2116

Heck, N. C., Flentje, A., & Cochran, B. N. (2013). Offsetting risks: High school gay–straight alliances and lesbian, gay, bisexual, and transgender (LGBT) youth. *Psychology of Sexual Orientation and Gender Diversity, 1*(S), 81–90.

Ioverno, S., Belser, A. B., Baiocco, R., Grossman, A. H., & Russell, S. T. (2016). The protective role of gay–straight alliances for lesbian, gay, bisexual, and questioning students: A prospective analysis. *Psychology of Sexual Orientation and Gender Diversity, 3*(4), 397–406. https://doi.org/10.1037/sgd0000193

Johns, M. M., Poteat, V. P., Horn, S. S., & Kosciw, J. (2019). Strengthening our schools to promote resilience and health among LGBTQ youth: Emerging evidence and research priorities from *The State of LGBTQ Youth Health and Wellbeing* symposium. *LGBT Health, 6*(4), 146–155. https://doi.org/10.1089/lgbt.2018.0109

Jones, B. A., Arcelus, J., Bouman, W. P., & Haycraft, E. (2017). Sport and transgender people: A systematic review of the literature relating to sport participation and competitive sport policies. *Sports Medicine, 47*(4), 701–716. https://doi.org/10.1007/s40279-016-0621-y

Kõiv, K. (2012). Social Skills Training as a mean of improving intervention for bullies and victims. *Procedia: Social and Behavioral Sciences, 45*, 239–246. https://doi.org/10.1016/j.sbspro.2012.06.560

Konishi, C., Saewyc, E., Homma, Y., & Poon, C. (2013). Population-level evaluation of school-based interventions to prevent problem substance use among gay, lesbian and bisexual adolescents in Canada. *Preventive Medicine, 57*(6), 929–933. https://doi.org/10.1016/j.ypmed.2013.06.031

Kosciw, J. G., Greytak, E. A., Zongrone, A. D., Clark, C. M., & Truong, N. L. (2018). *The 2017 National School Climate Survey: The experiences of lesbian, gay, bisexual and transgender youth in our nation's schools*. GLSEN. https://www.glsen.org/research/2017-national-school-climate-survey-0

Kull, R. M., Greytak, E. A., Kosciw, J. G., & Villenas, C. (2016). Effectiveness of school district antibullying policies in improving LGBT youths' school climate. *Psychology of Sexual Orientation and Gender Diversity*, *3*(4), 407–415. https://doi.org/10.1037/sgd0000196

LaCosse, J., & Plant, E. A. (2019). Imagined contact with famous gay men and lesbians reduces heterosexuals' misidentification concerns and sexual prejudice. *European Journal of Social Psychology*, *49*(1), 141–156. https://doi.org/10.1002/ejsp.2391

Marshall, A. (2016). Suicide prevention interventions for sexual & gender minority youth: An Unmet need. *Yale Journal of Biology and Medicine*, *89*, 205–213.

McGuire, J. K., Anderson, C. R., Toomey, R. B., & Russell, S. T. (2010). School climate for transgender youth: A mixed method investigation of student experiences and school responses. *Journal of Youth and Adolescence*, *39*(10), 1175–1188. https://doi.org/10.1007/s10964-010-9540-7

Minnesota Professional Educator Licensing and Standards Board. (n.d.). *Cultural competency training sessions*. Retrieved June 1, 2020, from https://mn.gov/pelsb/board/news/?id=1113-376976

National Center for Transgender Equality. (2016, August 15). *Fact sheet on U.S. Department of Education policy letter on transgender students*. https://transequality.org/issues/resources/fact-sheet-on-us-department-of-education-policy-letter-on-transgender-students

New York State Office of Children and Family Services. (n.d.). *Resources for LGBTQ adults*. https://ocfs.ny.gov/main/LGBTQ/resources_for_lgbtq_adults.asp

Orman, S., & Walsh, J. (2017, October 19–21). *Student privacy v. parent rights—Must we keep secrets from the parents? May We Keep Secrets from the Parents?* [Seminar]. COSA School Law Practice Seminar, Chicago, IL, United States. https://cdn-files.nsba.org/s3fs-public/Student_Privacy_v_Parent_Rights_Orman_Walsh.pdf

Polanin, J. R., Espelage, D. L., & Pigott, T. D. (2012). A meta-analysis of school-based bullying prevention programs' effects on bystander intervention behavior. *School Psychology Review*, *41*(1), 47–65.

Poteat, V. P., Calzo, J. P., & Yoshikawa, H. (2016). Promoting youth agency through dimensions of gay–straight alliance involvement and conditions that maximize associations. *Journal of Youth and Adolescence*, *45*(7), 1438–1451. https://doi.org/10.1007/s10964-016-0421-6

Poteat, V. P., Mereish, E. H., DiGiovanni, C. D., & Koenig, B. W. (2011). The effects of general and homophobic victimization on adolescents' psychosocial and educational concerns: The importance of intersecting identities and parent support. *Journal of Counseling Psychology*, *58*(4), 597–609. https://doi.org/10.1037/a0025095

Religious Freedom Restoration Act of 1993, 42 U.S.C. § 2000bb-1 (1994).

Rosenbaum, L., Anderson, C., Christopher, D., & Wright, T. (2018). *The Respect Workshop trainer manual* (3rd ed.). American Psychological Association.

Russell, S. T., Kosciw, J., Horn, S., & Saewyc, E. (2010). Safe schools policy for LGBTQ students. *Social Policy Report*, *24*(4), 1–25. https://doi.org/10.1002/j.2379-3988.2010.tb00065.x

Ryan, C., Huebner, D., Diaz, R. M., & Sanchez, J. (2009). Family rejection as a predictor of negative health outcomes in White and Latino lesbian, gay, and bisexual young adults. *Pediatrics*, *123*(1), 346–352. https://doi.org/10.1542/peds.2007-3524

Safe and Supportive Schools Act, Cal. Stat. Article 2.7, Section 218, Chapter 2, Part 1, Division 1, Title 1 of the Education Code (2019).

Slesaransky-Poe, G., Ruzzi, L., Dimedio, C., & Stanley, J. (2013). Is this the right elementary school for my gender nonconforming child? *Journal of LGBT Youth*, *10*(1–2), 29–44. https://doi.org/10.1080/19361653.2012.718521

State of New Jersey Department of Children and Families. (n.d.). *LBGTQI resources.* https://www.nj.gov/dcf/adolescent/lgbtqi/

Toomey, R. B., Huynh, V. W., Jones, S. K., Lee, S., & Revels-Macalinao, M. (2017). Sexual minority youth of color: A content analysis and critical review of the literature. *Journal of Gay & Lesbian Mental Health, 21*(1), 3–31. https://doi.org/10.1080/19359705.2016.1217499

Toomey, R. B., Ryan, C., Diaz, R. M., & Russell, S. T. (2011). High school gay–straight alliances (GSAs) and young adult well-being: An examination of GSA presence, participation, and perceived effectiveness. *Applied Developmental Science, 15*(4), 175–185. https://doi.org/10.1080/10888691.2011.607378

U.S. Department of Education, Office for Civil Rights. (n.d.). *Civil Rights Data Collection (CRDC).* https://www2.ed.gov/about/offices/list/ocr/frontpage/faq/crdc.html

van Verseveld, M. D. A., Fukkink, R. G., Fekkes, M., & Oostdam, R. J. (2019). Effects of antibullying programs on teachers' interventions in bullying situations. A meta-analysis. *Psychology in the Schools, 56*(9), 1522–1539. https://doi.org/10.1002/pits.22283

Vezzali, L., Stathi, S., Crisp, R. J., Giovannini, D., Capozza, D., & Gaertner, S. L. (2015). Imagined intergroup contact and common ingroup identity: An integrative approach. *Social Psychology, 46*(5), 265–276. https://doi.org/10.1027/1864-9335/a000242

Resources

ADVOCACY

Advocates for Youth (https://advocatesforyouth.org/)
- *LGBTQ Health and Rights* (https://advocatesforyouth.org/issue/lgbtq-health-and-rights/)

GLSEN (originally the Gay, Lesbian and Straight Education Network; https://www.glsen.org/)
- *Day of Silence* (https://www.glsen.org/day-of-silence)
- *Changing the Game: The GLSEN Sports Project* (https://www.glsen.org/sports)
- *No Name-Calling Week* (https://www.glsen.org/no-name-calling-week)

Live Out Loud (https://www.liveoutloud.info/)
- *LGBT Youth Organizations* (https://www.liveoutloud.info/resources/lgbt-youth-organizations/)

National Youth Advocacy Coalition (http://www.nyacyouth.org/)

Soulforce (https://www.soulforce.org/)

The Trevor Project (https://www.thetrevorproject.org/)
- *Trevor Advocacy* (https://www.thetrevorproject.org/get-involved/trevor-advocacy/)

ALLIES

GLAAD (originally the Gay & Lesbian Alliance Against Defamation; https://www.glaad.org/)
- *Be an Ally & a Friend* (https://www.glaad.org/resources/ally)

GLSEN (originally the Gay, Lesbian and Straight Education Network; https://www.glsen.org/)
- *How Can I Be an Ally?* (https://www.glsen.org/ally-week)
- *Key Concepts and Terms* (https://www.glsen.org/sites/default/files/GLSEN%20Terms%20and%20Concepts%20Thematic.pdf)

Human Rights Campaign (HRC; https://www.hrc.org/)
- *Explore: Allies* (https://www.hrc.org/explore/topic/allies)

PFLAG (originally Parents and Friends of Lesbians and Gays; https://pflag.org/)
- *Allies* (https://pflag.org/allies)

Stonewall (https://www.stonewall.org.uk/)
- *Come Out for LGBT: Becoming an Active LGBT Ally* (https://www.stonewall.org.uk/about-us/news/come-out-lgbt-becoming-active-lgbt-ally)

- *10 Ways to Step Up as an Ally to Non-Binary People* (https://www.stonewall.org.uk/about-us/blog/10-ways-step-ally-non-binary-people)

Straight for Equality (https://www.straightforequality.org/)
- *Resources for Allies* (https://www.straightforequality.org/allyresources)

Teaching Tolerance (https://www.tolerance.org/)
- *A Gender Spectrum Glossary* (https://www.tolerance.org/print/86569/print)

Transgender pride flag (https://pixabay.com/illustrations/trans-transgender-flag-pride-1792756/)

Youth Engaged 4 Change (https://engage.youth.gov/)
- *Being an Ally to LGBT People* (https://engage.youth.gov/resources/being-ally-lgbt-people)

FAMILY

American Library Association (ALA; http://www.ala.org/)
- *Resources for Parents and Families of LGBTQ Individuals* (http://www.ala.org/rt/sites/ala.org.rt/files/content/professionaltools/ResourcesforParentsandFamiliesofLGBTQIndividuals.pdf)

Children of Lesbians and Gays Everywhere (COLAGE; https://www.colage.org/)

Family Acceptance Project (FAP; https://familyproject.sfsu.edu/)

Family Diversity Projects (FDP; https://familydiv.org/)

Family Equality Council (https://www.familyequality.org/)

Human Rights Campaign (HRC; https://www.hrc.org/)
- *All Children—All Families: LGBTQ Resources for Child Welfare Professionals* (https://www.hrc.org/resources/all-children-all-families-additional-resources)

National Center for Transgender Equality (NCTE; https://transequality.org/)
- *Issues: Families* (http://transequality.org/issues/families)

PFLAG (originally Parents and Friends of Lesbians and Gays; https://pflag.org/)
- *Loving Families* (https://pflag.org/loving-families)

Strong Family Alliance (https://www.strongfamilyalliance.org/)
* *Parent Guide* (https://www.strongfamilyalliance.org/parent-guide/)

The Trevor Project (https://www.thetrevorproject.org/)
* *Trevor Support Center: Family* + Friends (https://www.thetrevorproject.org/trvr_support_center/family-friends/)

GENDER IDENTITY

Genders & Sexualities Alliance Network (GSA Network; https://gsanetwork.org)

Gender Odyssey (http://www.genderodyssey.org/)

Gender Spectrum (https://www.genderspectrum.org)
* *The Lounge* (https://lounge.genderspectrum.org/)

GLAAD (originally the Gay & Lesbian Alliance Against Defamation; https://www.glaad.org/)
* *Transgender Resources* (https://www.glaad.org/transgender/resources)

Human Rights Campaign (HRC; https://www.hrc.org/)
* *Explore: Transgender Children & Youth* (https://www.hrc.org/explore/topic/transgender-children-youth)

LGBT National Help Center (https://www.glbthotline.org/)
* *GLBT Near Me* (https://www.glbtnearme.org/)
* *LGBT National Hotline 888-843-4564* (https://www.glbthotline.org/national-hotline.html)
* *LGBT National Online Peer Support CHAT* (https://www.glbthotline.org/peer-chat.html)
* *Trans Youth Online Chat Group for 13 Years Old & Younger* (https://www.glbthotline.org/transyouth.html)
* *Trans Teens Online Talk Group* (https://www.glbthotline.org/transteens.html)
* *Youth CHAT ROOM Lounge* (https://www.glbthotline.org/youthchatrooms.html)

National Center for Transgender Equality (NCTE; https://transequality.org/)
* *Fact Sheet on U.S. Department of Education Policy Letter on Transgender Students* (http://www.transequality.org/sites/default/files/ED-DCL-Fact-Sheet.pdf)

Trans Student Educational Resources (TSER; https://www.transstudent.org/)
* *Queer Youth of Color* (https://www.transstudent.org/queeryouthofcolor)

Trans Youth Equality Foundation (TYEF; http://www.transyouthequality.org/)
* *For Youth* (http://www.transyouthequality.org/for-youth-1)

Tumblr (https://www.tumblr.com/)
* *The Gender Book* (https://thegenderbook.tumblr.com/ and https://thegenderbook.com/)

World Professional Association for Transgender Health (WPATH; http://www.wpath.org/)

GENERAL RESOURCES

7 Cups (https://www.7cups.com/)
- *LGBTQ+ Q&A* (https://www.7cups.com/qa-lgbtq--17/)

American Academy of Pediatrics (AAP; https://www.aap.org/en-us/Pages/Default.aspx)
- *LGBT Resources* (https://www.aap.org/en-us/advocacy-and-policy/aap-health-initiatives/Pages/LGBT-Resources.aspx)

American Civil Liberties Union (ACLU; https://www.aclu.org/)

Anti-Defamation League (ADL; https://www.adl.org/)

GLAAD (originally the Gay & Lesbian Alliance Against Defamation; https://www.glaad.org/)

GLSEN (originally Gay, Lesbian and Straight Education Network; https://www.glsen.org/)
- *How to Start a Community GSA* (http://live-glsen-website.pantheonsite.io/blog/how-start-community-gsa)
- *"No Pro Homo" Laws* (https://www.glsen.org/learn/policy/issues/nopromohomo)

GroundSpark (https://groundspark.org/)
- *RFAP [Respect for All Project] Films* (https://groundspark.org/respect-for-all/rfap-films)

Human Rights Campaign (HRC; https://www.hrc.org/)
- *Explore: Children & Youth* (https://www.hrc.org/explore/topic/children-youth)
- *Glossary of Terms* (https://www.hrc.org/resources/glossary-of-terms)

National LGBTQ Task Force (https://www.thetaskforce.org/)

PFLAG (originally Parents and Friends of Lesbians and Gays; https://pflag.org/)

MENTAL AND PHYSICAL HEALTH PROFESSIONALS

Counseling

American Counseling Association (ACA; https://www.counseling.org/)
- *2014 ACA Code of Ethics* (https://www.counseling.org/resources/aca-code-of-ethics.pdf)

- *Association for Lesbian, Gay, Bisexual, and Transgender Issues in Counseling (ALGBTIC) Competencies for Counseling With Lesbian, Gay, Bisexual, Queer, Questioning, Intersex and Ally Individuals* (https://www.counseling.org/docs/ethics/algbtic-2012-07)

American School Counselor Association (ASCA; https://www.schoolcounselor.org/)
- *ASCA Ethical Standards for School Counselors* (https://www.schoolcounselor.org/asca/media/asca/Ethics/EthicalStandards2016.pdf)

- *Best Practices for Creating an LGBTQ-Inclusive School Climate* (https://videos.schoolcounselor.org/best-practices-for-creating-an-lgbt-inclusive-school-climate)

- *Transgender and Gender Nonconforming Students: Advocate for Best Practices* (https://www.schoolcounselor.org/magazine/blogs/september-october-2015/transgender-and-gender-nonconforming-students-adv)

Medical

Act for Youth (http://actforyouth.net/)
- *Resources for Working With LGBT Patients* (http://actforyouth.net/adolescence/healthcare/lgbt.cfm)

Advocates for Youth (https://advocatesforyouth.org/)

American Medical Association (AMA; https://www.ama-assn.org/)
- *Advocating for the LGBTQ Community* (https://www.ama-assn.org/delivering-care/population-care/advocating-lgbtq-community)

- *Code of Medical Ethics Overview* (https://www.ama-assn.org/delivering-care/ethics/code-medical-ethics-overview)

- *Creating an LGBTQ-Friendly Practice* (https://www.ama-assn.org/delivering-care/population-care/creating-lgbtq-friendly-practice)

- *Policies on Lesbian, Gay, Bisexual, Transgender & Queer (LGBTQ) Issues* (https://www.ama-assn.org/delivering-care/population-care/policies-lesbian-gay-bisexual-transgender-queer-lgbtq-issues)

American Psychological Association (APA; https://www.apa.org/)
- *Respect Workshop* (https://www.apa.org/pi/lgbt/programs/safe-supportive/training/respect-workshop)

Centers for Disease Control and Prevention (CDC; https://www.cdc.gov/)
- *Healthy People.gov* (https://www.healthypeople.gov/)
  - *Health Considerations for LGBTQ Youth* (https://www.cdc.gov/healthyyouth/disparities/health-considerations-lgbtq-youth.htm)
  - *Lesbian, Gay, Bisexual, and Transgender Health* (https://www.cdc.gov/lgbthealth/index.htm)
  - *Lesbian, Gay, Bisexual, and Transgender Health* (https://www.healthypeople.gov/2020/topics-objectives/topic/lesbian-gay-bisexual-and-transgender-health)
  - *LGBT Youth* (https://www.cdc.gov/lgbthealth/youth.htm)

Gay and Lesbian Medical Association (GLMA; http://www.glma.org/)
- *GLMA Provider Directory* (https://glmaimpak.networkats.com/ members_online_new/members/dir_provider.asp)

Fenway Health (https://fenwayhealth.org/)

Human Rights Campaign (HRC, https://www.hrc.org/)
- *Healthcare Equality Index* (https://www.hrc.org/hei)

National LGBT Health Education Center (https://www.lgbthealtheducation.org/)
- *Learning Resources—LGBTQIA+* People of Color (https://www. lgbthealtheducation.org/resources/in/lgbtqia-people-of-color/)

Society for Adolescent Health and Medicine (SAHM; https://www. adolescenthealth.org/Home.aspx)
- *LGBT Health* (https://www.adolescenthealth.org/Resources/Clinical-Care-Resources/LGBT-Health.aspx)

Psychology

American Psychological Association (APA; https://www.apa.org/)
- *APA Highlights Books for LGBTQ+* Children & Families for Pride Month (https://www.apa.org/news/press/releases/2019/05/lgbtq-children-books)

- *APA LGBT Resources and Publications* (https://www.apa.org/pi/lgbt/resources/ index?tab=7)

- *APA Resolution on Support for the Expansion of Mature Minors' Ability to Participate in Research* (https://www.apa.org/about/policy/resolution-minors-research.pdf)

- *Bullying Resources & Safe Schools for LGBT Students* (https://www.apa.org/ pi/lgbt/programs/safe-supportive/bullying/resources)

- *Ethical Principles of Psychologists and Code of Conduct* (https://www.apa.org/ ethics/code/)

- *Facts About "Conversion Therapy"* (https://www.apadivisions.org/division-44/ resources/conversion-fact-sheet.pdf)

- *Gender Diversity and Transgender Identity in Adolescents* (https://www. apadivisions.org/division-44/resources/advocacy/transgender-adolescents.pdf)

- *Gender Diversity and Transgender Identity in Children* (https://www. apadivisions.org/division-44/resources/advocacy/transgender-children.pdf)

- *Guidelines for Psychological Practice With Transgender and Gender Nonconforming People* (https://www.apa.org/practice/guidelines/transgender.pdf)

- *Just the Facts About Sexual Orientation and Youth* (https://www.apa.org/pi/ lgbt/resources/just-the-facts)

- *Just the Facts About Sexual Orientation and Youth: A Primer for Principals, Educators and School Personnel* (https://www.apa.org/pi/lgbt/resources/just-the-facts?_ga=2.192839338.1896901160.1591401553-1038138390.1590194149)

- *Lesbian, Gay, Bisexual, & Transgender Concerns* (booklet of current APA policy statements; https://www.apa.org/about/policy/booklet.pdf)

- *Lesbian, Gay, Bisexual and Transgender Health* (https://www.apa.org/pi/lgbt/resources/lgbt-health)

- *LGBT Youth Resources* (https://www.apa.org/pi/lgbt/programs/safe-supportive/lgbt/index)

- *Non-Binary Gender Identities* (https://www.apadivisions.org/division-44/resources/advocacy/non-binary-facts.pdf)

- *Office on Sexual Orientation and Gender Diversity* (https://www.apa.org/pi/lgbt/)

- *Practice Guidelines for LGB Clients: Guidelines for Psychological Practice With Lesbian, Gay, and Bisexual Clients* (https://www.apa.org/pi/lgbt/resources/guidelines)

- *Society for the Psychology of Sexual Orientation and Gender Diversity* (https://www.apa.org/about/division/div44)

- *Resolution on Gender and Sexual Orientation Diversity in Children and Adolescents in Schools* (https://www.apa.org/about/policy/orientation-diversity)
  - *How Educators Can Support Families With Gender Diverse and Sexual Minority Youth: Promoting Resiliency for Gender Diverse and Sexual Minority Students in Schools* (https://www.apa.org/pi/lgbt/programs/safe-supportive/lgbt/educators-families.pdf)
  - *Key Terms and Concepts in Understanding Gender Diversity and Sexual Orientation Among Students* (https://www.apa.org/pi/lgbt/programs/safe-supportive/lgbt/key-terms.pdf)
  - *School-Based Risk and Protective Factors for Gender Diverse and Sexual Minority Children and Youth: Improving School Climate* (https://www.apa.org/pi/lgbt/programs/safe-supportive/lgbt/risk-factors.pdf)
  - *Supporting Transgender and Gender Diverse Students in Schools: Key Recommendations for School Administrators* (https://www.apa.org/pi/lgbt/programs/safe-supportive/lgbt/school-administrators.pdf)
  - *Supporting Transgender and Gender Diverse Students in Schools: Key Recommendations for School Health Personnel* (https://www.apa.org/pi/lgbt/programs/safe-supportive/lgbt/health-personnel.pdf)

- *Respect Workshop* (https://www.apa.org/pi/lgbt/programs/safe-supportive/training/respect-workshop)
  - *Planning Delivery of the Respect Workshop Training: A Guide for Sponsors* (https://www.apa.org/pi/lgbt/programs/safe-supportive/training/planning-respect-workshop.pdf)

– *The Respect Online Course* (https://www.apa.org/pi/lgbt/programs/safe-supportive/training/respect-online-course)

- *Toolbox to Promote Healthy LGBTQ Youth* (https://www.apa.org/pi/lgbt/programs/safe-supportive/training/toolbox)

- *Understanding Bisexuality* (https://www.apa.org/pi/lgbt/resources/bisexual)

- *Youth at Disproportionate Risk* (https://www.apa.org/pi/lgbt/programs/safe-supportive/disproportionate-risk)

National Association of School Psychologists (NASP; https://www.nasponline.org/)
- *Disclosure Experiences of Urban, Ethnically Diverse LGBT High School Students: Implications for School Personnel* (https://www.nasponline.org/publications/periodicals/spf/volume-10/volume-10-issue-1-(spring-2016)/disclosure-experiences-of-urban-ethnically-diverse-lgbt-high-school-students-implications-for-school-personnel)

- *LGBTQ Posters* (https://www.nasponline.org/resources-and-publications/resources-and-podcasts/diversity/lgbtq-youth/lgbtq-posters)

- *LGBTQ Youth* (https://www.nasponline.org/resources-and-publications/resources-and-podcasts/diversity/lgbtq-youth)

- *Organizations Supporting LGBTQ Youth* (https://www.nasponline.org/resources-and-publications/resources-and-podcasts/diversity/lgbtq-youth/organizations-supporting-lgbtq-youth)

- *Professional Ethics* (https://www.nasponline.org/standards-and-certification/professional-ethics)

- *Resolutions* (https://www.nasponline.org/research-and-policy/policy-priorities/resolutions)

Research

American Psychological Association (APA; https://www.apa.org/)
- *APA Resolution on Support for the Expansion of Mature Minors' Ability to Participate in Research* (https://www.apa.org/about/policy/resolution-minors-research.pdf)

- *Guidelines for Psychological Practice With Transgender and Gender Nonconforming People* (https://www.apa.org/practice/guidelines/transgender.pdf)

- *LGBT Science and Research Resources* (https://www.apadivisions.org/division-44/resources/research)

- *Practice Guidelines for LGB Clients: Guidelines for Psychological Practice With Lesbian, Gay, and Bisexual Clients* (https://www.apa.org/pi/lgbt/resources/guidelines)

Electronic Code of Federal Regulations (https://www.ecfr.gov/cgi-bin/ECFR?page=browse)

U.S. Department of Health & Human Services, Office for Human Research Protections (https://www.hhs.gov/ohrp/)

- *The Belmont Report: Ethical Principles and Guidelines for the Protection of Human Subjects of Research* (https://www.hhs.gov/ohrp/regulations-and-policy/belmont-report/index.html)

- *Regulations, Policy, & Posting* (https://www.hhs.gov/ohrp/regulations-and-policy)

PARENTS/GUARDIANS

American Academy of Pediatrics (AAP; https://www.aap.org/en-us/Pages/Default.aspx)

- *The AAP Parenting Website* (https://www.healthychildren.org/English/Pages/default.aspx)
  - *Coming Out: Information for Parents of LGBT Teens* (https://www.healthychildren.org/English/ages-stages/teen/dating-sex/Pages/Four-Stages-of-Coming-Out.aspx)

American Library Association (ALA; http://www.ala.org/)

- *Resources for Parents and Families of LGBTQ Individuals* (http://www.ala.org/rt/sites/ala.org.rt/files/content/professionaltools/ResourcesforParentsandFamiliesofLGBTQIndividuals.pdf)

Child Welfare Information Gateway (https://www.childwelfare.gov/)

- *Resources for Families of LGBTQ Youth* (https://www.childwelfare.gov/topics/systemwide/diverse-populations/lgbtq/lgbt-families/)

Genders & Sexualities Alliance Network (GSA Network; https://gsanetwork.org)

- *Supporting LGBTQ Youth Through Family Engagement* (https://gsanetwork.org/resources/supporting-lgbtq-youth-through-family-engagement/)

Human Rights Campaign (HRC; https://www.hrc.org/)

- *School Resources for Parents* (https://www.hrc.org/resources/school-resources-for-parents)

John Hopkins Medicine (https://www.hopkinsmedicine.org/)

- *Tips for Parents of LGBTQ Youth* (https://www.hopkinsmedicine.org/health/wellness-and-prevention/tips-for-parents-of-lgbtq-youth)

National Foster Parent Association (NFPA; https://nfpaonline.org/)

- *Supporting Your LGBTQ Youth: A Guide for Foster Parents* (https://www.childwelfare.gov/pubs/LGBTQyouth/)

PFLAG (originally Parents and Friends of Lesbians and Gays; https://pflag.org/)

- *Loving Families* (https://pflag.org/loving-families)

Strong Family Alliance (https://www.strongfamilyalliance.org/)
* *Parent Guide* (https://www.strongfamilyalliance.org/parent-guide/)

Substance Abuse and Mental Health Services Association (SAMHSA; https://www.samhsa.gov/)
* *A Practitioner's Resource Guide: Helping Families to Support Their LGBT Children* (https://store.samhsa.gov/sites/default/files/d7/priv/pep14-lgbtkids.pdf)

RACIALLY AND ETHNICALLY DIVERSE

The Brown Boi Project (http://www.brownboiproject.org/)

Center for Black Equity (CBE; https://centerforblackequity.org/)
* *Black LGBTQ+* Prides (https://centerforblackequity.org/black-prides/)

Desi lgbtQ Helpline for South Asians (DeQH; http://www.deqh.org/)

GAPA (originally the Gay Asian Pacific Alliance; https://www.gapa.org/)

GLSEN (originally the Gay, Lesbian and Straight Education Network; https://www.glsen.org/)
* *Some Considerations When Working With LGBT Students of Color* (https://www.glsen.org/sites/default/files/LGBT_studentsofcolor.pdf)

GroundSpark (https://groundspark.org/)
* *RFAP [Respect for All Project] Films* (https://groundspark.org/respect-for-all/rfap-films)

Human Rights Campaign (HRC; https://www.hrc.org/)
* *Being African American & LGBTQ: An Introduction* (https://www.hrc.org/resources/being-african-american-lgbtq-an-introduction)

* *Black and African American LGBTQ Youth Report* (https://www.hrc.org/resources/black-and-african-american-lgbtq-youth-report)

* *Explore: Communities of Color* (https://www.hrc.org/explore/topic/communities-of-color)

* *Society and Coming Out Issues for Asian Pacific Americans* (https://www.hrc.org/resources/society-and-coming-out-issues-for-asian-pacific-americans)

Latino GLBT History Project (https://www.latinoglbthistory.org/)

National Association of School Psychologists (NASP; https://www.nasponline.org/)
* *Disclosure Experiences of Urban, Ethnically Diverse LGBT High School Students: Implications for School Personnel* (https://www.nasponline.org/publications/periodicals/spf/volume-10/volume-10-issue-1-(spring-2016)/disclosure-experiences-of-urban-ethnically-diverse-lgbt-high-school-students-implications-for-school-personnel)

National Black Justice Coalition (NBJC; http://www.nbjc.org/)

National Public Radio (NPR; https://www.npr.org/)
- *Latino USA #1409—Queer* (https://www.latinousa.org/2014/02/28/1409-queer/)

PFLAG (originally Parents and Friends of Lesbians and Gays; https://pflag.org/)
- *Training Toolkit: Family Acceptance Within Families of Color* (https://pflag.org/familiesofcolor)

Safe Schools Coalition (http://www.safeschoolscoalition.org/index.html)
- *GLBT Youth of Color: Resources for Parents/Guardians, Family Members, Educators and Allies* (http://www.safeschoolscoalition.org/RG-glbt_youth_of_color.html)

Trans Student Educational Resources (TSER; https://www.transstudent.org/)
- *Queer Youth of Color* (https://www.transstudent.org/queeryouthofcolor)

Trikone (http://www.trikone.org/)

Zuna Institute (http://zunainstitute.org/)

RELIGION

Gay Buddhist Fellowship (GBF; http://gaybuddhist.org/v3-wp/)

Jewish Queer Youth (JQY; https://www.jqyouth.org/)

JQ (https://jqinternational.org/)
- *JQ Helpline* (https://jqinternational.org/helpline/)

Human Rights Campaign (HRC; https://www.hrc.org/)
- *Faith Resources* (https://www.hrc.org/resources/faith-resources)

PFLAG (originally Parents and Friends of Lesbians and Gays; https://pflag.org/)
- *Faith Resources for Christians and Catholics* (https://pflag.org/blog/faith-resources-christians-and-catholics)

- *Faith Resources for Jews* (https://pflag.org/jewish)

- *Faith Resources for Muslims* (https://pflag.org/resource/faith-resources-muslims)

- *Faith Resources for Non-Judeo-Christian/Abrahamic Denominations* (https://pflag.org/blog/faith-resources-non-judeo-christianabrahamic-denominations)

- *LDS Church and Suicide Prevention* (https://pflag.org/blog/lds-church-and-suicide-prevention)

- *Resources for Interfaith/Non-Denominational Communities* (https://pflag.org/nondenominational)

Public Broadcasting Service (PBS; https://www.pbs.org/)
- *LGBT Religious Organization Resource List* (https://www.pbs.org/independentlens/content/love-free-or-die_lgbt-religious-organizations-html/)

Soulforce (https://www.soulforce.org/)

Strong Family Alliance (https://www.strongfamilyalliance.org/)
- *Faith-Based Organizations* (https://www.strongfamilyalliance.org/hopeful-voices/faith-based-organizations/)

SCHOOLS

American Psychological Association (APA; https://www.apa.org/)
- *Safe & Supportive Schools Project* (https://www.apa.org/pi/lgbt/programs/safe-supportive/)

American Civil Liberties Union (ACLU; https://www.aclu.org/)
- *LGBTQ Youth & Schools Resource Library* (https://www.aclu.org/library-lgbt-youth-schools-resources-and-links?redirect=lgbt-rights_hivaids/library#filtering)

- *Open Letter to Schools About LGBT Student Privacy* (https://www.aclu.org/letter/open-letter-schools-about-lgbt-student-privacy)

American Library Association (ALA; http://www.ala.org/)
- *Rainbow Book List: GLBTQ Books for Children & Teens* (https://glbtrt.ala.org/rainbowbooks/)

GLSEN (originally the Gay, Lesbian and Straight Education Network; https://www.glsen.org/)
- *Advocate for Inclusive & Affirming Curriculum* (https://www.glsen.org/inclusive-curriculum)

- *Developing LGBTQ-Inclusive Classroom Resources* (https://www.glsen.org/sites/default/files/2019-11/GLSEN_LGBTQ_Inclusive_Curriculum_Resource_2019_0.pdf)

- *Educator Resources* (https://www.glsen.org/resources/educator-resources)

- *GLSEN Safe Space Kit* (https://www.glsen.org/activity/glsen-safe-space-kit-be-ally-lgbtq-youth)

- *Model Laws and Policies* [for LGBTQ school inclusion] (https://www.glsen.org/article/model-laws-policies)

- *Professional Development* (http://glsen.org/educate/professional-development)

- *School Climate Survey* (https://www.glsen.org/research/school-climate-survey)

- *Some Considerations When Working With LGBT Students of Color* (https://www.glsen.org/sites/default/files/LGBT_studentsofcolor.pdf)

- *Student and GSA Resources* (https://www.glsen.org/resources/student-and-gsa-resources)

- *Support for Student-Led Clubs* (http://live-glsen-website.pantheonsite.io/support-student-gsas)

- *10 Steps to Start Your GSA* (https://www.glsen.org/sites/default/files/2019-11/GLSEN-10-Steps-To-Start-Your-GSA.pdf)

- *The 2017 National School Climate Survey* (https://www.glsen.org/sites/default/files/2019-10/GLSEN-2017-National-School-Climate-Survey-NSCS-Full-Report.pdf)

Harvard Graduate School of Education, Making Caring Common Project (https://mcc.gse.harvard.edu/)
- *For Educators: Supporting LGBTQIA Youth Resource List* (https://mcc.gse.harvard.edu/resources-for-educators/supporting-lgbtqia-youth-resource-list)

Human Rights Campaign (HRC; https://www.hrc.org/)
- *Creating Safe and Welcoming Schools* (https://www.welcomingschools.org/)

- *Schools in Transition: A Guide for Supporting Transgender Students in K–12 Schools* (https://www.hrc.org/resources/schools-in-transition-a-guide-for-supporting-transgender-students-in-k-12-s)

- *Schools: Welcoming Schools* (https://www.hrc.org/resources/schools)

Los Angeles LGBT Center (https://lalgbtcenter.org/)
- *Out for Safe Schools®: About the Program* (https://schools.lalgbtcenter.org/out-for-safe-schools/)

Los Angeles Unified School District (https://achieve.lausd.net/domain/4)
- *Human Relations, Diversity and Equity* (https://achieve.lausd.net/Page/9867#spn-content)

National Center for Transgender Equality (NCTE; https://transequality.org/)
- *Fact Sheet on U.S. Department of Education Policy Letter on Transgender Students* (http://www.transequality.org/sites/default/files/ED-DCL-Fact-Sheet.pdf)

National Institutes of Health, Office of Equity, Diversity, and Inclusion (NIH EDI; https://www.edi.nih.gov/)
- *Sexual & Gender Minority: SafeZone Posters* (printable; https://www.edi.nih.gov/people/sep/lgbti/resources/safe-zone-posters)

SafeSchools (https://www.safeschools.com/)

Safe Schools Coalition (http://www.safeschoolscoalition.org/index.html)
- *GLBT Youth of Color: Resources for Parents/Guardians, Family Members, Educators and Allies* (http://www.safeschoolscoalition.org/RG-glbt_youth_of_color.html)

Safe Zone Project (SZP; https://thesafezoneproject.com/)

- *About* (https://thesafezoneproject.com/about/)

Scholastic (https://www.scholastic.com/home)
- *Create Inclusive, Affirming Schools for LGBTQ Students* (https://www.scholastic.com/teachers/blog-posts/john-depasquale/2017/Create-Inclusive-Affirming-Schools-for-LGBT-Students/)

Stonewall (https://www.stonewall.org.uk/)
- *Creating an LGBT-Inclusive Secondary Curriculum* (https://www.stonewall.org.uk/resources/creating-lgbt-inclusive-secondary-curriculum)

Teaching Tolerance (https://www.tolerance.org/)
- *Common Roadblocks* (https://www.tolerance.org/professional-development/common-roadblocks)

- *A Gender Spectrum Glossary* (https://www.tolerance.org/print/86569/print)

- *School Climate: Best Practices for Serving LGBTQ Students—A Teaching Tolerance Guide* (https://www.tolerance.org/sites/default/files/2018-10/TT-Best-Practices-for-Serving-LGBTQ-Students-Guide.pdf)

- *Toolkit for LGBT Best Practices* (https://www.tolerance.org/magazine/fall-2013/toolkit-for-lgbt-best-practices)

U.S. Department of Education (https://www.ed.gov/)
- *Family Educational Rights and Privacy Act (FERPA)* (https://www2.ed.gov/policy/gen/guid/fpco/ferpa/index.html)

U.S. Department of Education, Office of Elementary & Secondary Education (https://oese.ed.gov/)
- *Examples of Policies and Emerging Practices for Supporting Transgender Students* (https://www2.ed.gov/about/offices/list/oese/oshs/emergingpractices.pdf)

Elementary School

Accredited Online Schools (https://www.accreditedschoolsonline.org/)
- *LGBTQ Student Resources & Support* (https://www.accreditedschoolsonline.org/resources/lgbtq-student-support/)

- *Online Elementary School* (https://www.accreditedschoolsonline.org/k-12/online-elementary-school/)

Anti-Defamation League (ADL; https://www.adl.org/)
- *Beyond the Binary: Discussing Transgender and Gender Non-Conforming Identity in K–12 Schools* (https://www.adl.org/education/resources/tools-and-strategies/beyond-the-binary-discussing-transgender-and-gender-non)

- *Identity-Based Bullying* (https://www.adl.org/sites/default/files/documents/assets/pdf/education-outreach/identity-based-bullying.pdf)

GLSEN (originally the Gay, Lesbian and Straight Education Network; https://www.glsen.org/)
- *Advocate for Inclusive & Affirming Curriculum* (https://www.glsen.org/inclusive-curriculum)

LGBT National Help Center (https://www.glbthotline.org/)
- *GLBT Near Me* (https://www.glbtnearme.org/)
- *LGBT National Hotline 888-843-4564* (https://www.glbthotline.org/national-hotline.html)
- *Trans Youth Online Chat Group for 13 Years Old & Younger* (https://www.glbthotline.org/transyouth.html)
- *Youth CHAT ROOM Lounge* (https://www.glbthotline.org/youthchatrooms.html)

Middle School

Accredited Online Schools (https://www.accreditedschoolsonline.org/)
- *LGBTQ Student Resources & Support* (https://www.accreditedschoolsonline.org/resources/lgbtq-student-support/)

- *Online Middle School* (https://www.accreditedschoolsonline.org/k-12/online-middle-school/)

Anti-Defamation League (ADL; https://www.adl.org/)
- *Beyond the Binary: Discussing Transgender and Gender Non-Conforming Identity in K–12 Schools* (https://www.adl.org/education/resources/tools-and-strategies/beyond-the-binary-discussing-transgender-and-gender-non)

- *What Is Marriage Equality?* (https://www.adl.org/sites/default/files/documents/assets/pdf/education-outreach/What-Is-Marriage-Equality.pdf)

GLSEN (originally the Gay, Lesbian and Straight Education Network; https://www.glsen.org/)
- *Advocate for Inclusive & Affirming Curriculum* (https://www.glsen.org/inclusive-curriculum)

LGBT National Help Center (https://www.glbthotline.org/)
- *GLBT Near Me* (https://www.glbtnearme.org/)
- *LGBT National Hotline 888-843-4564* (https://www.glbthotline.org/national-hotline.html)
- *LGBT National Online Peer Support CHAT* (https://www.glbthotline.org/peer-chat.html)
- *LGBT National Youth Talkline* (1-800-246-7743; https://www.glbthotline.org/youth-talkline.html)
- *LGBTQ Teens Online Talk Group* (https://www.glbthotline.org/lgbtqteens.html)
- *LGBT Teens Online Talk Group* [Facebook] (https://www.facebook.com/LGBT-Teens-Online-Talk-Group-362230117838175/)
- *Trans Teens Online Talk Group* (https://www.glbthotline.org/transteens.html)
- *Trans Teens Online Talk Group* [Facebook] (https://www.facebook.com/TransTeensOnlineTalkGroup)
- *Trans Youth Online Chat Group for 13 Years Old & Younger* (https://www.glbthotline.org/transyouth.html)
- *Youth CHAT ROOM Lounge* (https://www.glbthotline.org/youthchatrooms.html)

High School

Accredited Online Schools (https://www.accreditedschoolsonline.org/)
- *LGBTQ Student Resources & Support* (https://www.accreditedschoolsonline.org/resources/lgbtq-student-support/)

- *Accredited Online High School* (https://www.accreditedschoolsonline.org/k-12/online-high-school/)

Anti-Defamation League (ADL; https://www.adl.org/)
- *Analyzing Hate Crimes Statistics* (https://www.adl.org/sites/default/files/documents/assets/pdf/education-outreach/analyzing-hate-crimes-statistics.pdf)

- *Beyond the Binary: Discussing Transgender and Gender Non-Conforming Identity in K–12 Schools* (https://www.adl.org/education/resources/tools-and-strategies/beyond-the-binary-discussing-transgender-and-gender-non)

- *Caitlyn Jenner and the Power of Coming Out* (https://www.adl.org/education/educator-resources/lesson-plans/caitlyn-jenner-and-the-power-of-coming-out#.VUplufm6fcs)

- *Unheard Voices: Stories of LGBT History* (https://www.adl.org/sites/default/files/documents/assets/pdf/education-outreach/curriculum-connections-fall-2011.pdf)

GLSEN (originally the Gay, Lesbian and Straight Education Network; https://www.glsen.org/)
- *Advocate for Inclusive & Affirming Curriculum* (https://www.glsen.org/inclusive-curriculum)

LGBT National Help Center (https://www.glbthotline.org/)
- *GLBT Near Me* (https://www.glbtnearme.org/)
- *LGBT National Hotline 888-843-4564* (https://www.glbthotline.org/national-hotline.html)
- *LGBT National Online Peer Support CHAT* (https://www.glbthotline.org/peer-chat.html)
- *LGBT National Youth Talkline* (1-800-246-7743; https://www.glbthotline.org/youth-talkline.html)
- *LGBTQ Teens Online Talk Group* (https://www.glbthotline.org/lgbtqteens.html)
- *LGBT Teens Online Talk Group* [Facebook] (https://www.facebook.com/LGBT-Teens-Online-Talk-Group-362230117838175/)
- *Trans Teens Online Talk Group* (https://www.glbthotline.org/transteens.html)
- *Trans Teens Online Talk Group* [Facebook] (https://www.facebook.com/TransTeensOnlineTalkGroup)
- *Youth CHAT ROOM Lounge* (https://www.glbthotline.org/youthchatrooms.html)

Q Chat Space (https://www.qchatspace.org/)

Stonewall (https://www.stonewall.org.uk/)
- *Creating an LGBT-Inclusive Secondary Curriculum* (https://www.stonewall.org.uk/resources/creating-lgbt-inclusive-secondary-curriculum)

SEXUAL ORIENTATION

Accredited Online Schools (https://www.accreditedschoolsonline.org/)
- *LGBTQ Student Resources & Support* (https://www.accreditedschoolsonline.org/resources/lgbtq-student-support/)

American Institute of Bisexuality (AIB; http://www.americaninstituteofbisexuality.org/)

BiNet USA (http://www.binetusa.org/)

Bi.org (originally bisexual.org; https://bi.org/en)

Bisexual Resource Center (BRC; http://biresource.org/)
- *Bi Youth* (https://biresource.org/resources/youth/)

Human Rights Campaign (HRC; https://www.hrc.org/)
- *Bi+* Youth Report (https://www.hrc.org/resources/bi-youth-report)

LGBT National Help Center (https://www.glbthotline.org/)
- *GLBT Near Me* (https://www.glbtnearme.org/)
- *LGBT National Hotline 888-843-4564* (https://www.glbthotline.org/national-hotline.html)
- *LGBT National Online Peer Support CHAT* (https://www.glbthotline.org/peer-chat.html)
- *LGBT National Youth Talkline* (1-800-246-7743; https://www.glbthotline.org/youth-talkline.html)
- *LGBTQ Teens Online Talk Group* (https://www.glbthotline.org/lgbtqteens.html)
- *LGBT Teens Online Talk Group* [Facebook] (https://www.facebook.com/LGBT-Teens-Online-Talk-Group-362230117838175/)
- *Youth CHAT ROOM Lounge* (https://www.glbthotline.org/youthchatrooms.html)

National Center for Lesbian Rights (NCLR; http://www.nclrights.org/)
- *Youth* (http://www.nclrights.org/our-work/youth/)

We Are the Youth (http://wearetheyouth.org/)
- *Resources* (http://wearetheyouth.org/resources/)

SPORTS

Athlete Ally (https://www.athleteally.org/)

National Collegiate Athletic Association (NCAA; http://www.ncaa.org/)
- *NCAA Inclusion of Transgender Student-Athletes* (https://www.ncaa.org/sites/default/files/Transgender_Handbook_2011_Final.pdf)

You Can Play (http://www.youcanplayproject.org/)

STATE BY STATE

Center Link (https://www.lgbtcenters.org/)

Colorado One (https://one-colorado.org/)

Human Rights Campaign (HRC; https://www.hrc.org/)
- *State Maps of Laws & Policies* (https://www.hrc.org/state-maps)

Lambda Legal (https://www.lambdalegal.org/)
- *Direct Service Providers for LGBTQIA Youth: Resources for LGBTQ+* Youth by State (https://docs.google.com/document/d/1YC-iPkJAwFTexQ-huUNHep5WCQyTj12tldQj3_fD8Mg/edit)

Massachusetts Department of Elementary and Secondary Education, Office of Student and Family Support (SFS; http://www.doe.mass.edu/sfs/)
- *Safe Schools Program for LGBTQ Students* (http://www.doe.mass.edu/sfs/lgbtq/)

Yale University, Office of LGBTQ Resources (https://lgbtq.yale.edu/)
- *True Colors Sexual Minority and Youth Family Services* (https://lgbtq.yale.edu/resources/true-colors-sexual-minority-youth-and-family-services)

SUICIDE AND CRISIS PREVENTION

Desi lgbtQ Helpline for South Asians (DeQH, http://www.deqh.org/)

It Gets Better Project (https://itgetsbetter.org/)

JQ (https://jqinternational.org/)
- *JQ Helpline* (https://jqinternational.org/helpline/)

LGBT National Help Center (https://www.glbthotline.org/)
- *GLBTNearMe.org* (https://www.glbtnearme.org/)
- *LGBT National Hotline 888-843-4564* (https://www.glbthotline.org/national-hotline.html)
- *LGBT National Online Peer-Support CHAT* (https://www.glbthotline.org/peer-chat.html)

PFLAG (originally Parents and Friends of Lesbians and Gays; https://pflag.org/)
- *LDS Church and Suicide Prevention* (https://pflag.org/blog/lds-church-and-suicide-prevention)

Sources of Strength (https://sourcesofstrength.org/)

Trans Lifeline (https://www.translifeline.org/)

The Trevor Project (https://www.thetrevorproject.org/)
- *Education* (https://www.thetrevorproject.org/education/)
- *Get Help Now* (https://www.thetrevorproject.org/get-help-now/)

INDEX

ABOUT THE EDITORS

Megan C. Lytle, PhD, is an assistant professor in the Department of Psychiatry at the University of Rochester Medical Center (URMC). Dr. Lytle's clinical and research expertise is in multiculturalism with a particular focus on the health and suicide disparities that are experienced by many lesbian, gay, bisexual, transgender, and queer or questioning (LGBTQ) individuals. She completed two research-based internships: one with the International Association of Applied Psychology nongovernmental organization at the United Nations and a predoctoral internship in the Program of Research and Innovation in Disparities Education track at the URMC. Dr. Lytle received her PhD in counseling psychology from Seton Hall University. As a National Research Service Award Fellow and KL2 Scholar, she began developing a research portfolio on the prevention of suicide, attempted suicide, risk-related deaths, and antecedent risks amid transgender and gender-diverse communities. She is a licensed psychologist and, until 2018, was cochair of the Committee on Children, Youth and Families of American Psychological Association (APA) Division 44, Society for the Psychology of Sexual Orientation and Gender Diversity.

Richard A. Sprott, PhD, received his degree in developmental psychology from the University of California, Berkeley (UC Berkeley), in 1994. His early work was on social and language development in early childhood, and he has a long history of evaluating educational programs for migrant farmworker families in the Midwest. Dr. Sprott is currently directing research projects focused on issues facing homeless lesbian, gay, bisexual, transgender, and queer or questioning youth and on identity development and health and well-being in people who express alternative sexualities and nontraditional relationships. He also teaches in the Department of Human Development and Women's

Studies at California State University, East Bay, and teaches graduate-level courses at various universities in the San Francisco Bay Area, including UC Berkeley, the California Institute of Integral Studies, and Holy Names University. He is cochair of the Committee on Children, Youth and Families of APA Division 44. All of these efforts highlight the ways in which stigma, prejudice, minority dynamics, health, language, identity development, and community development intersect and affect each other.